UNDERCOVER GENIE

THE
IRREVERENT
CONJURINGS
OF AN
ILLUSTRATIVE
ALADDIN

KYLE BAKER

VERTIGO COMICS   NEW YORK. NEW YORK

AG
BAK

By Kyle Baker

TRY THESE SIMPLE MANLY EXERCISES!

DC COMICS

Karen Berger VP-EXECUTIVE EDITOR

Steve Bunche EDITOR

Amie Brockway-Metcalf ART DIRECTOR

Paul Levitz PRESIDENT & PUBLISHER

Georg Brewer VP-DESIGN & RETAIL PRODUCT DEVELOPMENT

Richard Bruning VP-CREATIVE DIRECTOR

Patrick Caldon SENIOR VP-FINANCE & OPERATIONS

Chris Caramalis VP-FINANCE

Terri Cunningham VP-MANAGING EDITOR

Dan DiDio VP-EDITORIAL

Alison Gill VP-MANUFACTURING

Lillian Laserson SENIOR VP & GENERAL COUNSEL

David McKillips VP-ADVERTISING

John Nee VP-BUSINESS DEVELOPMENT

Cheryl Rubin VP-LICENSING & MERCHANDISING

Bob Wayne VP-SALES & MARKETING

UNDERCOVER GENIE: THE IRREVERENT CONJURINGS OF AN ILLUSTRATIVE ALADDIN.

Published by DC Comics, 1700 Broadway, New York, NY 10019.
Cover, introduction, and compilation copyright © 2003 Kyle Baker.
All Rights Reserved. VERTIGO is a trademark of DC Comics.
DC Comics does not read or accept unsolicited
submissions of ideas, stories or artwork.
Printed in Canada.
DC Comics, a Warner Bros. Entertainment Company.
Cover art by Kyle Baker.

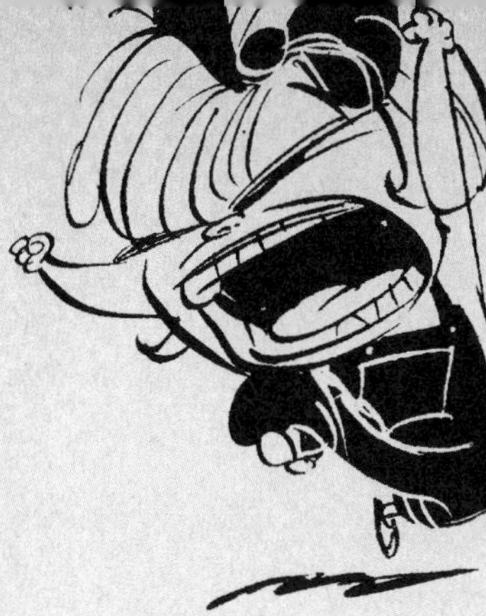

I have been told by my publisher to provide a written introduction to this volume. The publisher's expressed goal of this introduction is to inform the reader of who I am. My first draft of this intro, consisting of eight words, "If you don't know, you better ask somebody," was rejected, so I will elaborate.

INTRODUCTION

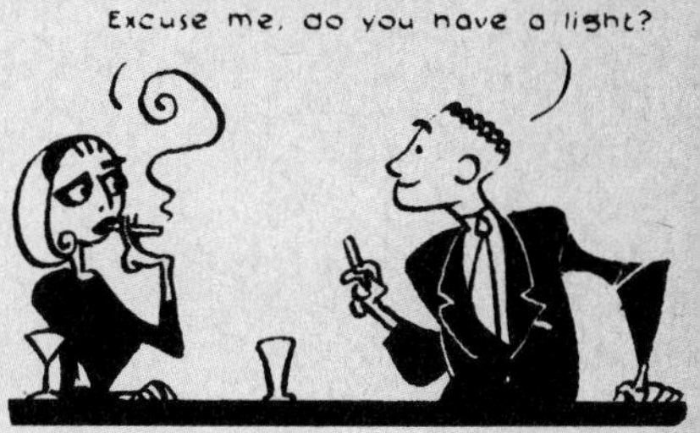
Excuse me, do you have a light?

Comic book professionals are an interesting breed. They don't seem to know that there is any sort of graphic communication in the world other than comic books. This attitude produces some interesting perceptual anomalies:

☞ Because there is no other form of graphic communication in the world, it is assumed that if an illustrator or writer is not working in comic books, he or she must be unemployed.

☞ Comic books are the only graphic medium that has remained more or less stylistically unchanged for over a century. Comic books are still drawn with the same tools that Outcault used to create the Yellow Kid back at the dawn of comics; a crow-quill dip pen and an inkwell! Who else on EARTH still uses an inkwell and quill pen? That's like going to a modern doctor and having him put leeches on you! Can you imagine picking up a newspaper today in 2003, and instead of photos, finding carefully etched woodcuts on every page? Comic books are still lettered by hand, and even when the type is set on a computer, every effort is expended to make it look like it was lettered by hand. Do digital movie theatres add scratches and dust to the image to simulate film? Are digital movie monsters rendered to simulate stop-motion animation or puppetry?

☞ The primary subject matter of comic books also remains unchanged since 1938. Muscular young men in tight, colorful Spandex. Since 1938! Imagine that MTV only played Tin-Pan Alley music today, and the performers all wore waxed moustaches, top hats and bustles. They'd go broke!

By contrast, animation, another form of cartooning, stays competitive by continually updating styles and imitating the most successful current hits and trends. *Ice Age* doesn't look or sound like *Snow White*.

Similarly, the advertising industry always seeks out and utilizes the most cutting-edge, up-to-the-minute graphic styles to stay hip and appealing to the masses. Why? To make money. Because being hip and fashionable SELLS.

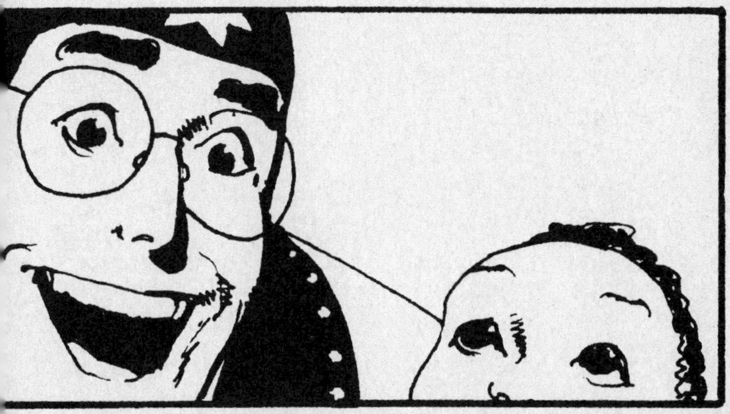

As a professional graphic artist, I am always on the lookout for the latest styles and techniques. I study current magazines, CD covers, movies, TV, even video games and art galleries to see what the most successful of my contemporaries are doing, then I imitate it and attempt to improve on it. I even use 3-D and digital photography in my cartoons today, just like a lot of graphics pros.

As a result of my diligence, my cartoons have appeared in major national magazines like *The New Yorker, The New York Times Magazine, Parade* and *TV Guide*. My work appears regularly on television, in movies, on music CDs, video games, clothing, and home furnishings. I get paid lots of money, and my work is seen by literally millions of people every year. Clients hire me because my style is fresh, appealing, and it SELLS, making more money for them as well.

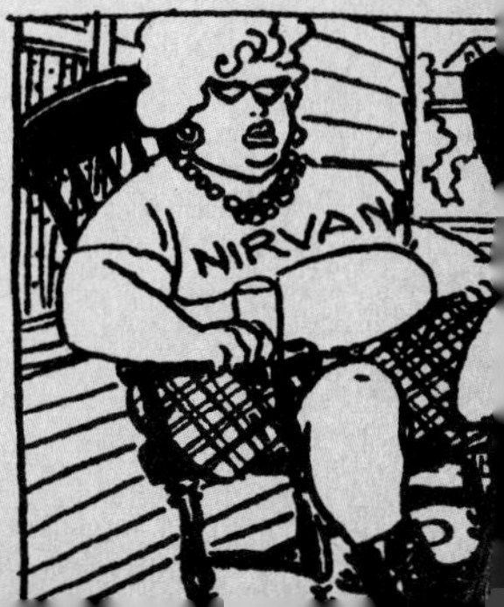
NIRVAN

Yet, comic book professionals still insist my stuff is "uncommercial."

Most of the work in this book was done in the 1990s. Comic book professionals will describe that decade as a "Golden Era," when books were selling in the millions and everyone was getting rich.

Throughout this "Golden Era" I couldn't get much work in comic books. Everyone wanted to publish McFarlane ripoffs, or overpriced "collectable" comics with foil covers and holograms. Since I produced neither of those, I couldn't get a comic book published, except for a couple books I did for free, and even then the publisher (not DC, but a rival) argued about letting me keep the reprint rights for work I was doing for free! (That stuff's in this book, so obviously I won that battle.)

I invite you to put yourself in my shoes for a moment; if you had a choice between working for high-profile, high-paying clients who were begging you to work for them, or a small network of hobby shops who don't want your work and don't pay much anyway, which would you choose?

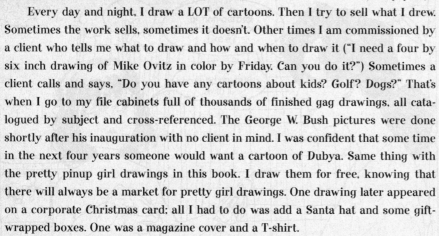

So I had to content myself with huge paychecks and an audience of millons.

Here's a lot of the work I did during that period. Some of the drawings in this book have been reprinted in many publications, and some are seeing print here for the first time (lucky you)!

TO CONQUER OTHER PLANETS!
EARTH IS NUMBER ONE!

Every day and night, I draw a LOT of cartoons. Then I try to sell what I drew. Sometimes the work sells, sometimes it doesn't. Other times I am commissioned by a client who tells me what to draw and how and when to draw it ("I need a four by six inch drawing of Mike Ovitz in color by Friday. Can you do it?") Sometimes a client calls and says, "Do you have any cartoons about kids? Golf? Dogs?" That's when I go to my file cabinets full of thousands of finished gag drawings, all catalogued by subject and cross-referenced. The George W. Bush pictures were done shortly after his inauguration with no client in mind. I was confident that some time in the next four years someone would want a cartoon of Dubya. Same thing with the pretty pinup girl drawings in this book. I draw them for free, knowing that there will always be a market for pretty girl drawings. One drawing later appeared on a corporate Christmas card; all I had to do was add a Santa hat and some gift-wrapped boxes. One was a magazine cover and a T-shirt.

I draw lots of character sketches and cartoons, just hoping to develop new ideas and techniques. The drawings on pages 16 and 69 are examples of this search for an idea or funny character. I chose not to develop them further, but I still like the drawings, so here they are.

LESTER FENTON'S DAUGHTERS and BOUNTY HUNTER DAD are two projects I'm working on, but I won't be using what's in this book. These drawings are some of the best I've done, so folks should see them anyway.

There're a few drawings of my kids in here also. Why? No reason. The idea of drawing something for no reason mystifies some folks, but a lot of the cartoons in this book were done for no reason. Everything does not have to be for money. Do you sing in the car? Why? No reason, just to sing! When you play sports, are you being paid? Probably not. (If you are a sports professional, hire me to draw you! Special rate for Venus and Serena!) Even if you are a professional athlete or singer, you still need to practice, and practice is for free. A practice drawing is still a drawing, and often a good one.

So that's the introduction. The publisher has also asked me to mention my other five Vertigo books, the COWBOY WALLY SHOW, WHY I HATE SATURN, YOU ARE HERE, I DIE AT MIDNIGHT, and KING DAVID, all still available in stores, and the complete set of six makes a unique, affordable gift. I have also been instructed to mention that I've won a bunch of awards. So I'm done here.

In conclusion, please let me say, "If you don't know, you better ask somebody."

KYLE BAKER

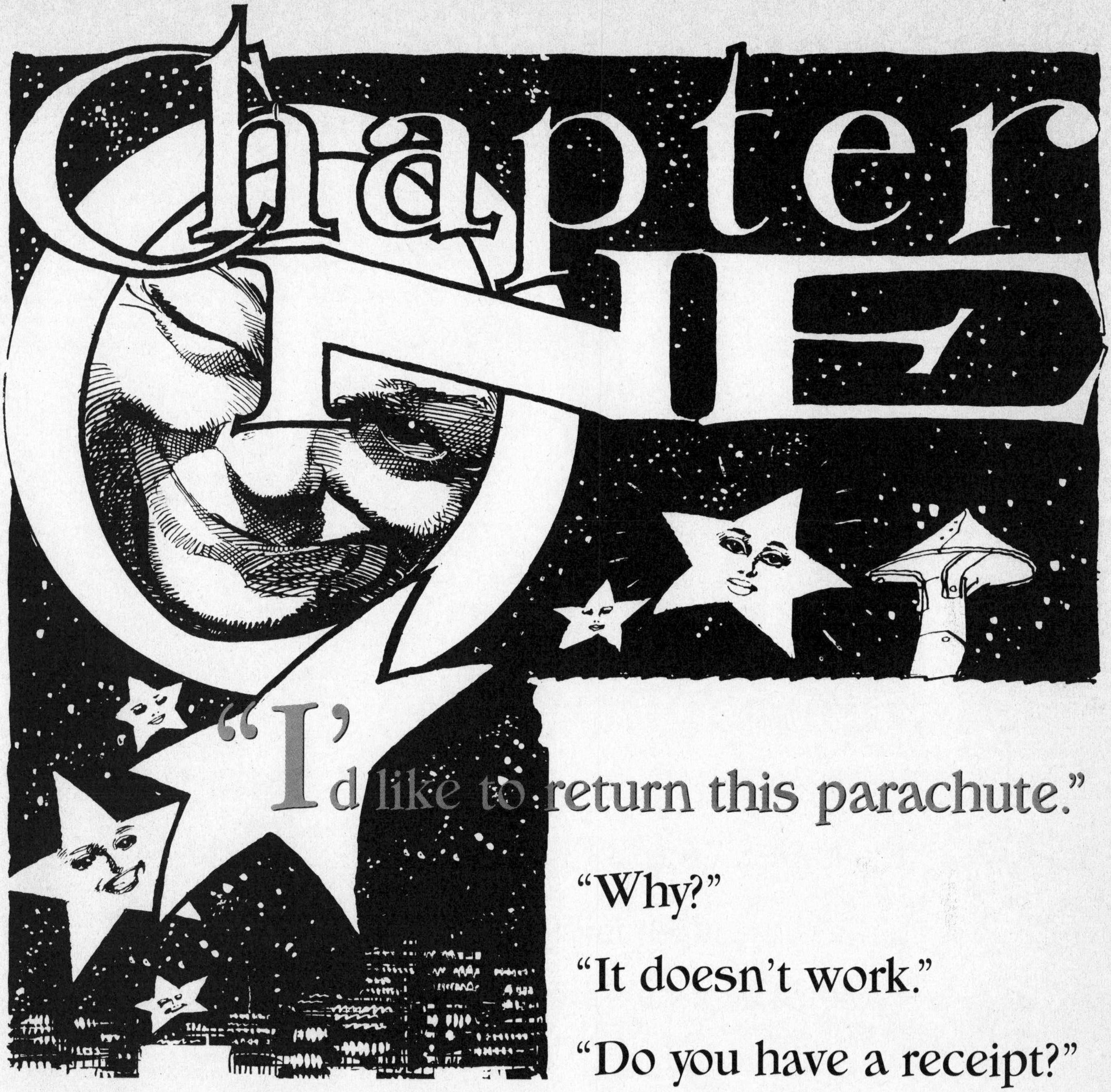
Chapter 12

"I'd like to return this parachute."

"Why?"

"It doesn't work."

"Do you have a receipt?"

A new tattoo, and Harley, too.

Some boots, a scar, and airplane glue.

A headband and a tambourine,

A pinkie ring and Vaseline.

A waterpipe shaped like a skull

Would make my shit job seem less dull.

SOMEDAY, YOU WILL WEAR PLAID.

When I was a teenager, I was a moody, maladjusted kid with a leather jacket and model cars. Those were the happiest days of my life.

Of course. When I was in high school, I was studious and friendly. Naturally, I never had a date.

My first serious girlfriend, Michelle, made me throw out my model cars. I thought we were in love. She dumped me when she left for college. I still carry a picture of those cars.

I figured that boys didn't ask me out because something was wrong with me. I worked on improving myself.

I'm basically lazy. I let others improve myself for me. In college, my girlfriend, Carla, wouldn't let me eat junk food. I became a vegetarian. She left me a year later, but I'm still a vegetarian. Mainly because I've never learned to cook.

As a result of my quest for self-improvement, I started college with a straight "A" average, a part-time job at a newspaper, and improved social skills and self-confidence. I considered it a waste of effort when I discovered I still didn't get any dates.

My next girlfriend, Sharon, got me to start showering and shaving regularly. I also got a haircut.

Grooming's important. I realized that men were only interested in stupid women with lots of makeup.

My next girlfriend, Christine, said I should stop dressing like a kid. I bought some suits that she picked out, and gave my leather jacket to Goodwill.

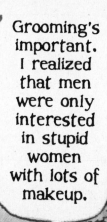

I started wearing lots of makeup and tight dresses, bought a second-hand leather jacket, and learned to keep my mouth shut. I married Tony a year later.

I moved in with Vanessa, who redecorated my apartment and got me to buy a bunch of appliances and a dog. She left me after two years. I still feel like I'm living in someone else's apartment. Probably the dog's.

I was so happy to finally have a man. I quit my job, and stopped seeing my old friends, except for the married ones.

Natalie got me to read a lot of books by women and give up what she viewed as "sexist" thought. She dumped me for an Italian. Now I wake up in Vanessa's apartment, with Natalie's brain, and put on Christine's clothes.

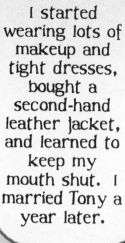

I'm 26, divorced, socially retarded, and trying to find an entry-level journalism job.

I have a lovely, decorated apartment full of appliances and a dog. I dress well, smell nice, eat right, and treat women with respect. I haven't had a date in two years. Women don't find me attractive anymore.

I feel I wasted a lot of time and potential on men. I'm not interested in a relationship at this point in my life.

I love you.

Suddenly every man wants me. You're all alike.

I can change.

My Last Conversation With Jack.

by Kyle Baker

I was back in town on a visit. I'd moved away years ago.

"Hey Jack."

No answer. I sat down to work.

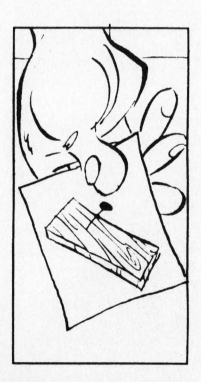

"I'm a little board."

"You know, I didn't recognize you with the hair."

MY LAST CONVERSATION WITH JACK

I didn't have the heart to tell him he'd said the same thing to me the day before.

"How's it goin', Jack?"

"Not so good."

"You'll be okay."

"I had another stroke."

"You told me."

He'd told me yesterday. And he'd told me a month before that, the last time I was in town.

"I did, huh? I forget things now. I'm pretty bad off."

"You told me. I heard. But you're better, things are looking up!"

"I still can't— I'm not what I was."

"Yes, but look how far you've come! You're walking, you went through the physical therapy—"

MY LAST CONVERSATION WITH JACK

"Physical therapy's the worst."

"You told me. And you made it! Not many guys could come back the way you've done! You'll be great! You're lucky you're–"

"GOD DAMN IT NO! I'm sick of everybody telling me how lucky I am! I don't feel lucky! I feel like shit! Everybody keeps telling me, lucky, lucky–Bullshit! I'm not lucky, it's terrible what's happened to me!"

"Fine, Jack. It's terrible. You're right."

I guess I was rude to him, but I'd heard that damn depressing story three times already, and I didn't see the point of sitting sympathetically through it again when he wasn't even going to remember it. I wanted to tell him, you're here now, you're alive now, it's all any of us have. None of our lives turn out the way we wanted, we have to be happy with whatever we get. I wanted to tell him, but I figured he'd just yell at me again. He wouldn't get it.

"You know, after all these years of marriage...I still find my wife to be the sexiest woman in the world...Does that seem sick to you?"

"I think it's wonderful, Jack."

OH, LE HUMANITY!
I weep for myself; I weep for beauty. Oh, Love!

AND NOW, LADIES AND GENTLEMEN, THE AMAZING ROLLO.
HE WILL PERFORM A DEATH-DEFYING ESCAPE FROM A SAFE FILLED WITH DYNAMITE.
HOW DO YOU PLAN TO ACCOMPLISH THIS SPECTACULAR FEAT?
WELL, I FIGURE I'LL BLOW THE DOOR OFF WITH THE DYNAMITE...
BAKER-

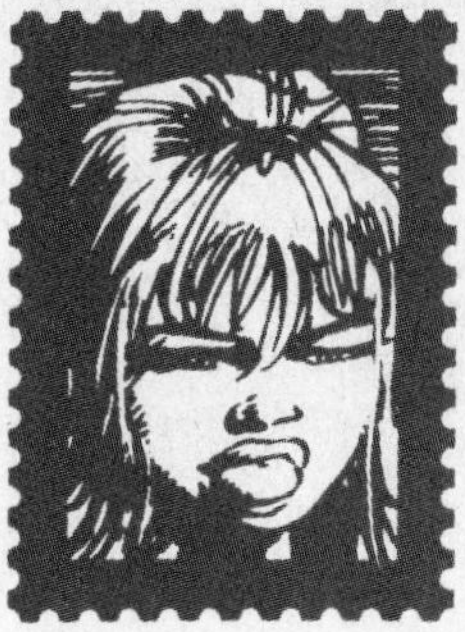

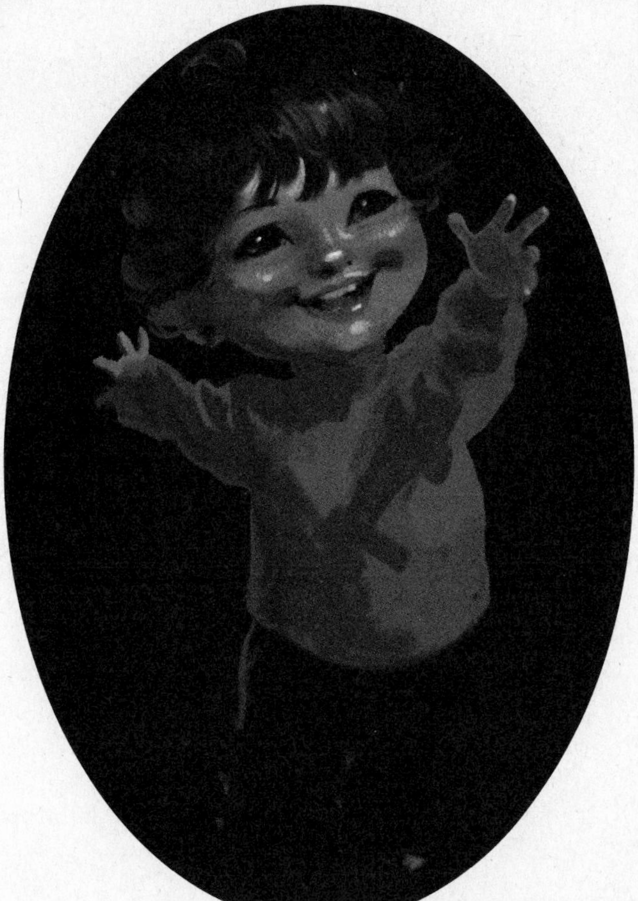

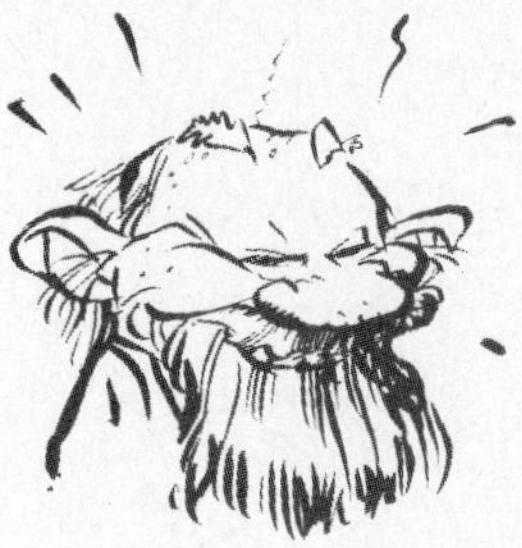

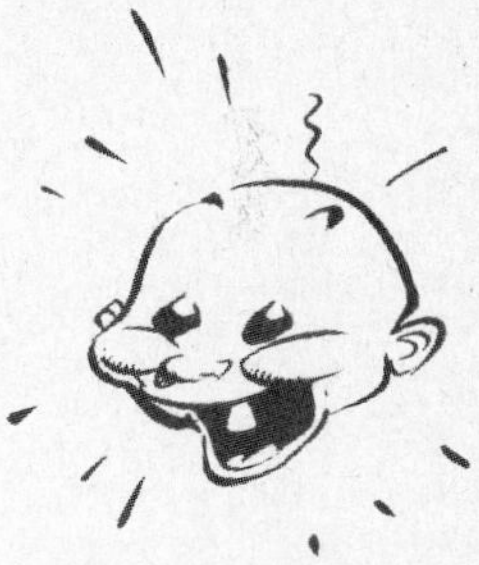

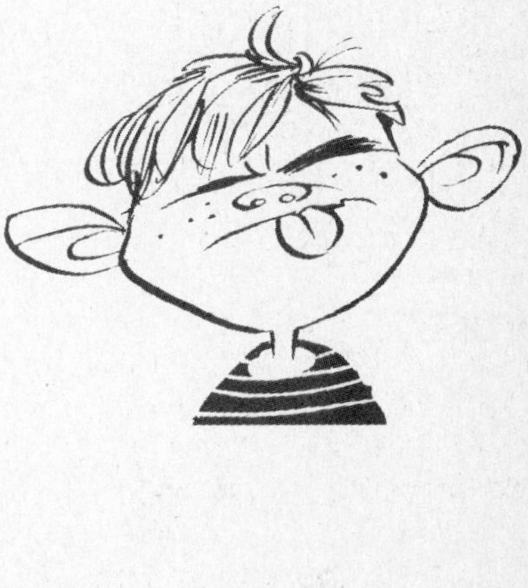

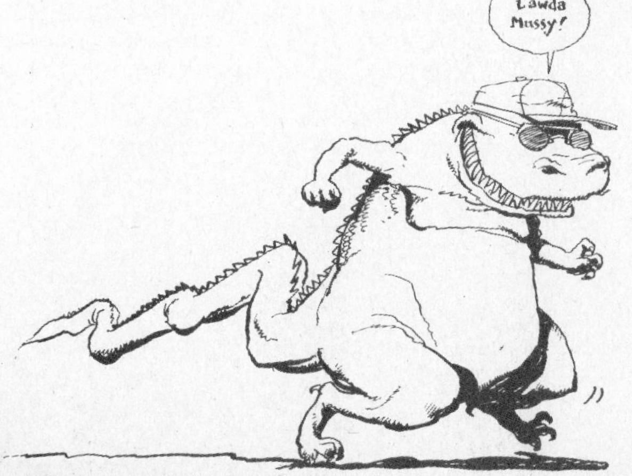
Lawda Mussy!

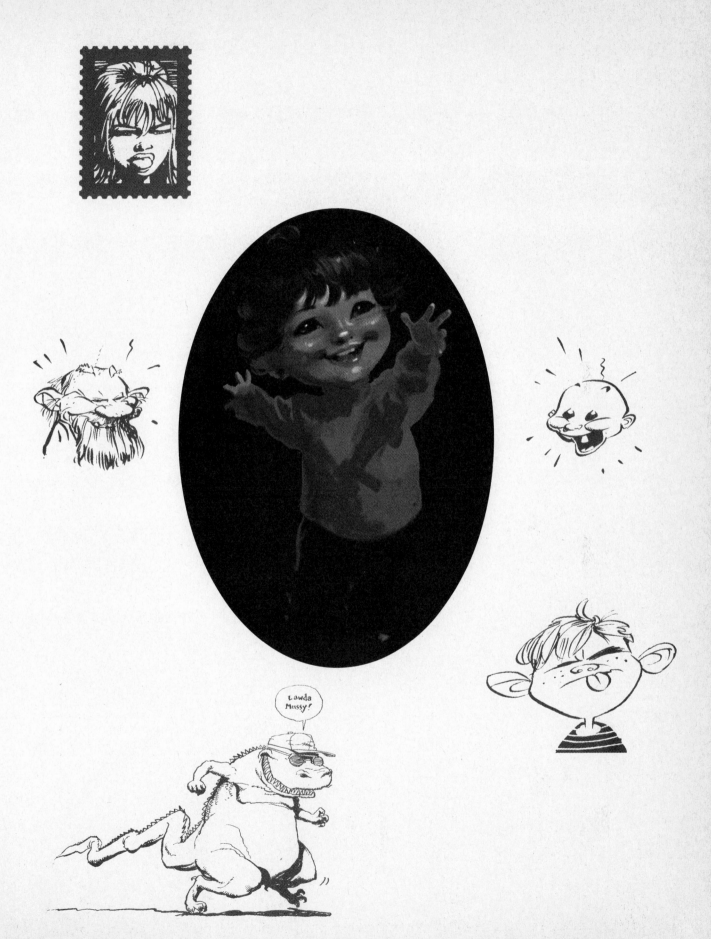

ISAAC 4-7-01
KB

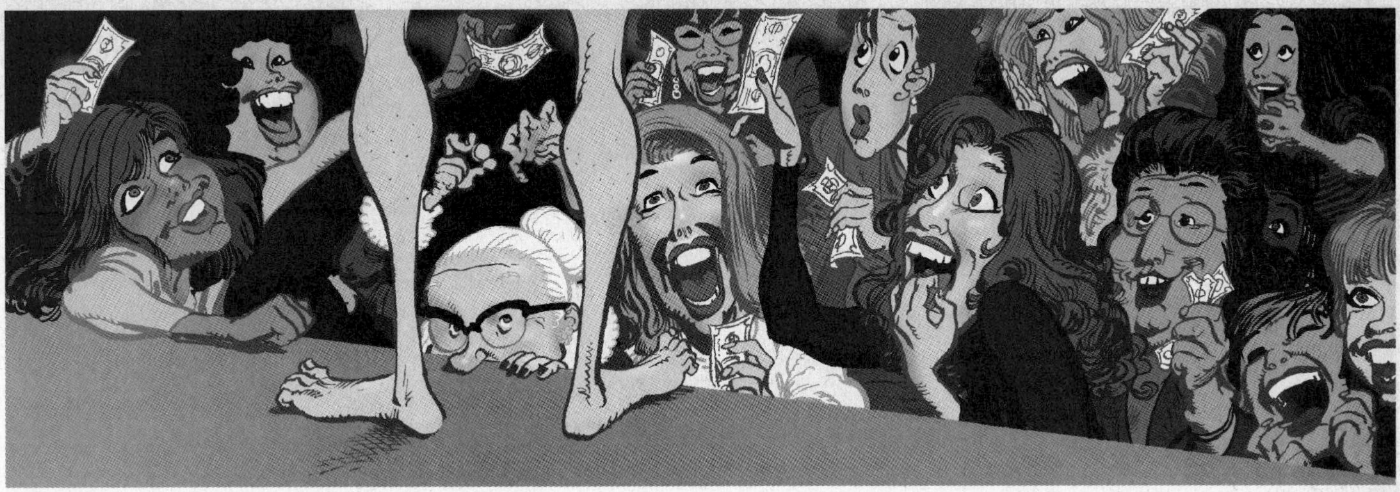

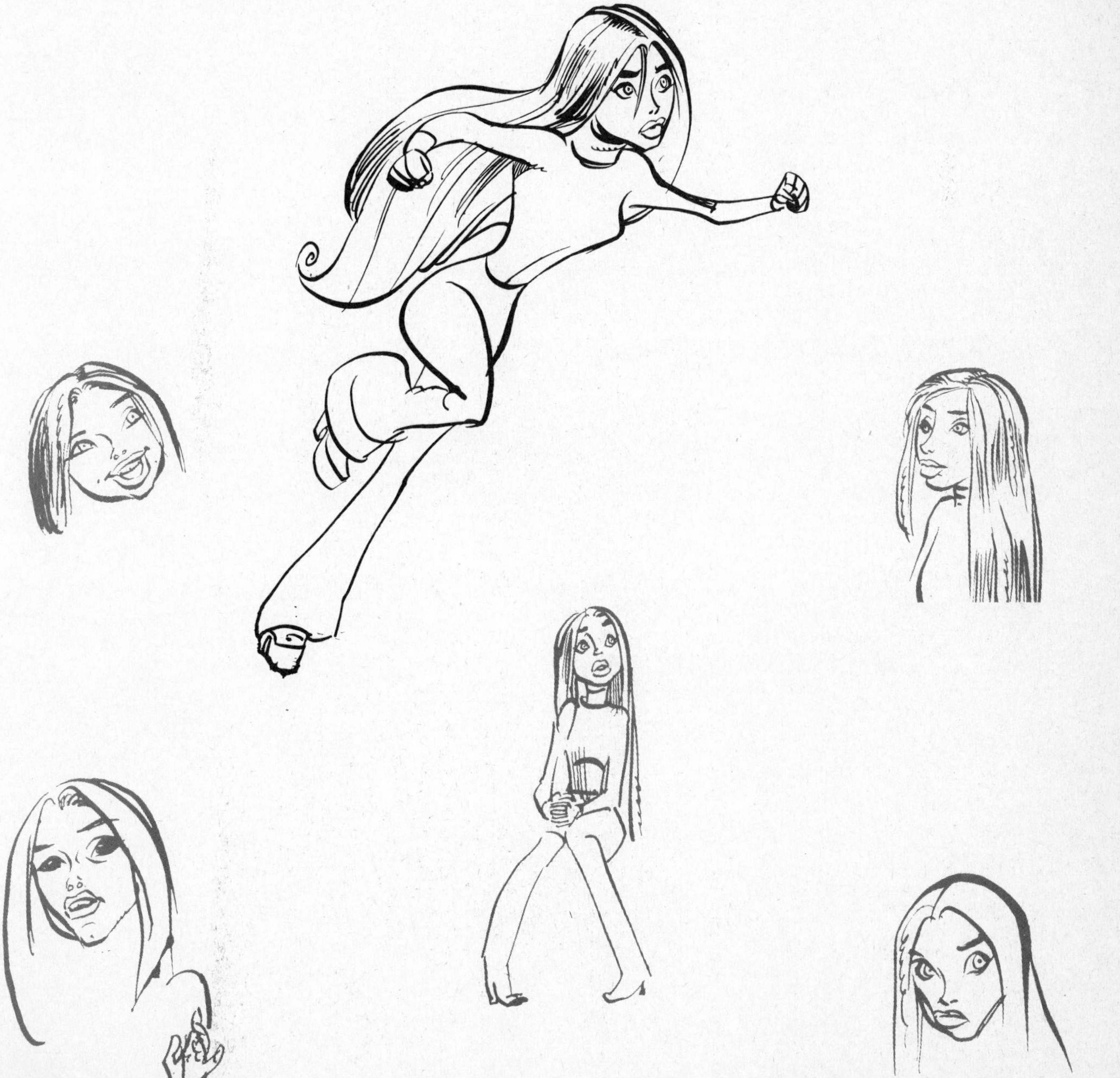

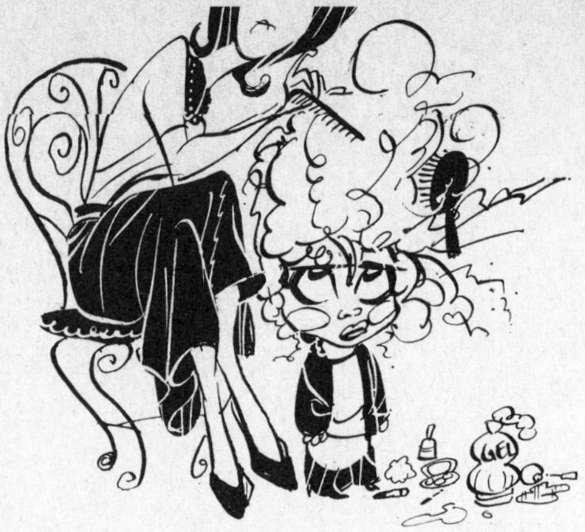
GEL

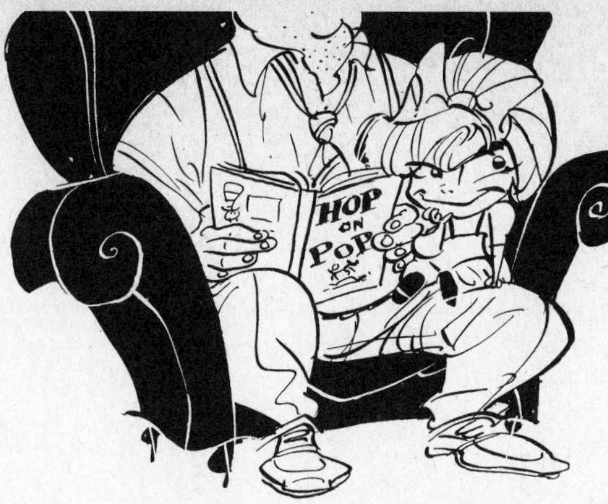
HOP ON POP

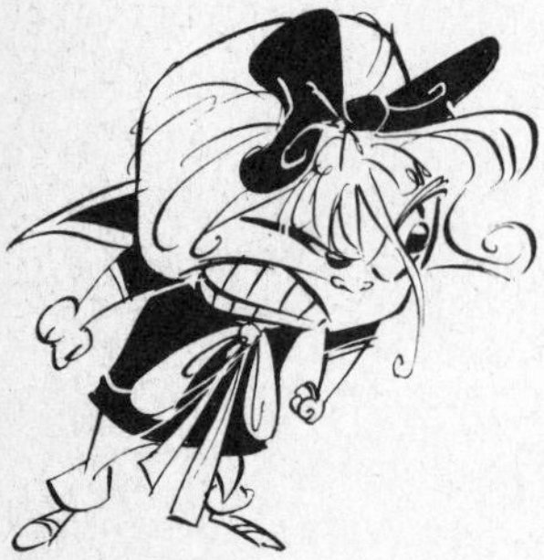

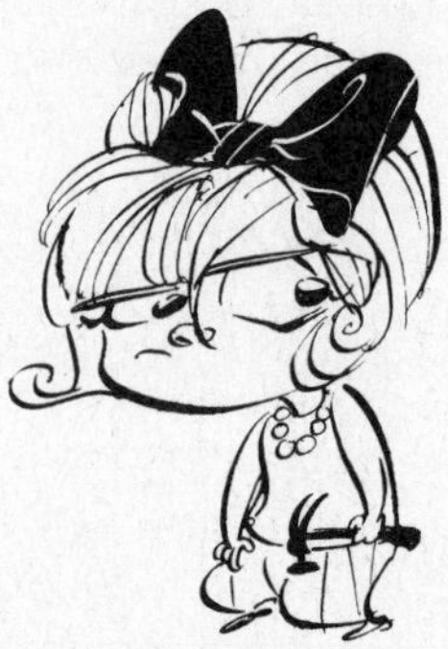

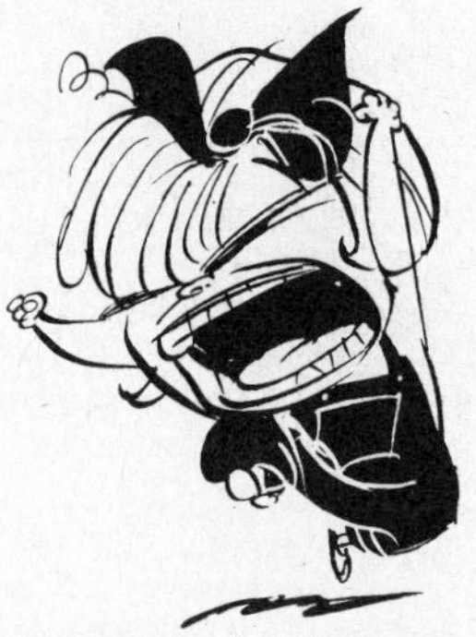

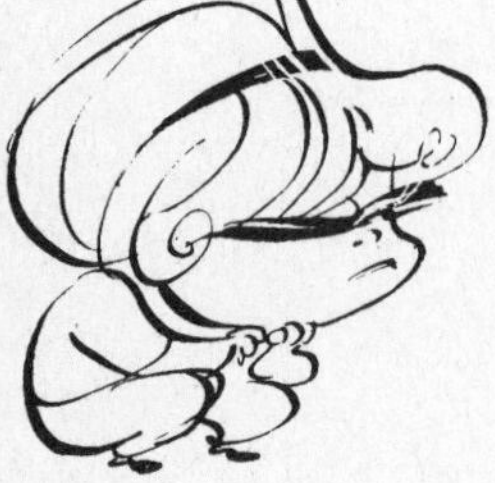

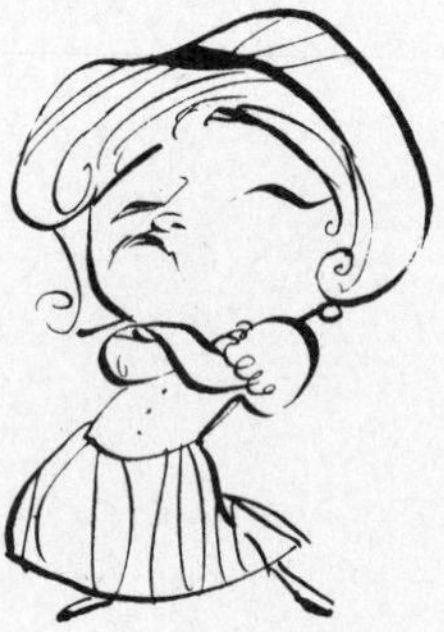

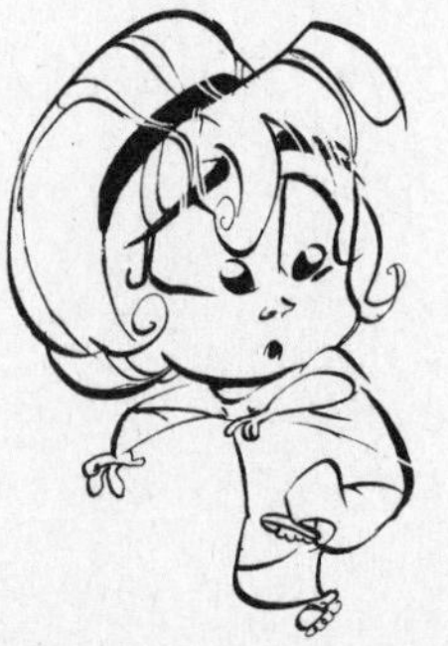

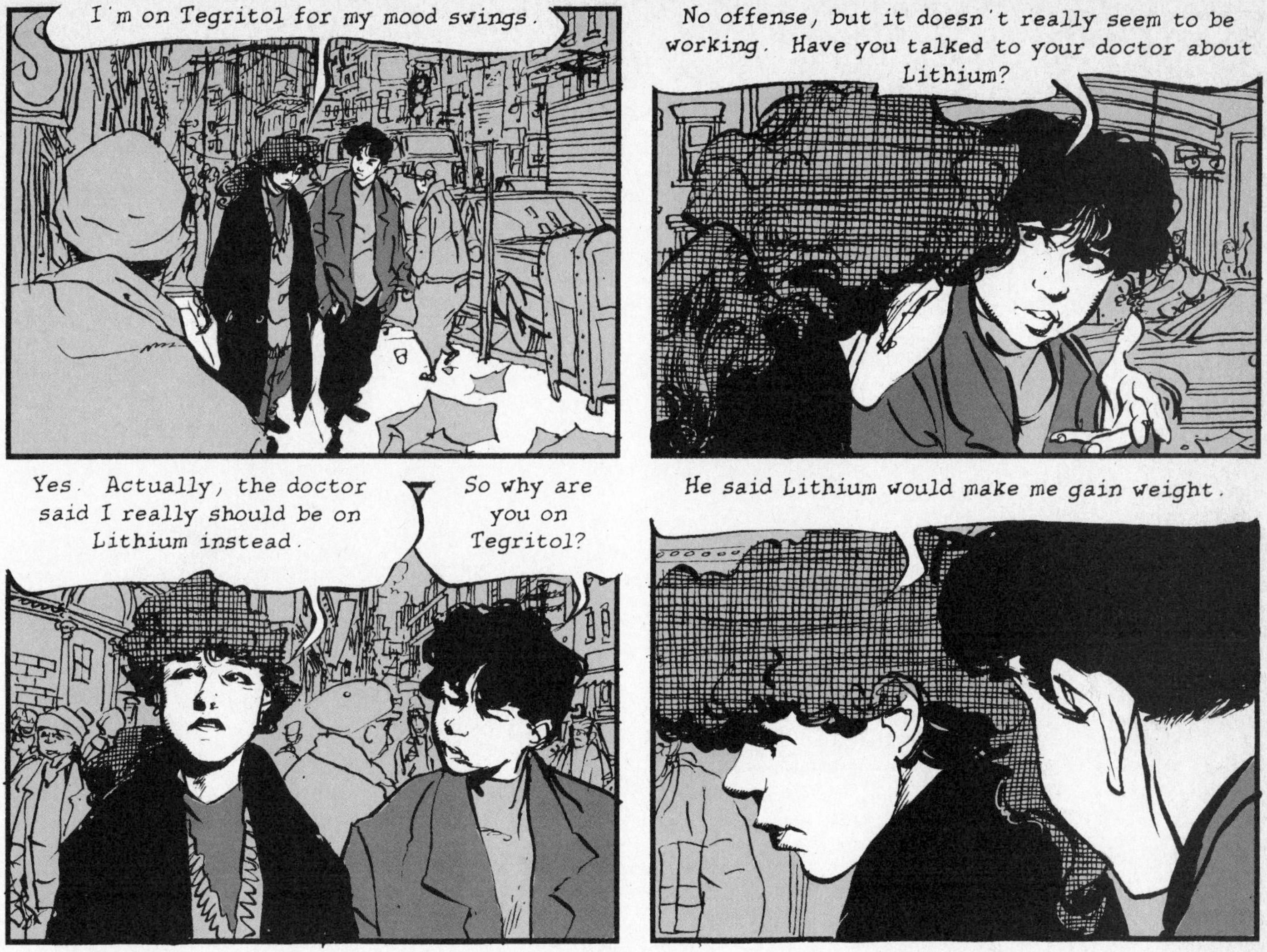
I'm on Tegritol for my mood swings.
No offense, but it doesn't really seem to be working. Have you talked to your doctor about Lithium?
Yes. Actually, the doctor said I really should be on Lithium instead.
So why are you on Tegritol?
He said Lithium would make me gain weight.

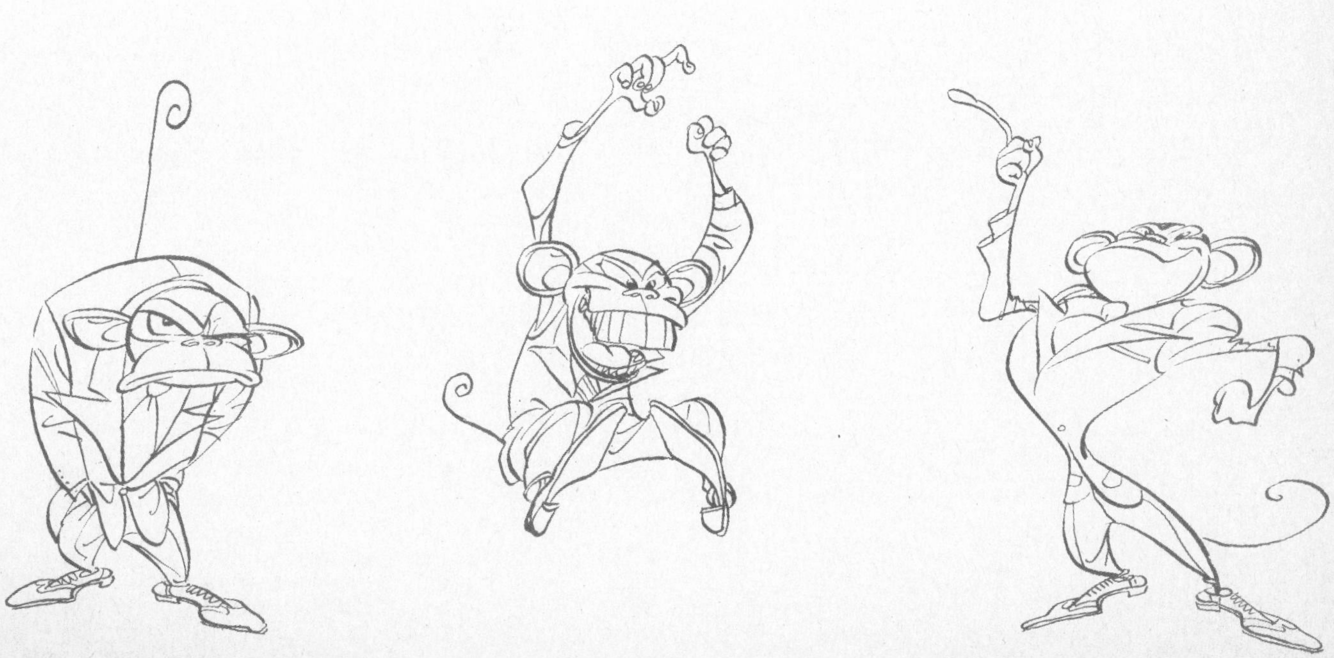

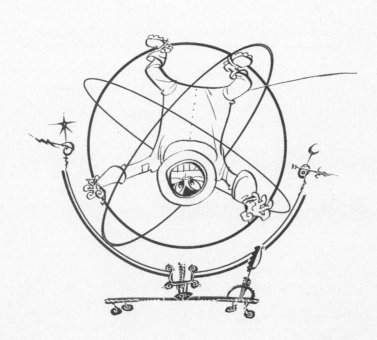

Kyle Baker

THE ADVENTURES OF GOD!

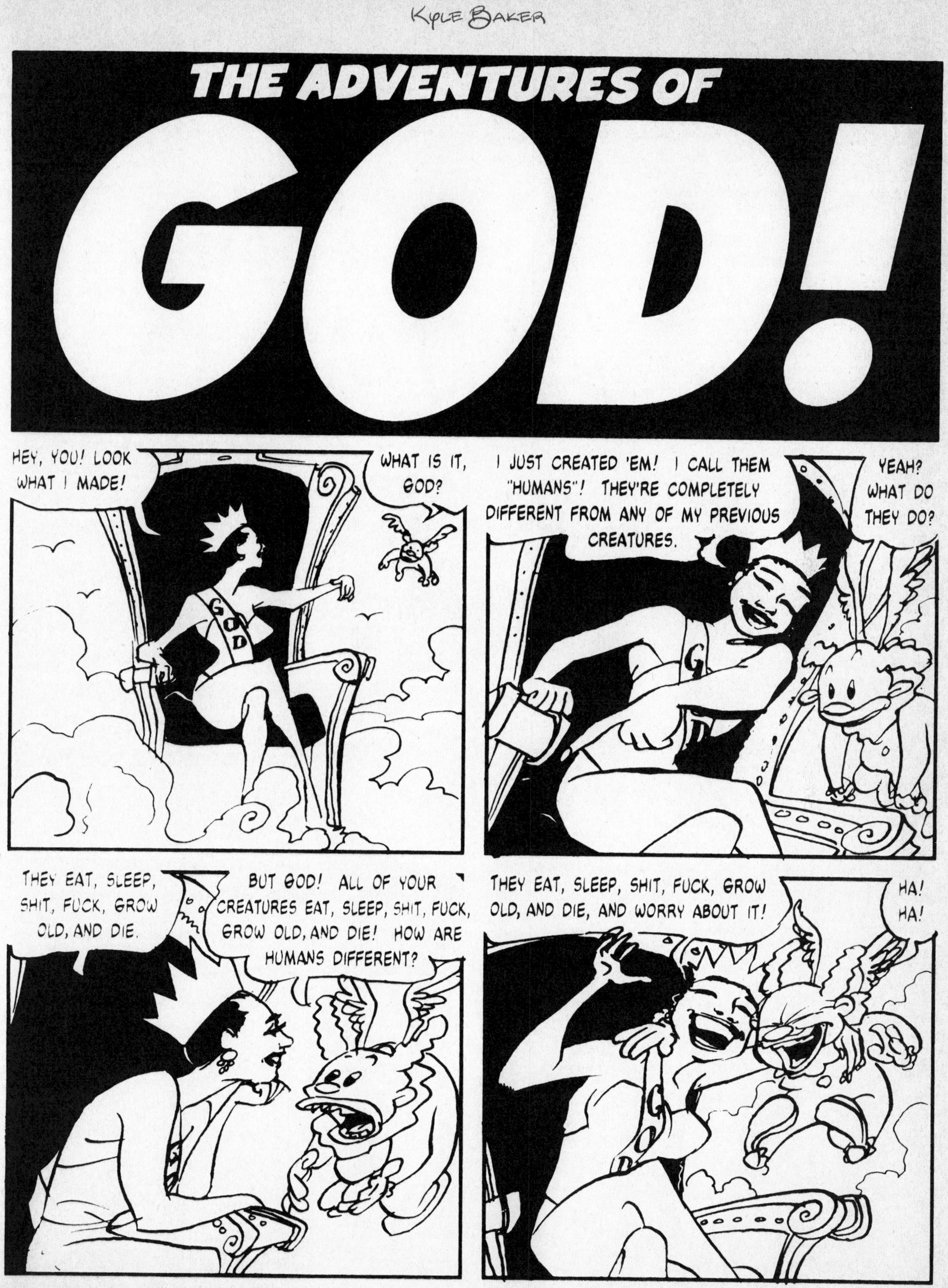

HEY, YOU! LOOK WHAT I MADE!
WHAT IS IT, GOD?
I JUST CREATED 'EM! I CALL THEM "HUMANS"! THEY'RE COMPLETELY DIFFERENT FROM ANY OF MY PREVIOUS CREATURES.
YEAH? WHAT DO THEY DO?
THEY EAT, SLEEP, SHIT, FUCK, GROW OLD, AND DIE.
BUT GOD! ALL OF YOUR CREATURES EAT, SLEEP, SHIT, FUCK, GROW OLD, AND DIE! HOW ARE HUMANS DIFFERENT?
THEY EAT, SLEEP, SHIT, FUCK, GROW OLD, AND DIE, AND WORRY ABOUT IT!
HA! HA!

KYLE BAKER

MEN!

Are you unhappy? Alone? Insecure and unsure of your place in the world, universe and grand scheme of things? ***OH, FOR CHRISSAKES,***

BE A MAN,

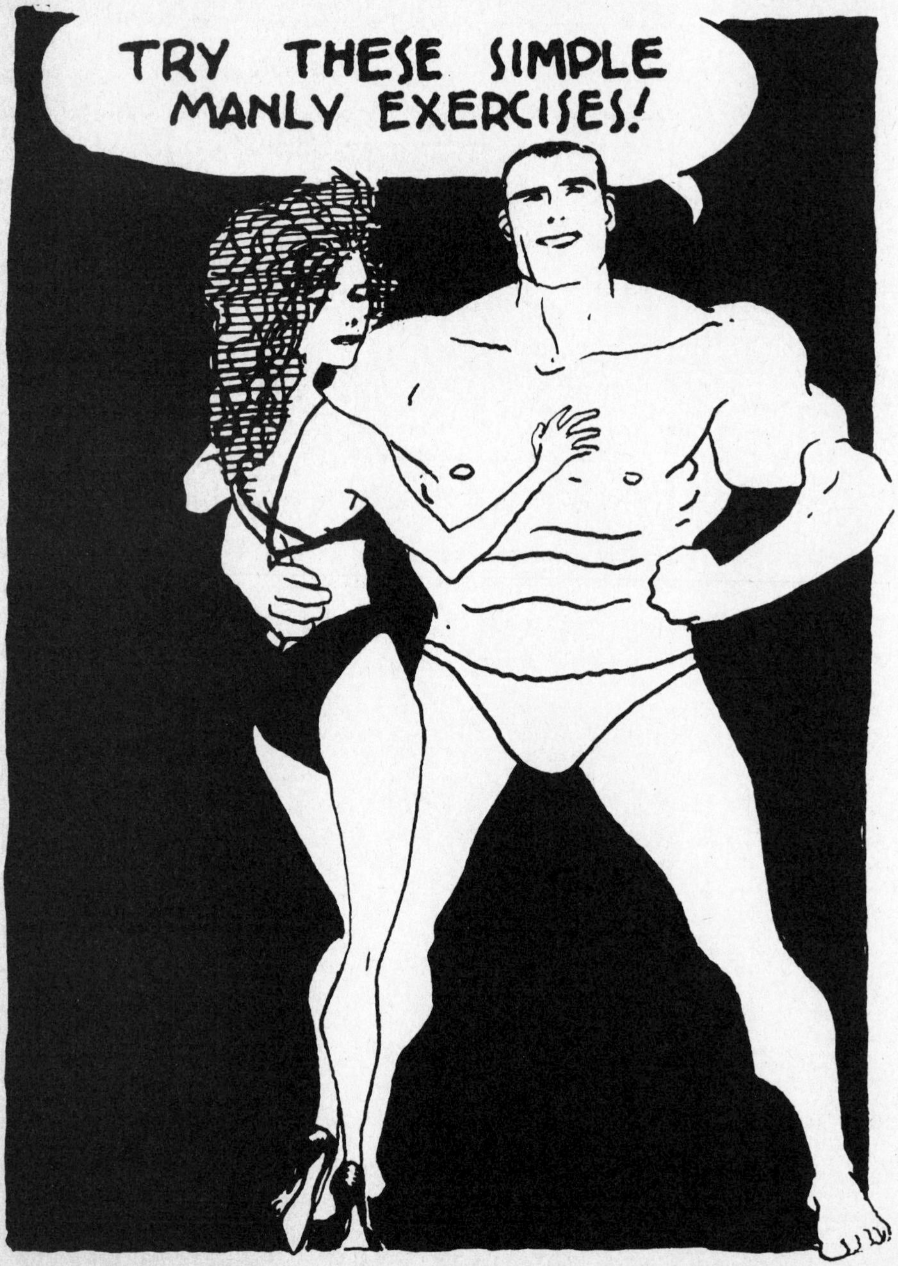
TRY THESE SIMPLE MANLY EXERCISES!

1

Have really passionate sex with a woman two or three times, then date her for a couple of weeks, acting just as friendly as ever, but now without having sex. Don't tell her you've stopped having sex with her. When she finally mentions it, you say,

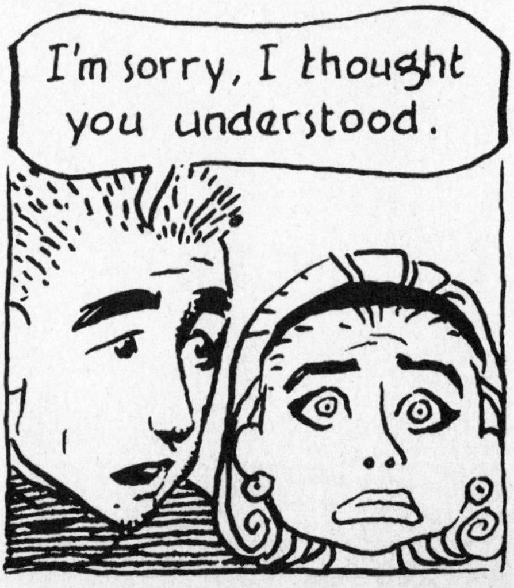
I'm sorry, I thought you understood.

DAMN YOU!

2

Never socialize with any man you consider to be your equal.

Let me offer you a thinly veiled reminder of the fact that I am more successful than you, phrasing my derision as advice.

3

Never accept responsibility for your actions. Nothing is ever your fault.

Ah, I'm forty years old, overweight, saddled with a wife, kids, lousy job. How do these things happen to me?

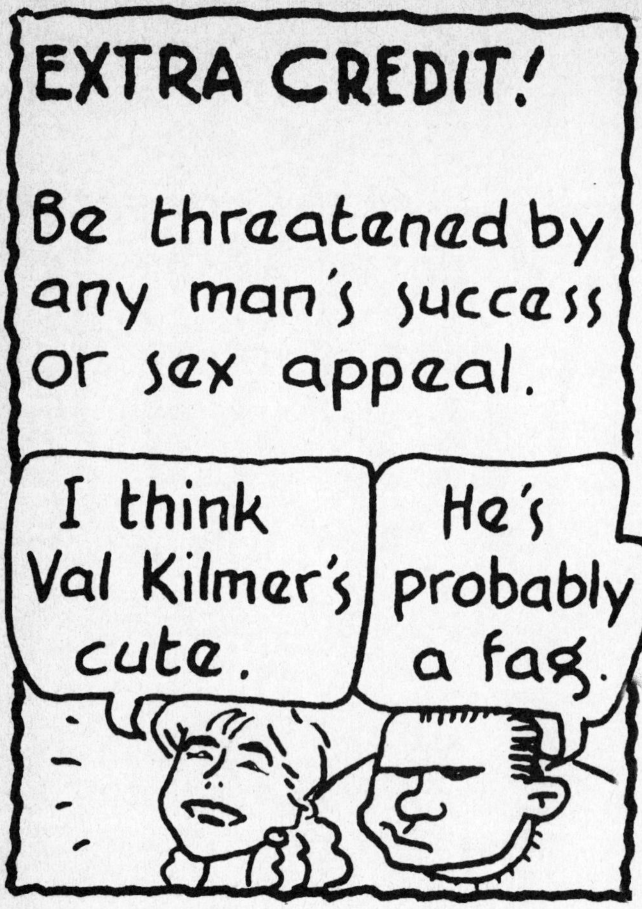
EXTRA CREDIT!
Be threatened by any man's success or sex appeal.
I think Val Kilmer's cute.
He's probably a fag.

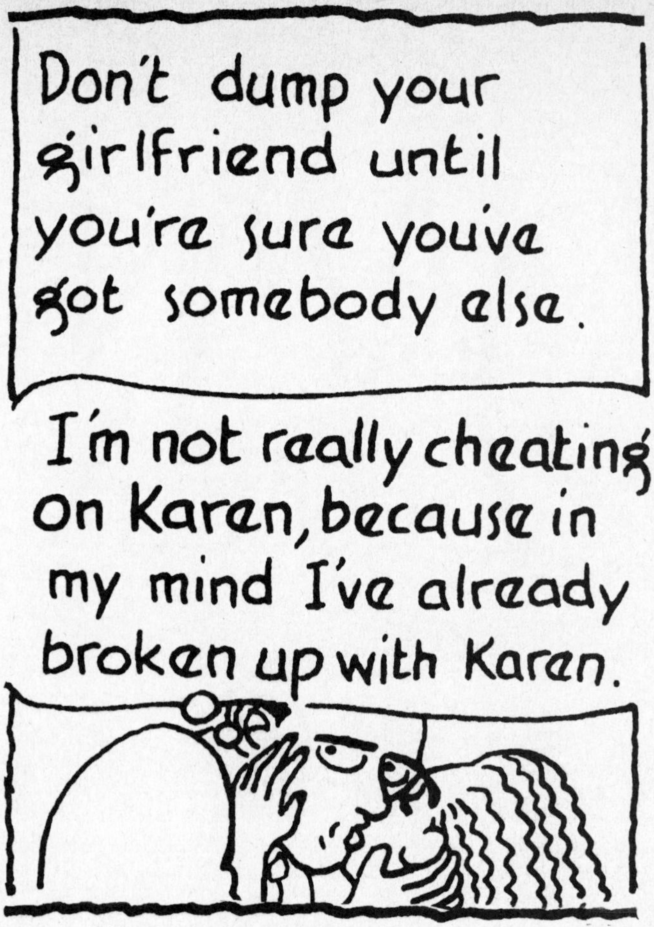
Don't dump your girlfriend until you're sure you've got somebody else.
I'm not really cheating on Karen, because in my mind I've already broken up with Karen.

DON'T GET MARRIED!
If you're not married you're not really cheating on her.

OKAY, SO YOU'RE MARRIED.
You're not really cheating as long as the other woman means nothing to you.

ATTENTION TEENAGERS!

Only old men drink to get drunk. **YOU** should be drinking to test your **stamina!**

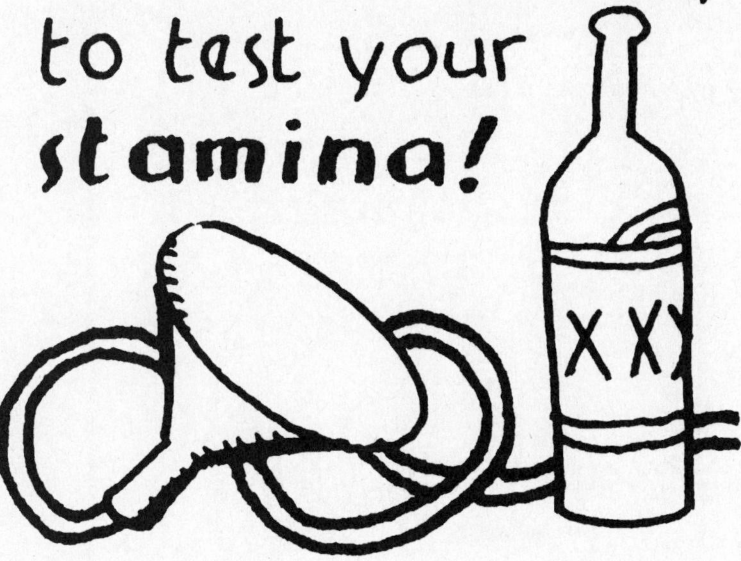

REMEMBER, FELLAS!

GROOMING is for ***Girls!***

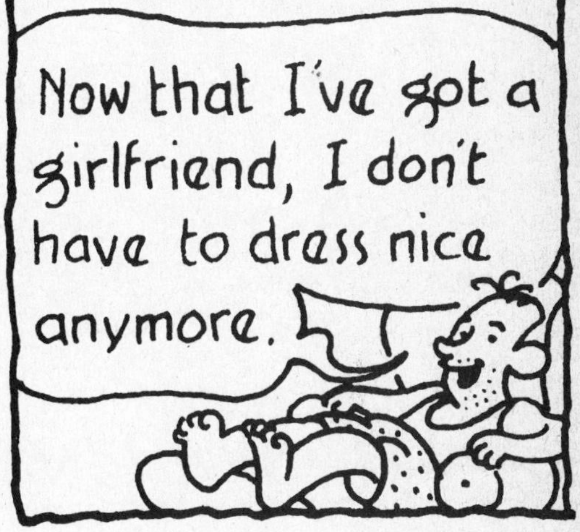
Now that I've got a girlfriend, I don't have to dress nice anymore.

SO YOU'RE FORTY!

Jesus, that means you're married to a woman old enough to be your **mother!**

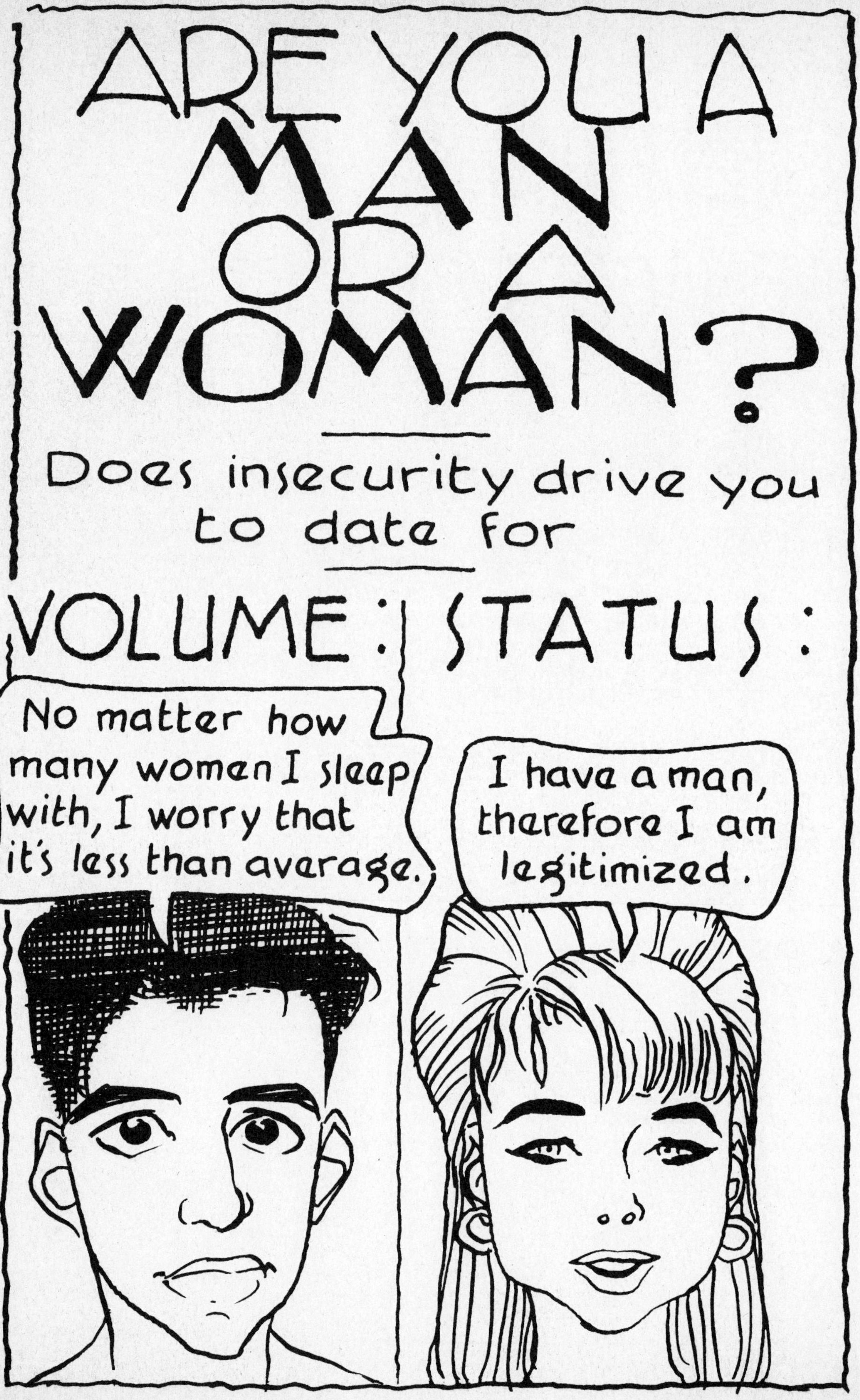
ARE YOU A MAN OR A WOMAN?
Does insecurity drive you to date for
VOLUME:
STATUS:
No matter how many women I sleep with, I worry that it's less than average.
I have a man, therefore I am legitimized.

Kyle Baker

EVERYBODY HATES HIM

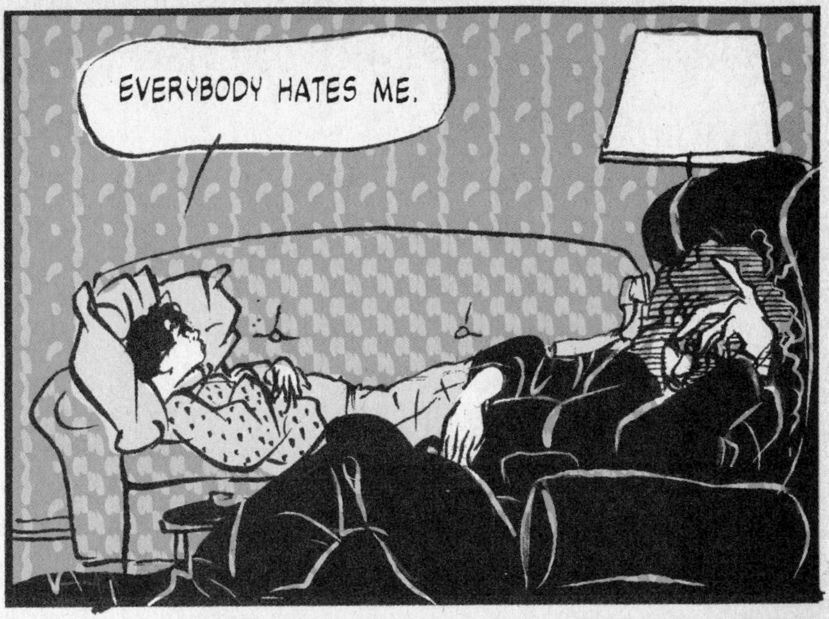

EVERYBODY HATES ME.

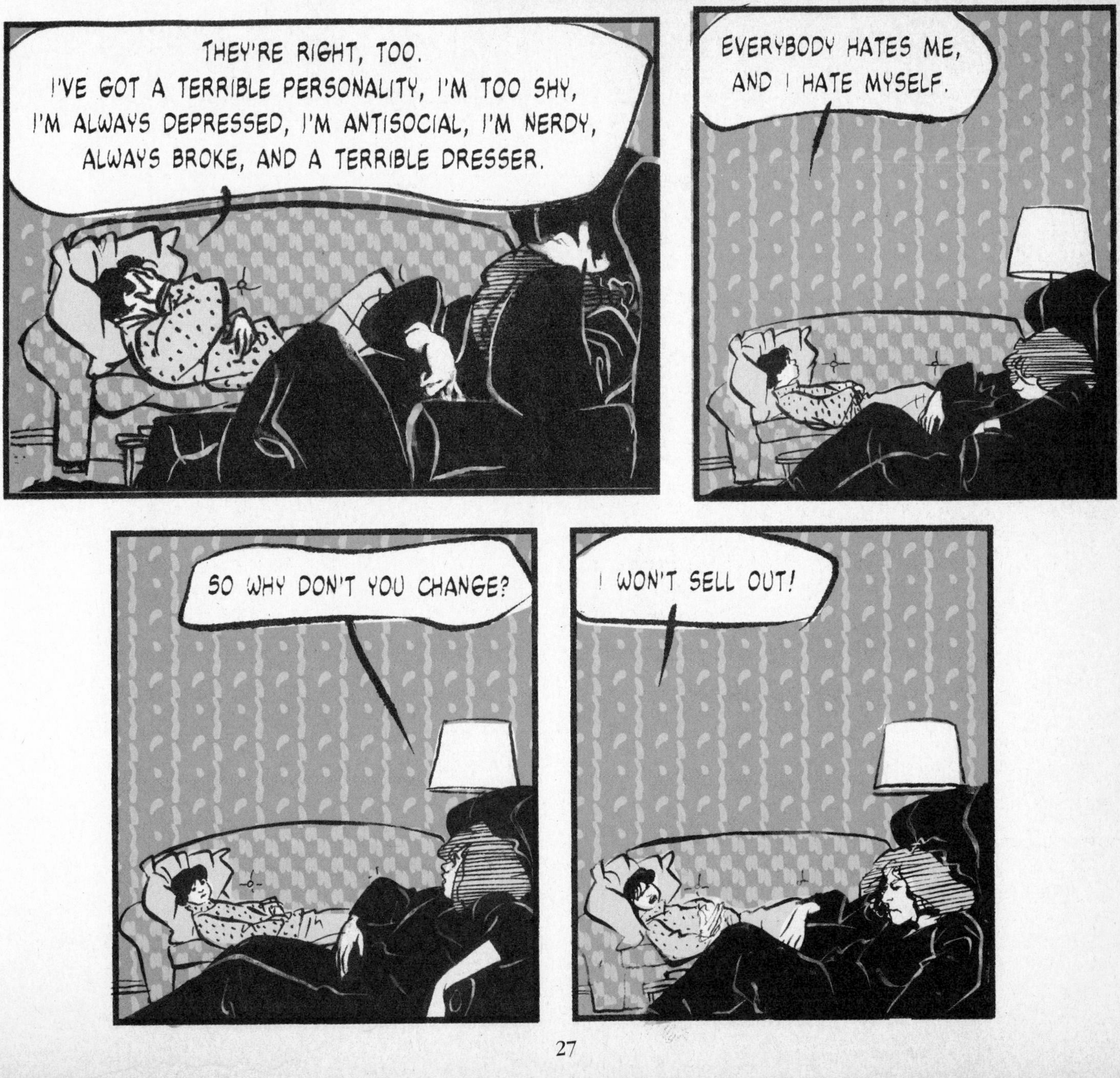

THEY'RE RIGHT, TOO. I'VE GOT A TERRIBLE PERSONALITY, I'M TOO SHY, I'M ALWAYS DEPRESSED, I'M ANTISOCIAL, I'M NERDY, ALWAYS BROKE, AND A TERRIBLE DRESSER.
EVERYBODY HATES ME, AND I HATE MYSELF.
SO WHY DON'T YOU CHANGE?
I WON'T SELL OUT!

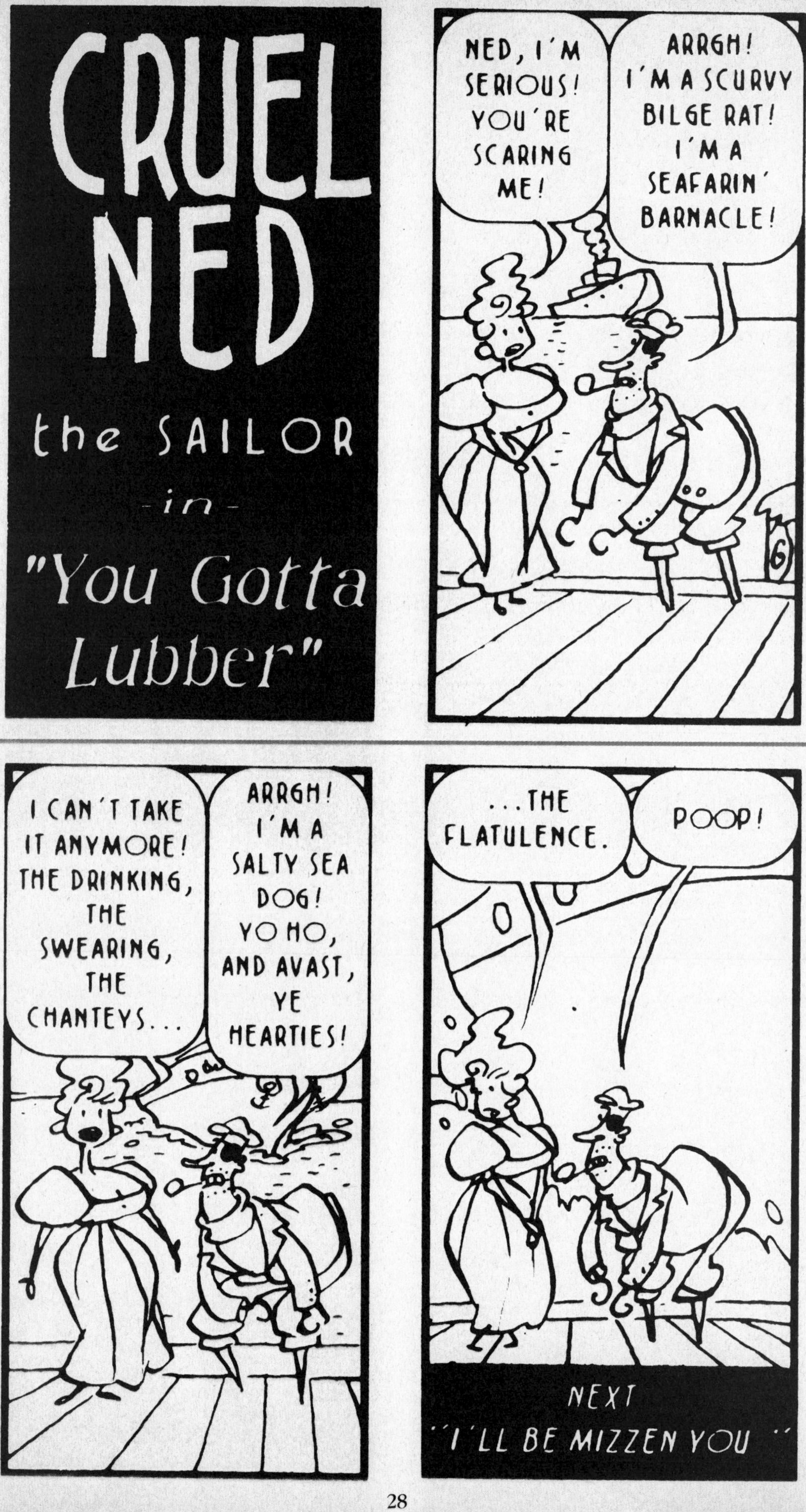
CRUEL NED
the SAILOR
-in-
"You Gotta Lubber"
NED, I'M SERIOUS! YOU'RE SCARING ME!
ARRGH! I'M A SCURVY BILGE RAT! I'M A SEAFARIN' BARNACLE!
I CAN'T TAKE IT ANYMORE! THE DRINKING, THE SWEARING, THE CHANTEYS...
ARRGH! I'M A SALTY SEA DOG! YO HO, AND AVAST, YE HEARTIES!
...THE FLATULENCE.
POOP!
NEXT
"I'LL BE MIZZEN YOU"

KYLE BAKER

MADAME OONA
The Fighting Teen Psychic
PREDICTS YOUR FUTURE!

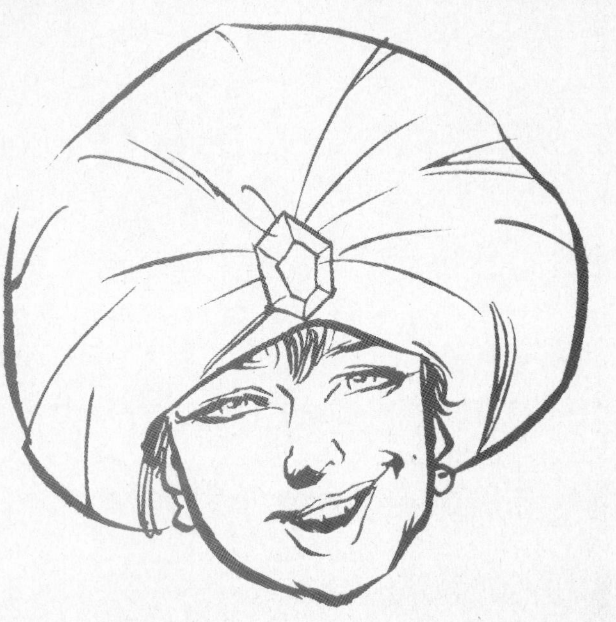

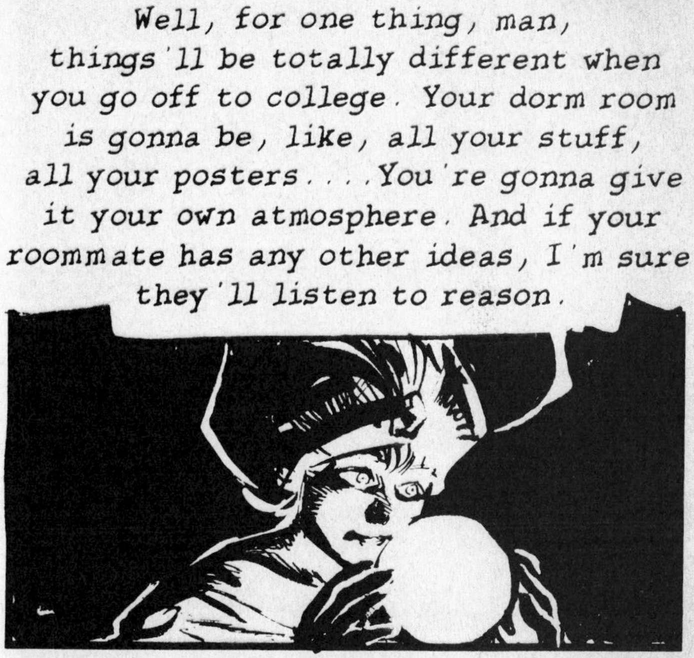
Well, for one thing, man, things'll be totally different when you go off to college. Your dorm room is gonna be, like, all your stuff, all your posters....You're gonna give it your own atmosphere. And if your roommate has any other ideas, I'm sure they'll listen to reason.

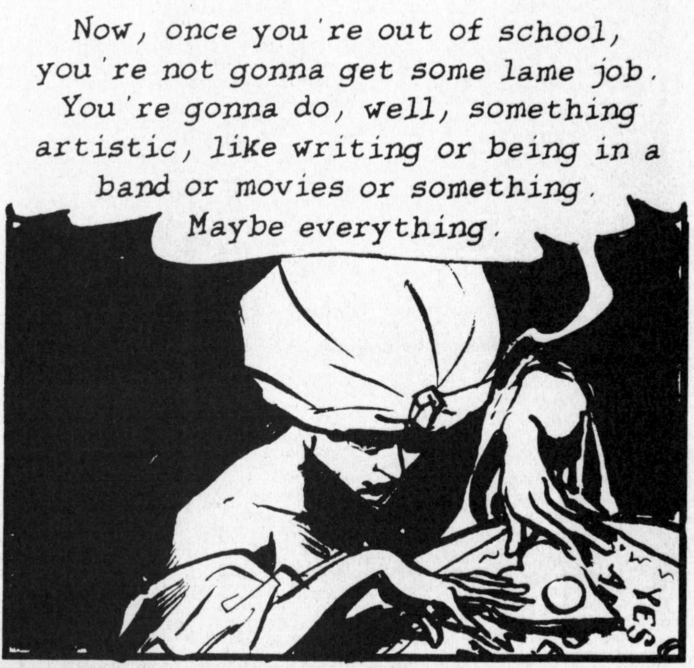
Now, once you're out of school, you're not gonna get some lame job. You're gonna do, well, something artistic, like writing or being in a band or movies or something. Maybe everything.
YES

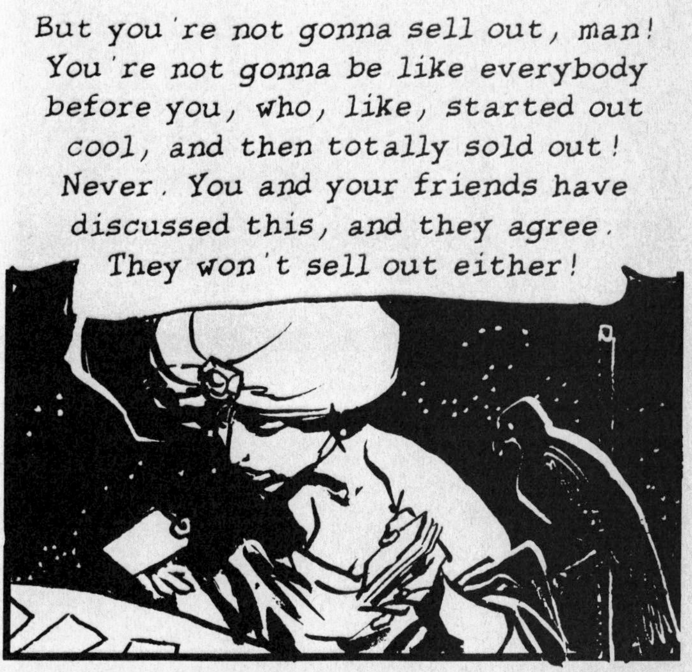
But you're not gonna sell out, man! You're not gonna be like everybody before you, who, like, started out cool, and then totally sold out! Never. You and your friends have discussed this, and they agree. They won't sell out either!

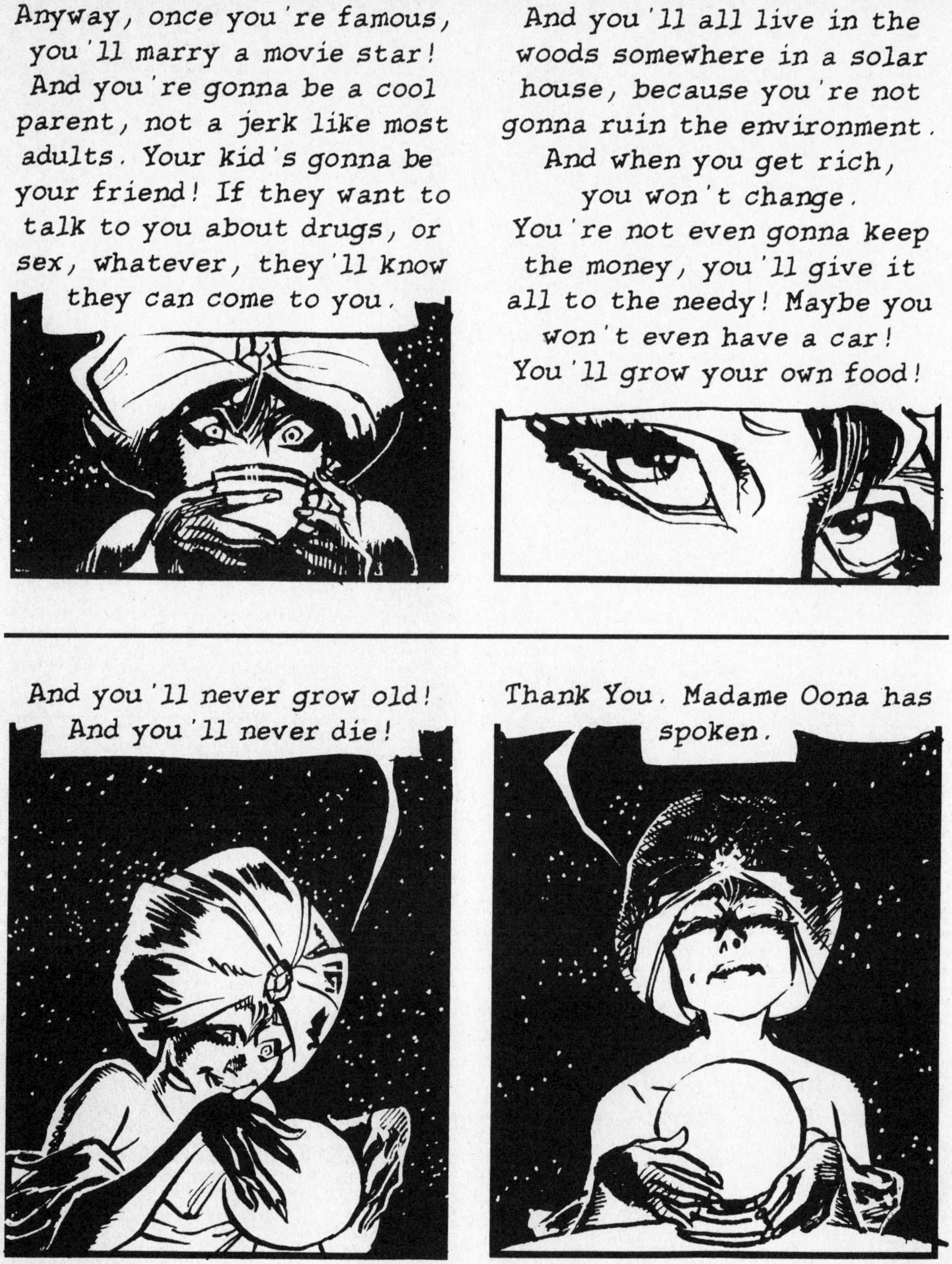
Anyway, once you're famous, you'll marry a movie star! And you're gonna be a cool parent, not a jerk like most adults. Your kid's gonna be your friend! If they want to talk to you about drugs, or sex, whatever, they'll know they can come to you.
And you'll all live in the woods somewhere in a solar house, because you're not gonna ruin the environment. And when you get rich, you won't change. You're not even gonna keep the money, you'll give it all to the needy! Maybe you won't even have a car! You'll grow your own food!
And you'll never grow old! And you'll never die!
Thank You. Madame Oona has spoken.

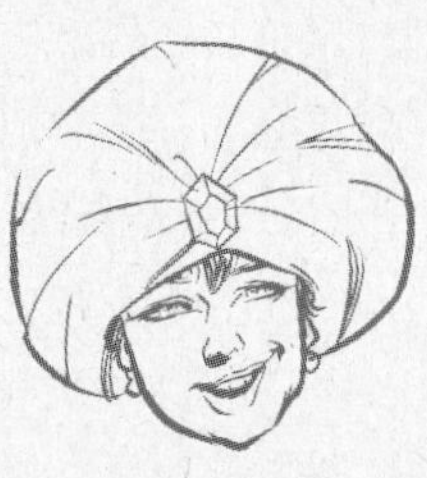

EVERYTHING'S FINE

GET BACK TO WORK

WISH YOU WERE A BLACK MAN!

Yes, *every white man secretly yearns to be black!* Mailer did it! Kerouac, too!

Now *you* can utter this ludicrous phrase with a straight face:

"Actually, I think of myself as a black man trapped in a white man's body."

Buy some *black guy* clothes! Play some *rap* or *jazz* records! Call your friends "Homeboy" and "Mon" while smoking dope!

Go up to one of your black friends and say,

"You know, man, when I look at you, I don't think of you as a black guy, you're just a normal guy, you know?"

BLACK MEN! Don't be left out of this exciting new trend! Remember- *every black man secretly yearns to be black also!*

I know what you're thinking: "But Kyle, I already *am* black!"

33

You FOOL! If lineage or pigmentation were the sole determinants of blackness, white guys wouldn't stand a chance! White people's constant assertion that *anybody* can be black implies that, more than color, it is class, slang, and musicality that determine one's race.

"But Kyle," you ask, "shouldn't I be offended by the implication that all one needs to do to be black is steal, play music, take drugs, play basketball, or speak bad English?"

Of course not, silly! That's why the African-American is the only race that has been in this country for over ten generations without losing its accent! Blacks wear their ability to speak in eighteenth-century sharecropper's dialect as a badge of honor! Blacks are the only people who voluntarily write songs depicting their race as gangsters and pimps!

"But Kyle," you try again, feebly, "all I really want to do is use my college education to get a good-paying job so I can buy a decent house for my wife and kids."

What are you, **white?**

KYLE BAKER

BE LESS GULLIBLE!

SEND $5,000.00 C/O THIS ADDRESS.
ALLOW 6-8 MONTHS FOR DELIVERY.

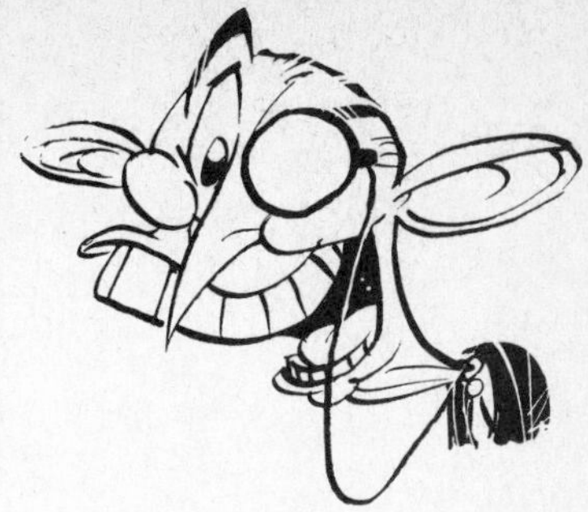

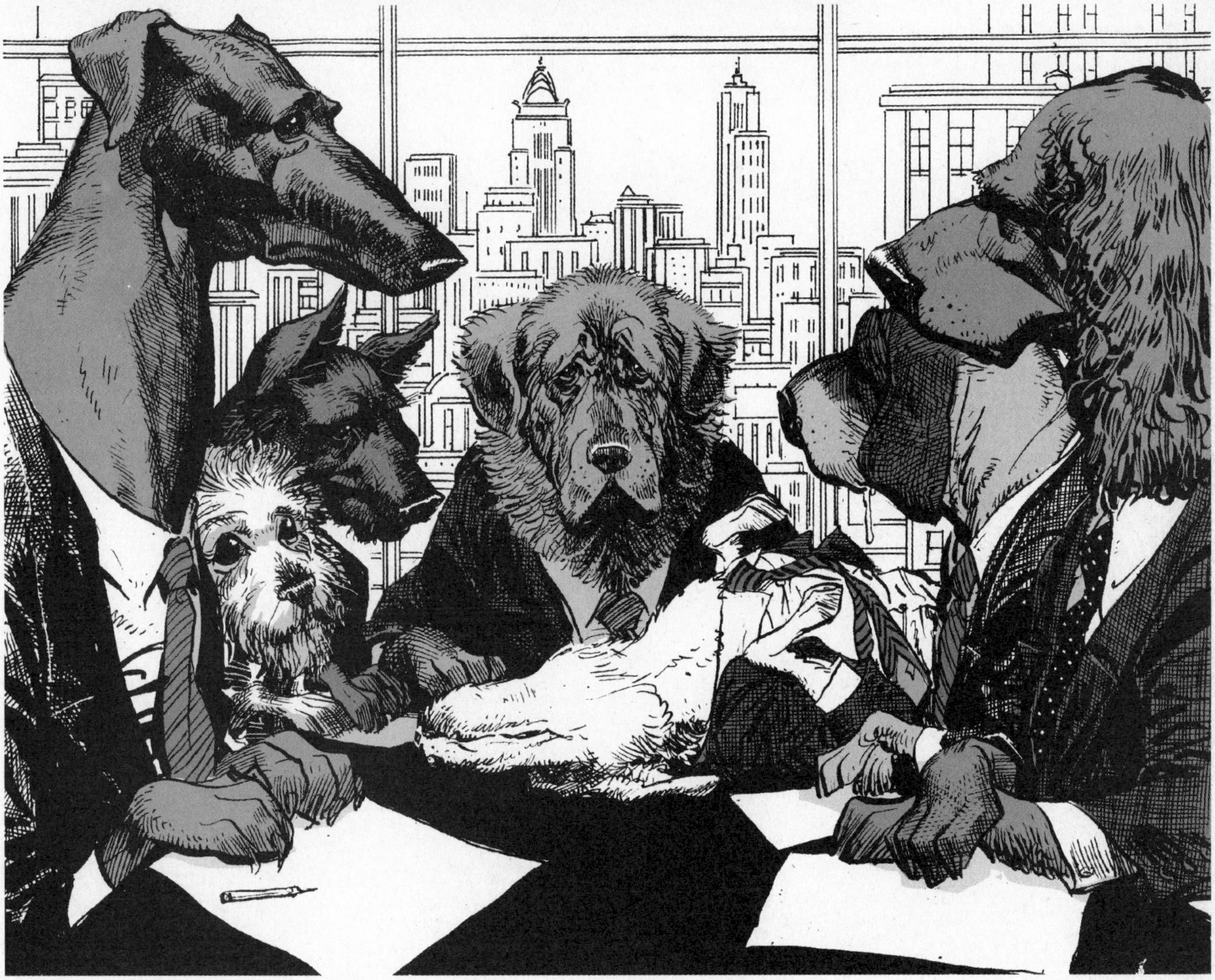

AND NOW, WE PROUDLY PRESENT—

A MAN EATING LIKE THERE'S NO TOMORROW

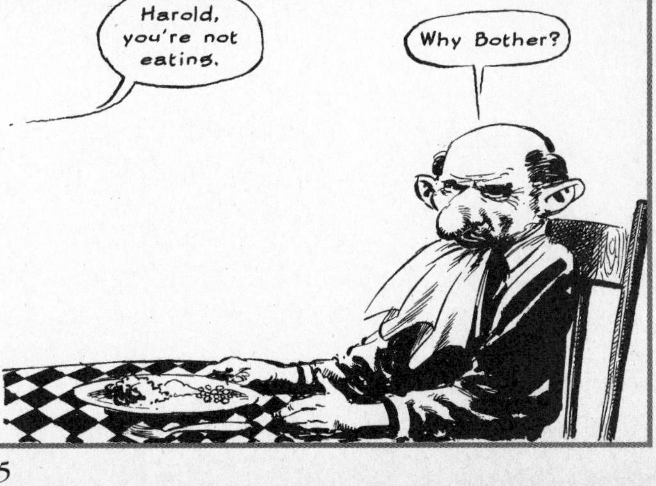
Harold, you're not eating.
Why Bother?

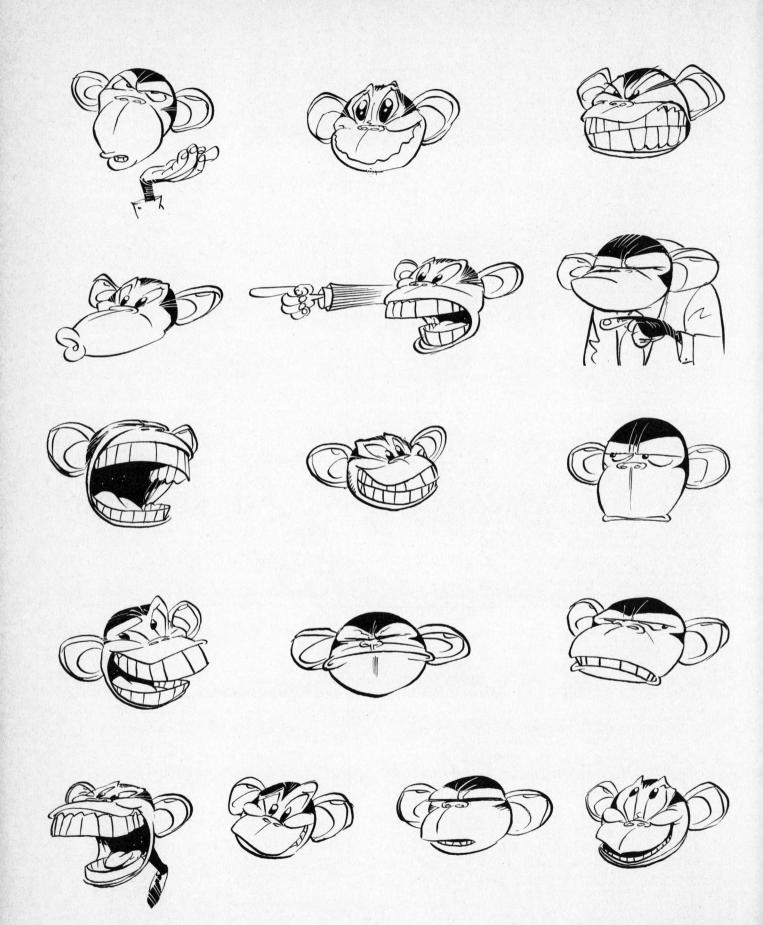

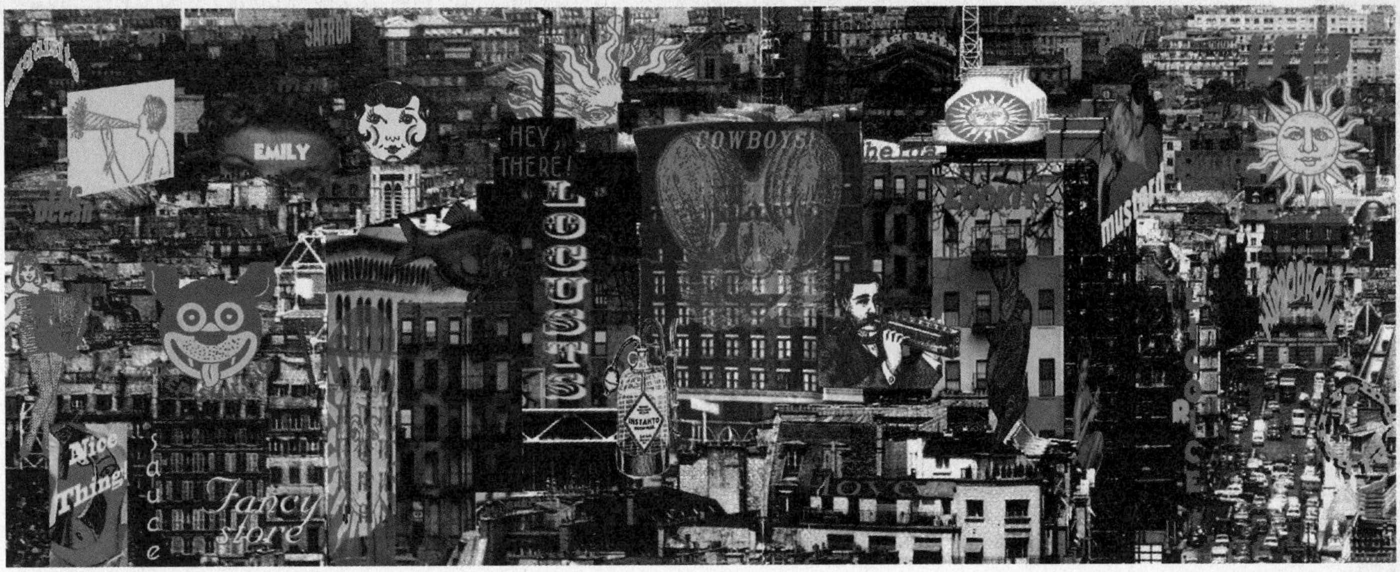
SAFRON
EMILY
HEY, THERE!
LOCUSTS
COWBOYS!
Nice Things
Fancy store

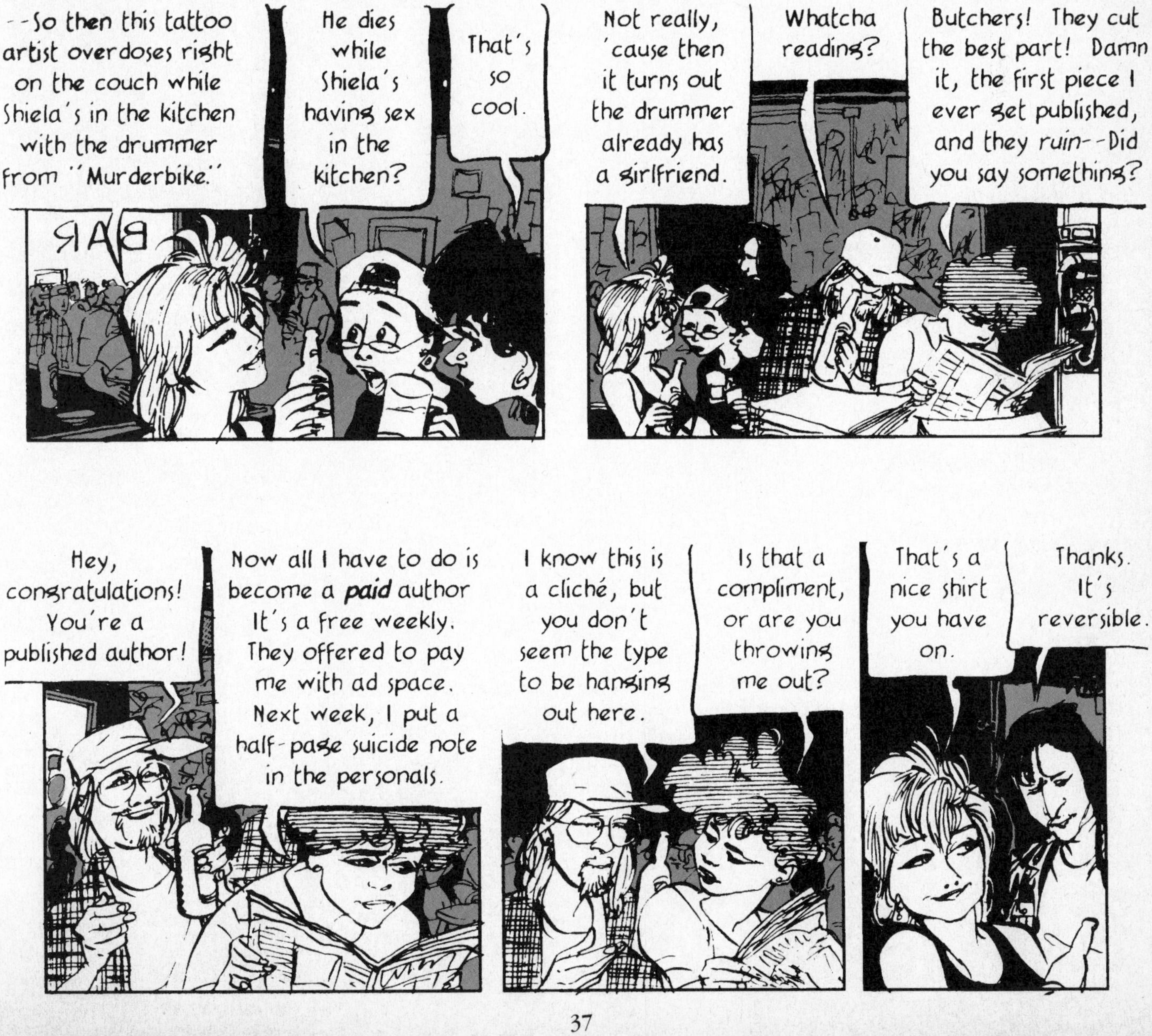
--So then this tattoo artist overdoses right on the couch while Shiela's in the kitchen with the drummer from "Murderbike."
He dies while Shiela's having sex in the kitchen?
That's so cool.
BAR
Not really, 'cause then it turns out the drummer already has a girlfriend.
Whatcha reading?
Butchers! They cut the best part! Damn it, the first piece I ever get published, and they *ruin*--Did you say something?
Hey, congratulations! You're a published author!
Now all I have to do is become a ***paid*** author. It's a free weekly. They offered to pay me with ad space. Next week, I put a half-page suicide note in the personals.
I know this is a cliché, but you don't seem the type to be hanging out here.
Is that a compliment, or are you throwing me out?
That's a nice shirt you have on.
Thanks. It's reversible.

Reversible? | Yeah, it's white when I wash it. | Well, he is one of my favorite authors, but I kind of see your point-- | I mean, don't you think that the Beat writers were actually trading one fraudulent value system for another, equally spurious, standard? | Yes, but at the same time, their physical wanderings were symbolic representations of internal, spiritual journeys-- | I'm tellin' you, man, you haven't really read "Where's Waldo" until you've read it on acid. | Really?

Yeah, man. I couldn't speak or make a fist for three weeks, but it's totally worth it! | You don't know what a joy it is to have an intelligent conversation for a change! | I know what you mean. Sometimes I think there's got to be more than this. All people seem to care about here is how somebody looks, or-- | You know, I've been wanting to ask you something. | Yes? | Your friend, the blonde, is she seeing anyone?

THE NEXT DAY Look at this place! It's like all they had in the fifties was Elvis and Coca-Cola! Christ, a fifties nostalgia joint. I thought New Yorkers were hipper than this. | The fifties were America's one and only golden era. | In the fifties, dissidents were branded Communists and blacklisted, we were at the brink of nuclear war, and women and minorities had no rights whatsoever.

38

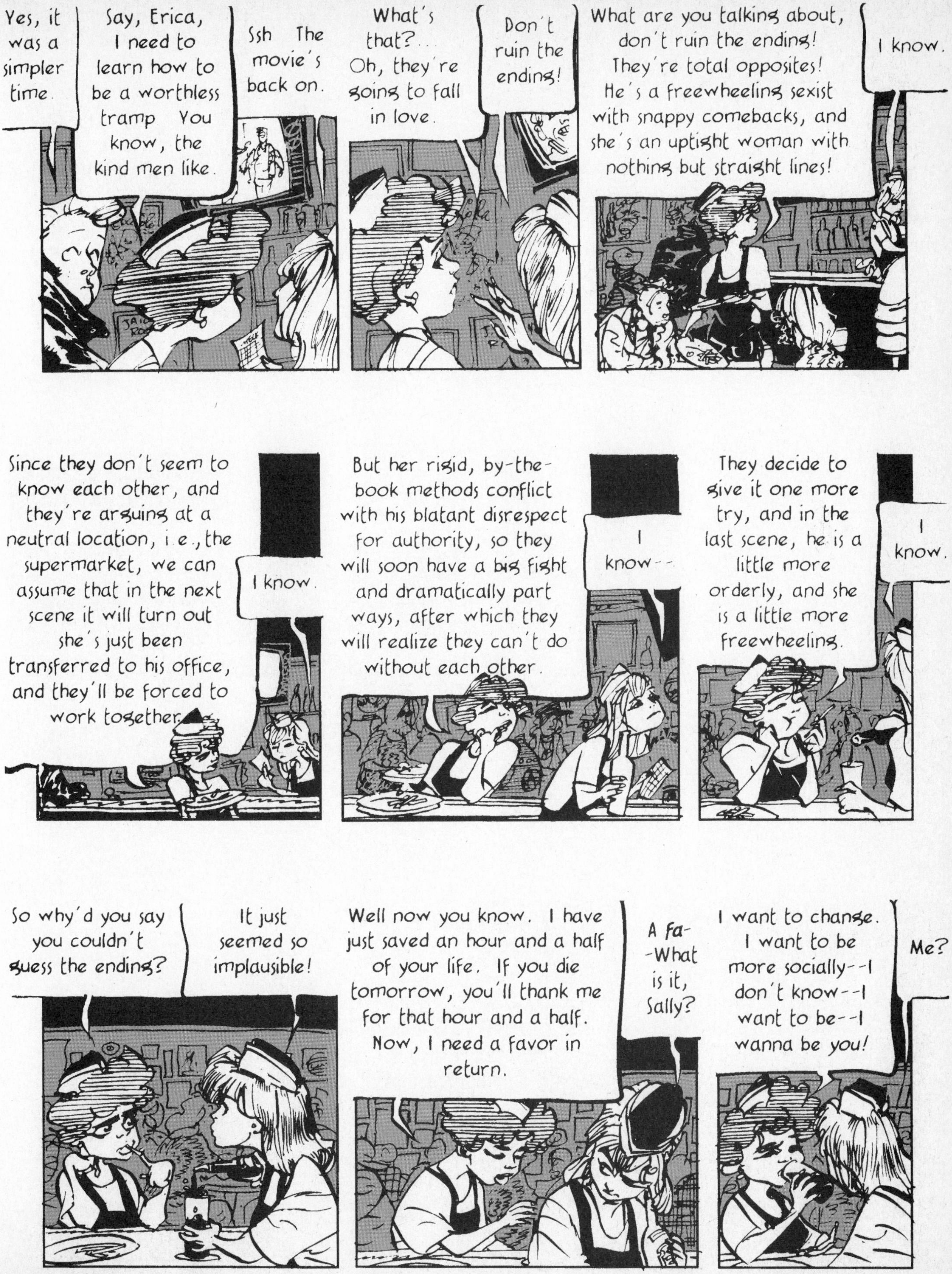
Yes, it was a simpler time.
Say, Erica, I need to learn how to be a worthless tramp. You know, the kind men like.
Ssh. The movie's back on.
What's that?... Oh, they're going to fall in love.
Don't ruin the ending!
What are you talking about, don't ruin the ending! They're total opposites! He's a freewheeling sexist with snappy comebacks, and she's an uptight woman with nothing but straight lines!
I know.
Since they don't seem to know each other, and they're arguing at a neutral location, i.e., the supermarket, we can assume that in the next scene it will turn out she's just been transferred to his office, and they'll be forced to work together.
I know.
But her rigid, by-the-book methods conflict with his blatant disrespect for authority, so they will soon have a big fight and dramatically part ways, after which they will realize they can't do without each other.
I know--
They decide to give it one more try, and in the last scene, he is a little more orderly, and she is a little more freewheeling.
I know.
So why'd you say you couldn't guess the ending?
It just seemed so implausible!
Well now you know. I have just saved an hour and a half of your life. If you die tomorrow, you'll thank me for that hour and a half. Now, I need a favor in return.
A Fa- -What is it, Sally?
I want to change. I want to be more socially--I don't know--I want to be--I wanna be *you!*
Me?

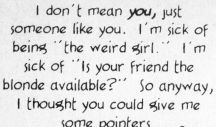

I don't mean **you,** just someone like you. I'm sick of being "the weird girl." I'm sick of "Is your friend the blonde available?" So anyway, I thought you could give me some pointers.

Excuse me, I know it's none of my business, but I think your only real problem is a lack of self-esteem.

She's right You don't have to act like somebody else just to be liked.

Really?

And you don't have to go along with the crowd to be cool.

Yeah?

Just be yourself. Everyone has something that makes them special. What is it that makes **you** special?

Well, um...

I just had my first story published!

I got my dick pierced.

Wow!

That's so cool!

So, like, f'rinstance, those shoes Where would I get shoes like those?

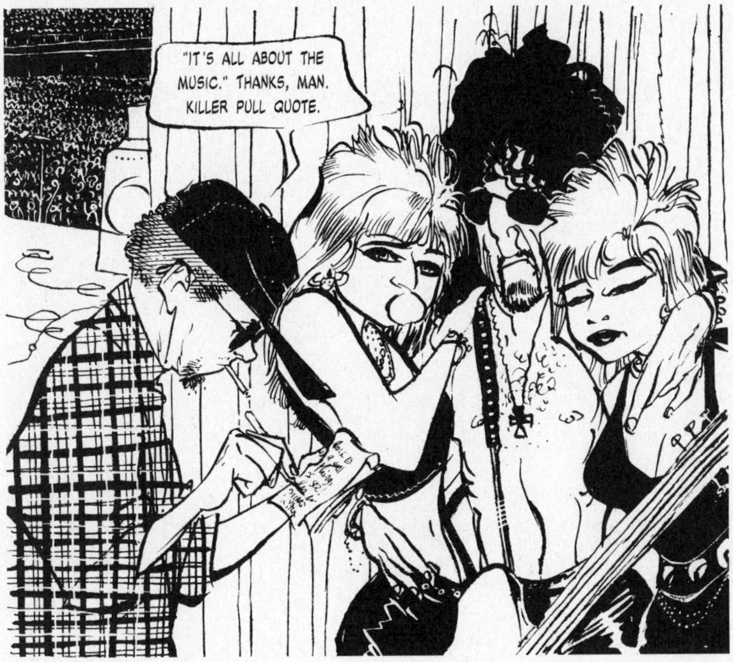
"IT'S ALL ABOUT THE MUSIC." THANKS, MAN. KILLER PULL QUOTE.

I'm gonna get a guitar, man,
And never learn to play.
No one will know it's just for show,
A way to get a lay.
I'm gonna get an earring, man,
And grow my hair real long.
I'll hit the string and start to sing
My groovy rebel song.
I'll be a phony rebel, see,
A hippie like my dad.
And get to dick suburban chicks
Who want to think they're bad.

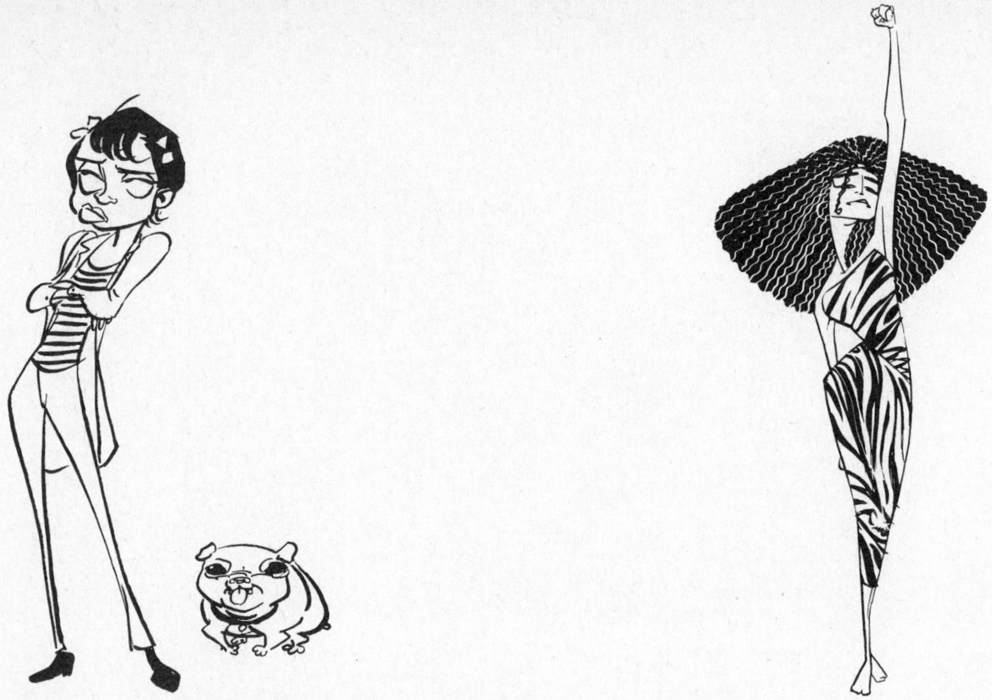

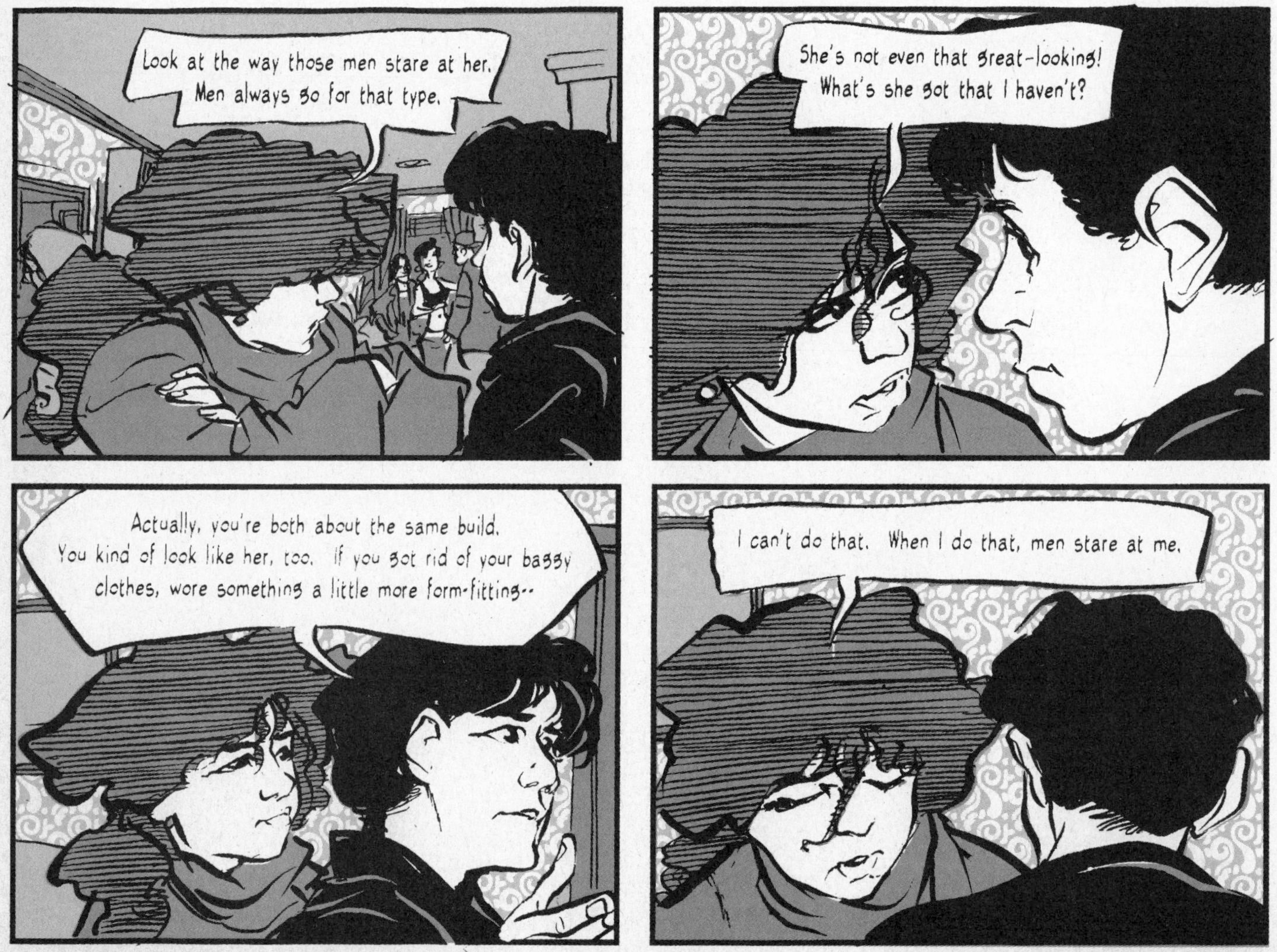
Look at the way those men stare at her. Men always go for that type.
She's not even that great-looking! What's she got that I haven't?
Actually, you're both about the same build. You kind of look like her, too. If you got rid of your baggy clothes, wore something a little more form-fitting--
I can't do that. When I do that, men stare at me.

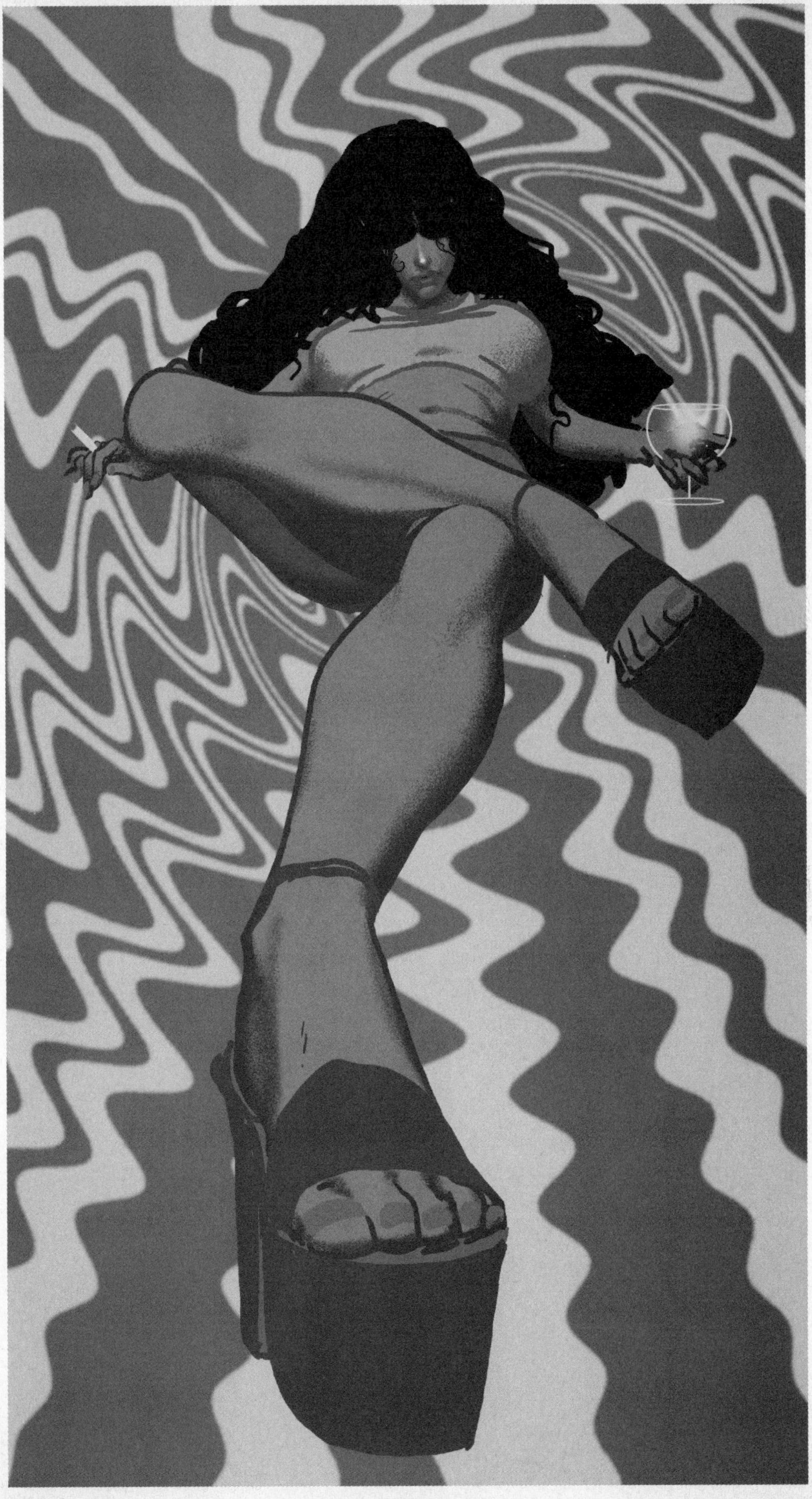

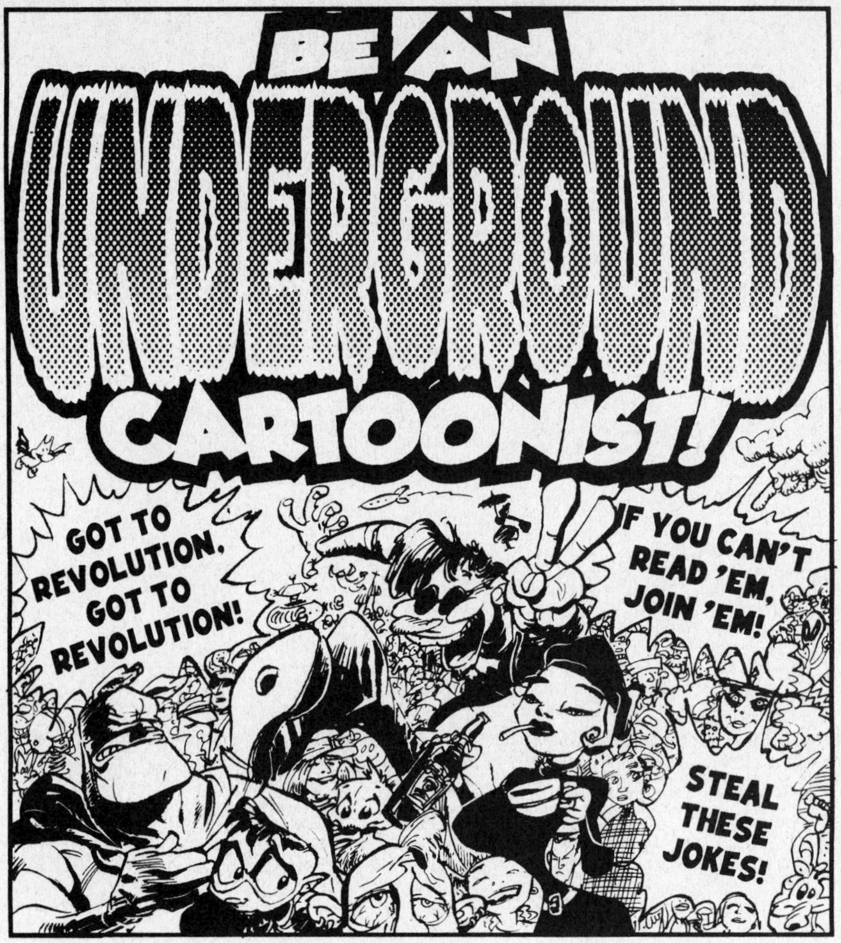
BE AN
UNDERGROUND
CARTOONIST!
GOT TO REVOLUTION, GOT TO REVOLUTION!
IF YOU CAN'T READ 'EM, JOIN 'EM!
STEAL THESE JOKES!

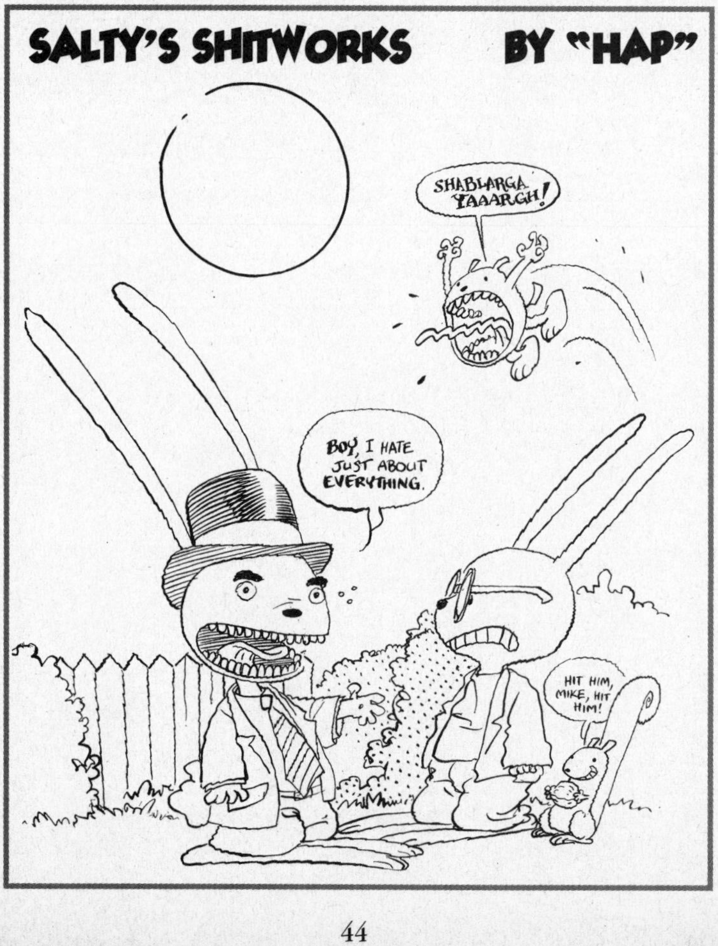
SALTY'S SHITWORKS BY "HAP"
SHABLARGA YAAARGH!
BOY, I HATE JUST ABOUT EVERYTHING.
HIT HIM, MIKE, HIT HIM!

Oh, there will come a day when all
  Our suffering will cease.
Yes, there will come a day when all
  The world will be at peace.
Some day it will not matter if
  You're yellow, brown or red,
For some day, people, some day
  Everyone will be quite dead.
Oh, if you're poor or ill or maimed
  Or even brokenhearted,
Remember that you soon will be
  Among the dear departed.
But if you're graced with wealth and strength,
  And nothing seems beyond you,
Your flesh will rot, your spirit fade,
  Back to the love that spawned you.

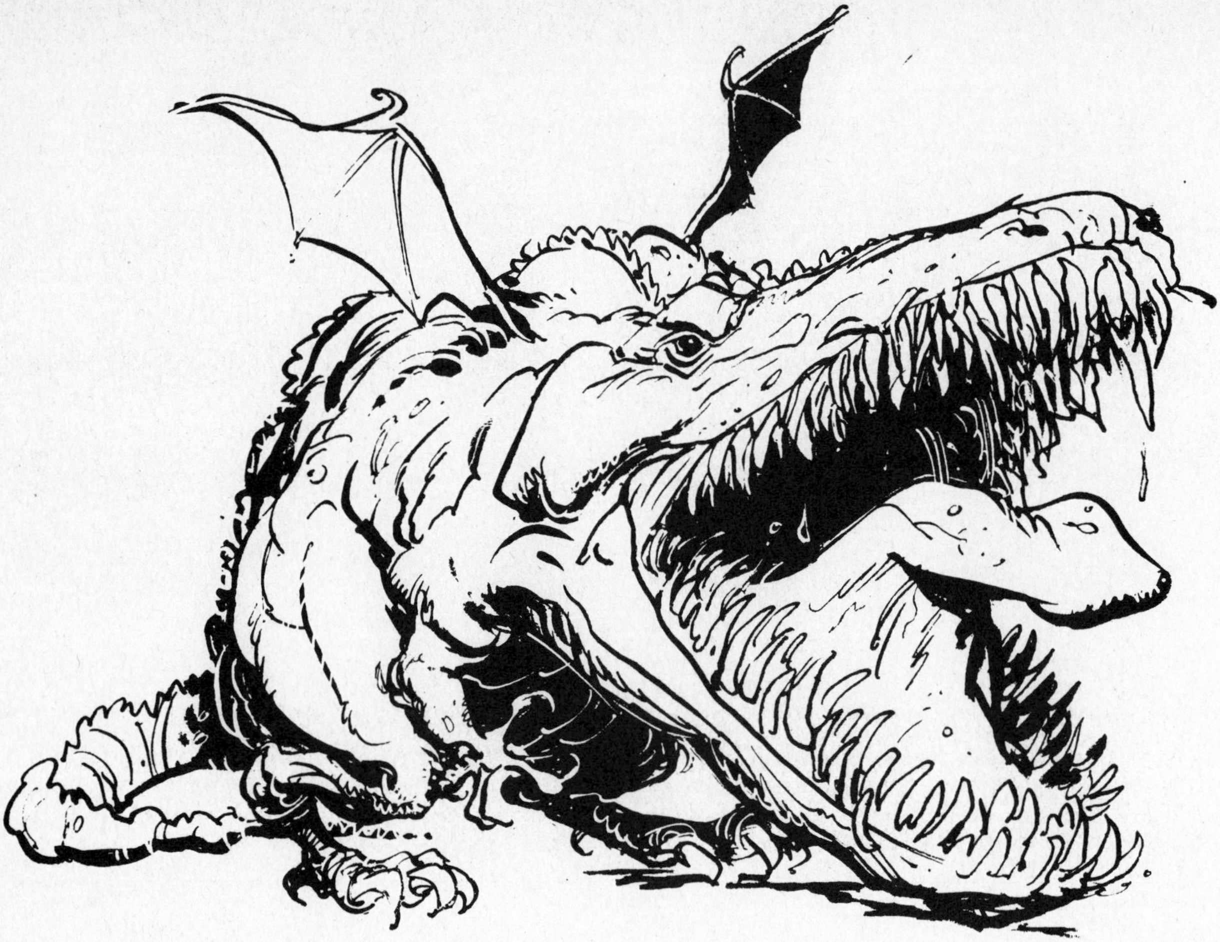

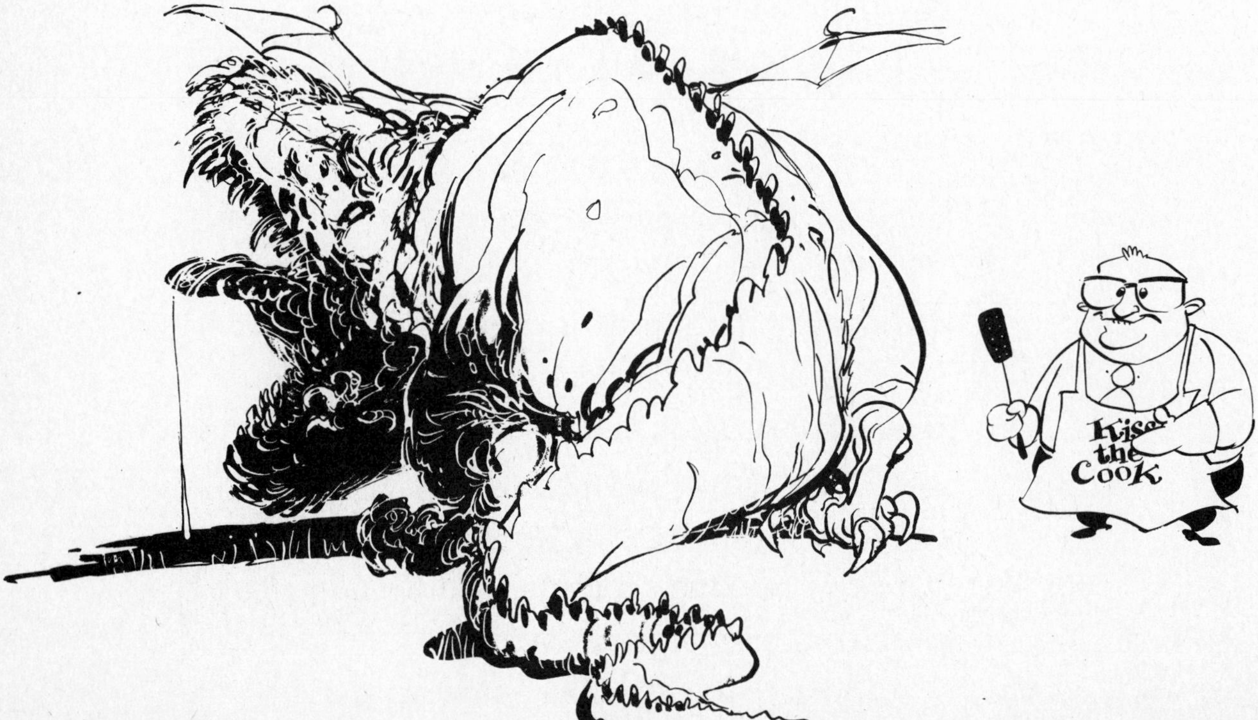
Kiss the Cook

POLITICS!

Dubya

Bill Clinton

The Nixons

Dubya

Jesse Helms

Newt Gingrich

Pat Robertson

Louis Farrakhan

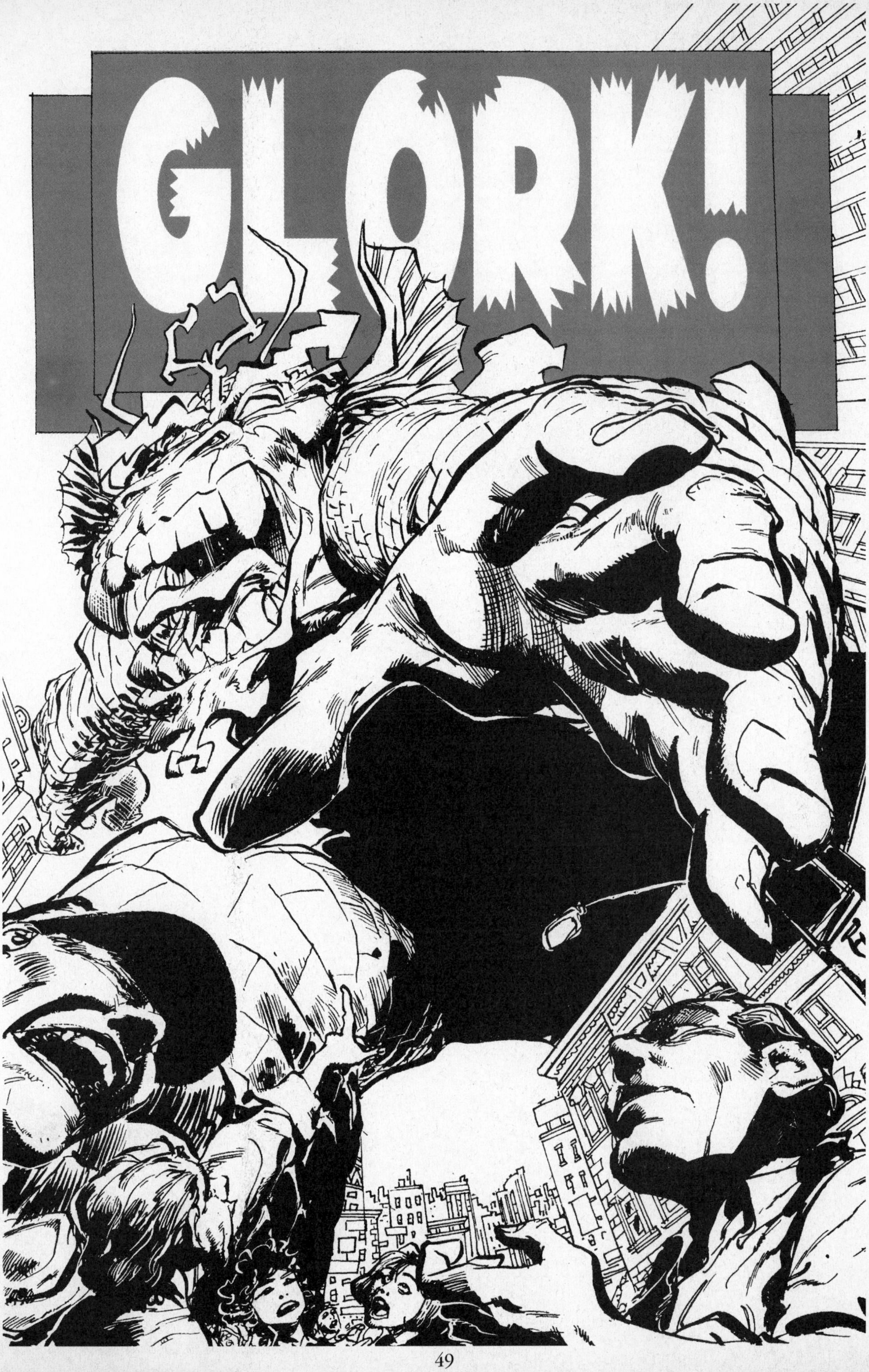
GLORK!

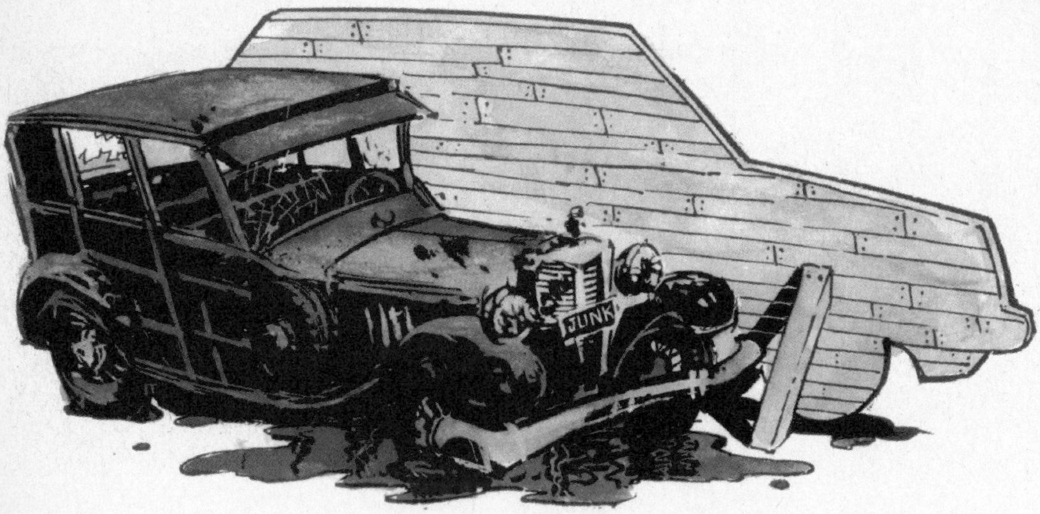
JUNK

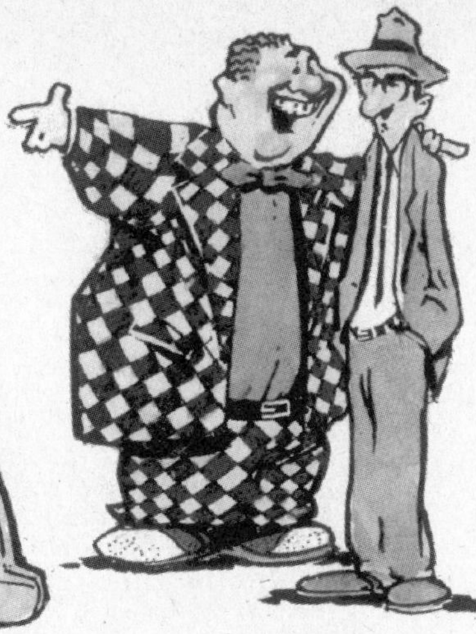

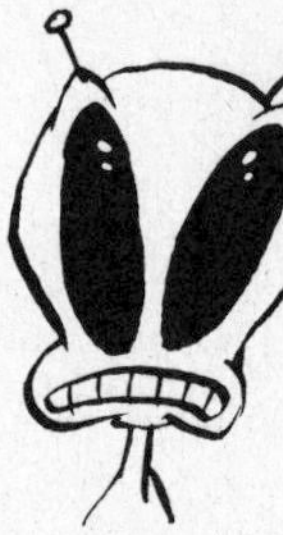

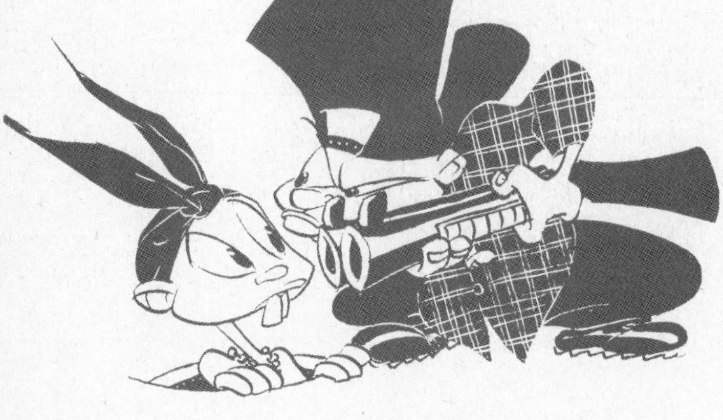

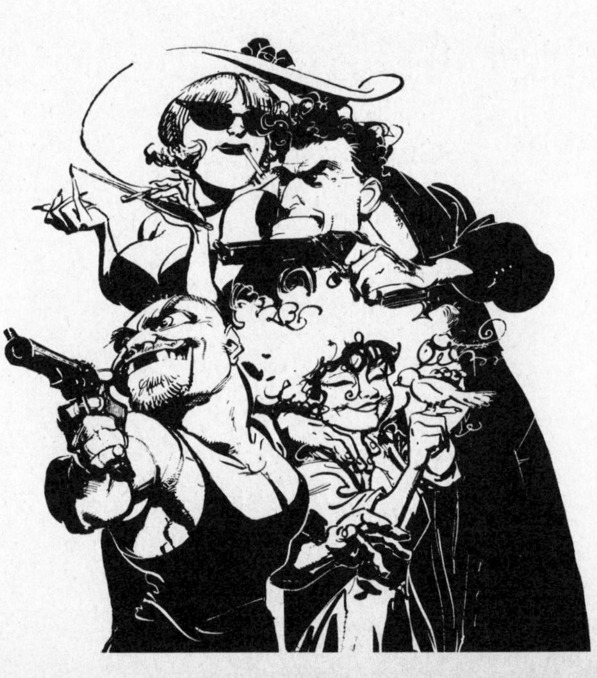

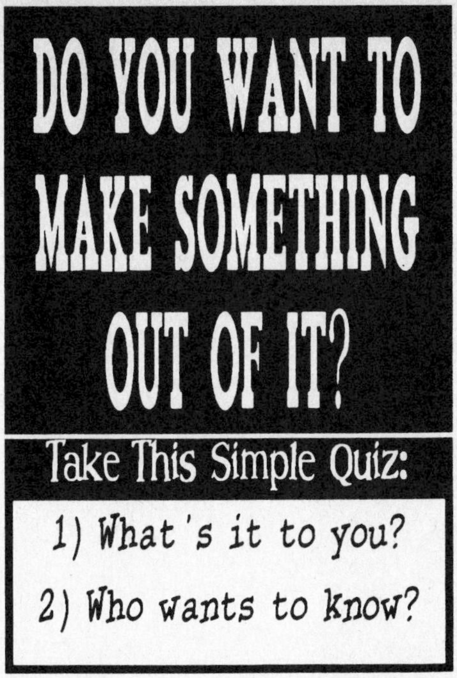
DO YOU WANT TO MAKE SOMETHING OUT OF IT?
Take This Simple Quiz:
1) What's it to you?
2) Who wants to know?

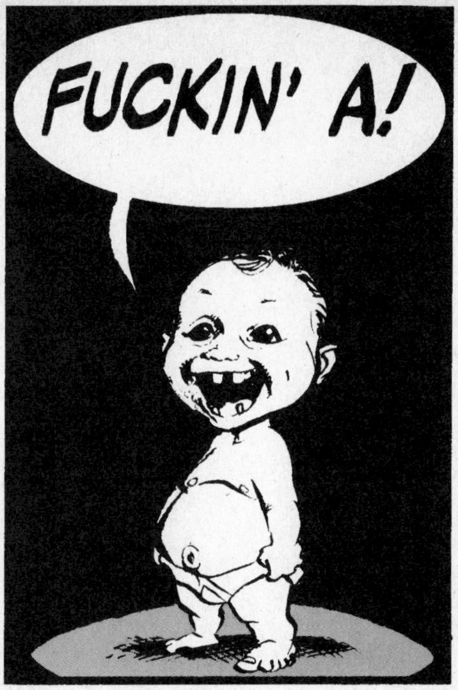
FUCKIN' A!

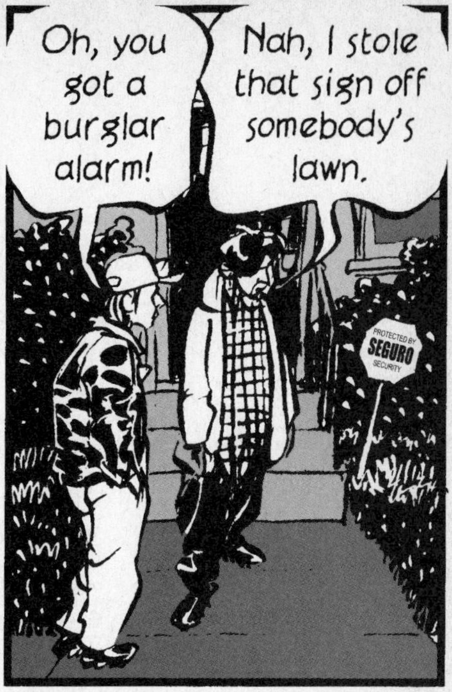
Oh, you got a burglar alarm!
Nah, I stole that sign off somebody's lawn.
PROTECTED BY SEGURO SECURITY

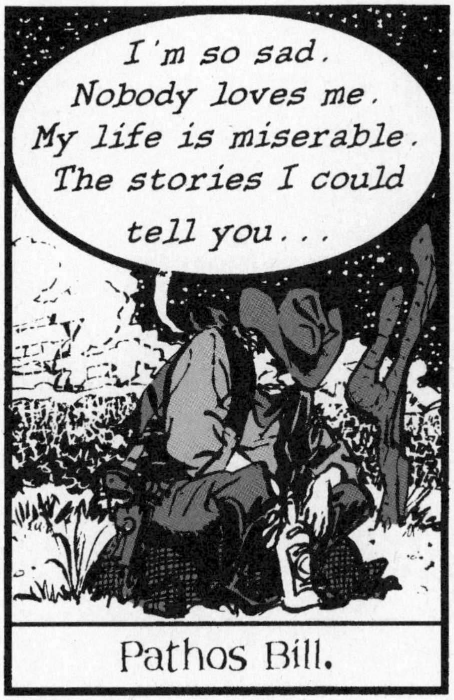
I'm so sad. Nobody loves me. My life is miserable. The stories I could tell you...
Pathos Bill.

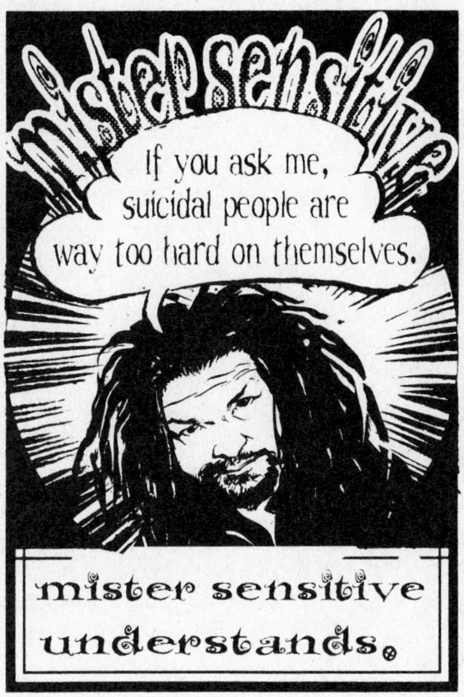
mister sensitive
If you ask me, suicidal people are way too hard on themselves.
mister sensitive understands.

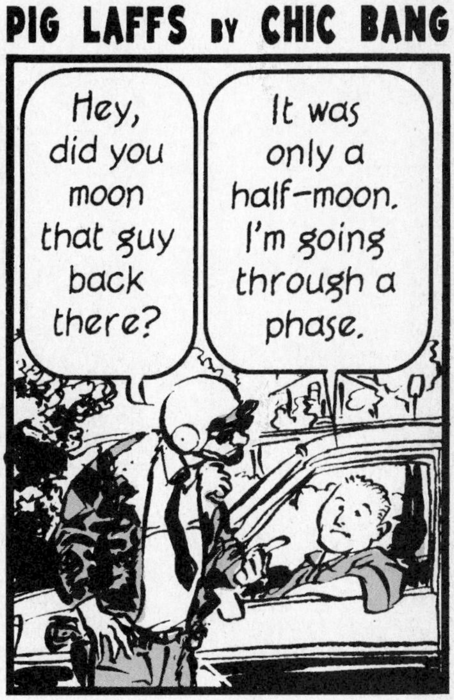
PIG LAFFS BY CHIC BANG
Hey, did you moon that guy back there?
It was only a half-moon. I'm going through a phase.

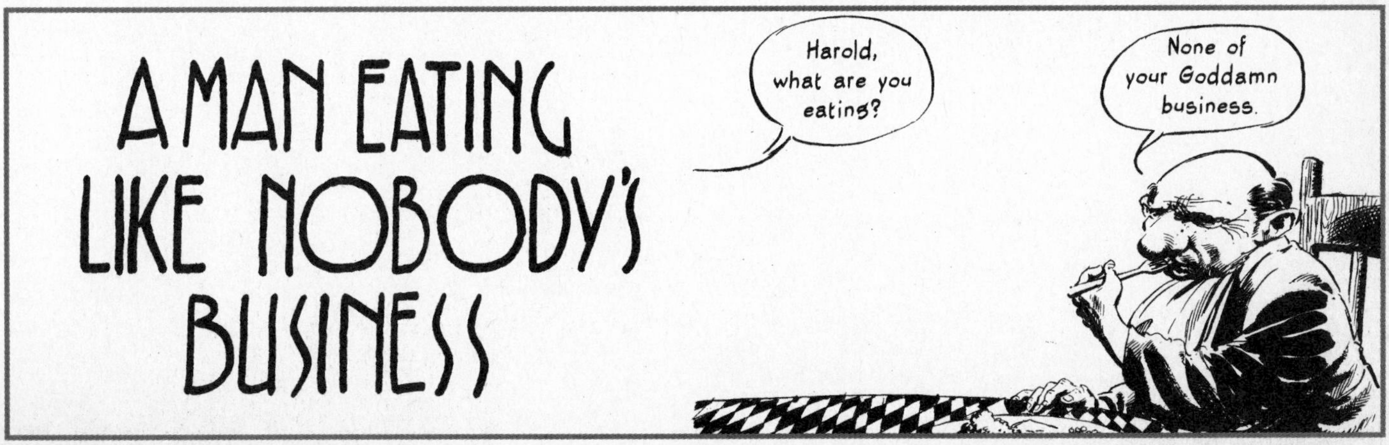
A MAN EATING LIKE NOBODY'S BUSINESS
Harold, what are you eating?
None of your Goddamn business.

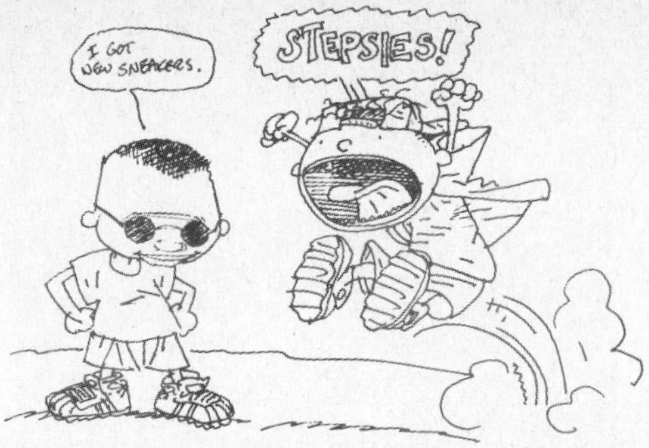
I GOT NEW SNEAKERS.
STEPSIES!

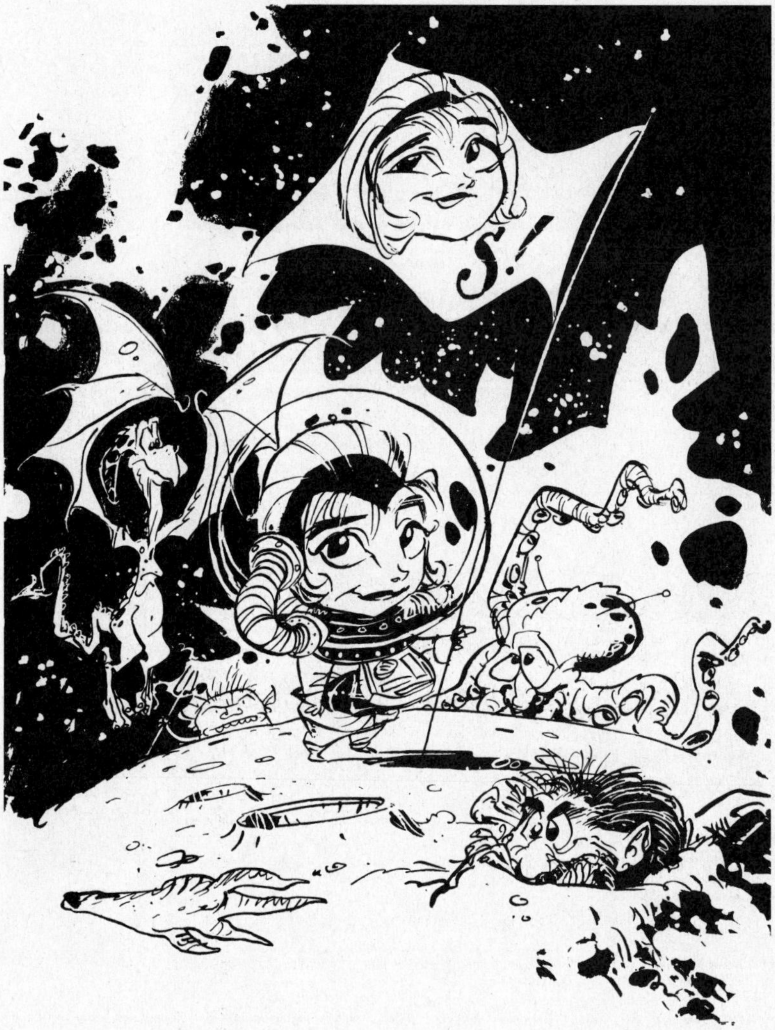
S!

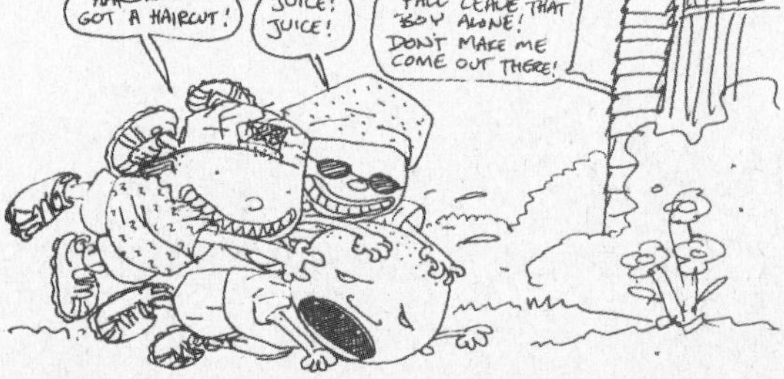
AARON GOT A HAIRCUT!
JUICE! JUICE!
Y'ALL LEAVE THAT BOY ALONE! DON'T MAKE ME COME OUT THERE!

Kyle Baker

LESTER FENTON'S DAUGHTERS

Kyle Baker

HAPPY HOUR

Excuse me, do you know what time it is?

Excuse me, do you have a light?

Uh. 7:30.

Thanks.

Hm. He's gone back to reading his magazine. That means either he's not interested, or he didn't understand that my question was actually a veiled, though transparent, come-on. Either that, or he did understand, and is just too shy to follow up. I'd better try again.

I notice you're reading the Gallery Guide. Are you an artist?

What? Oh, yeah, uh...wait, I've got one somewhere-- hold on. No, really, I had it a minute ago...

Wow, she's completely thrown by that request. That means either she digs me, or she's a flake. Her attempt to convince me that she really does have a light, in spite of the fact that she's holding a lit cigarette, as though she were afraid that I might think less of her if it turned out that she didn't have one, could be construed as a fear of missing an opportunity to talk to me, or she could just be insane.

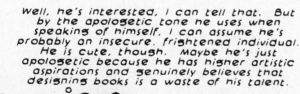

What? Oh, uh--no, not really. Well, kind of. I un I design books.

Well, he's interested, I can tell that. But by the apologetic tone he uses when speaking of himself, I can assume he's probably an insecure, frightened individual. He is cute, though. Maybe he's just apologetic because he has higher artistic aspirations and genuinely believes that designing books is a waste of his talent.

Oh, really? What kind of books?

Here you go, I'm sorry. I had a lighter, but I don't know what happened to it. I'm not usually this disorganized, you know. Okay, actually, I am, but--

Good grief. In spite of her fashionable clothes and good looks, she is obviously insecure. Of course, maybe she's just had a few drinks, maybe she's not totally nuts.

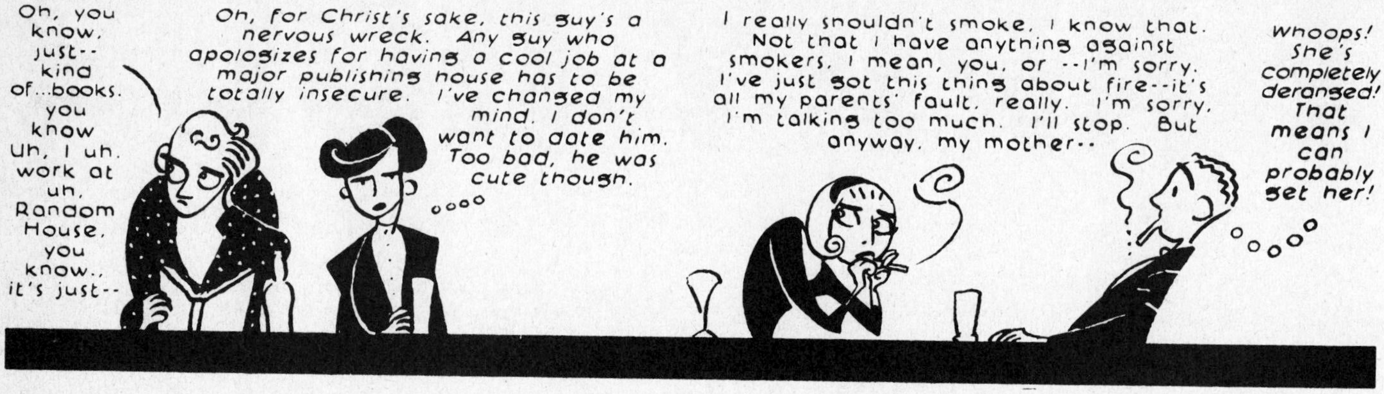
Oh, you know, just--kind of...books. you know Uh, I uh. work at uh, Random House, you know., it's just--
Oh, for Christ's sake, this guy's a nervous wreck. Any guy who apologizes for having a cool job at a major publishing house has to be totally insecure. I've changed my mind. I don't want to date him. Too bad, he was cute though.
I really shouldn't smoke. I know that. Not that I have anything against smokers, I mean, you, or --I'm sorry. I've just got this thing about fire--it's all my parents' fault, really. I'm sorry, I'm talking too much. I'll stop. But anyway, my mother--
Whoops! She's completely deranged! That means I can probably get her!

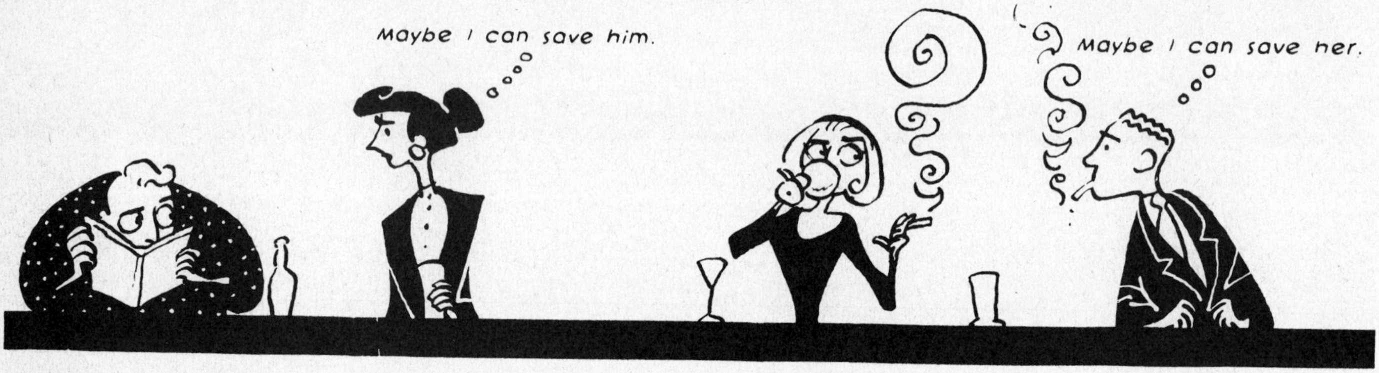
Maybe I can save him.
Maybe I can save her.

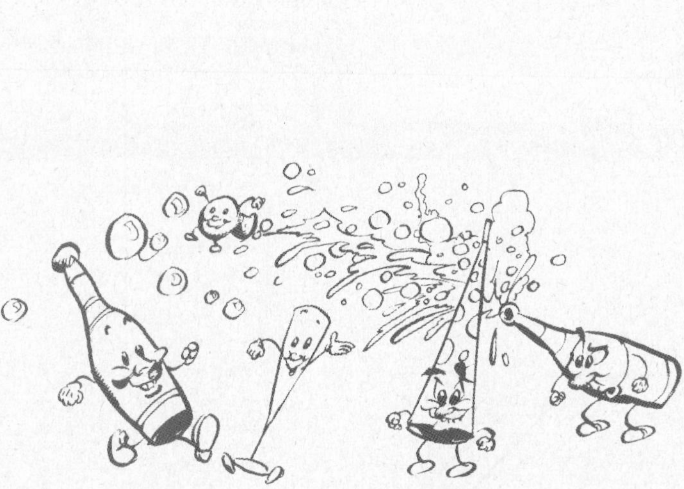

KYLE BAKER

Ghost Chimp, M.D.

Bring me wishes, I shall grant them.
Let's all sing the Ghost Chimp anthem.

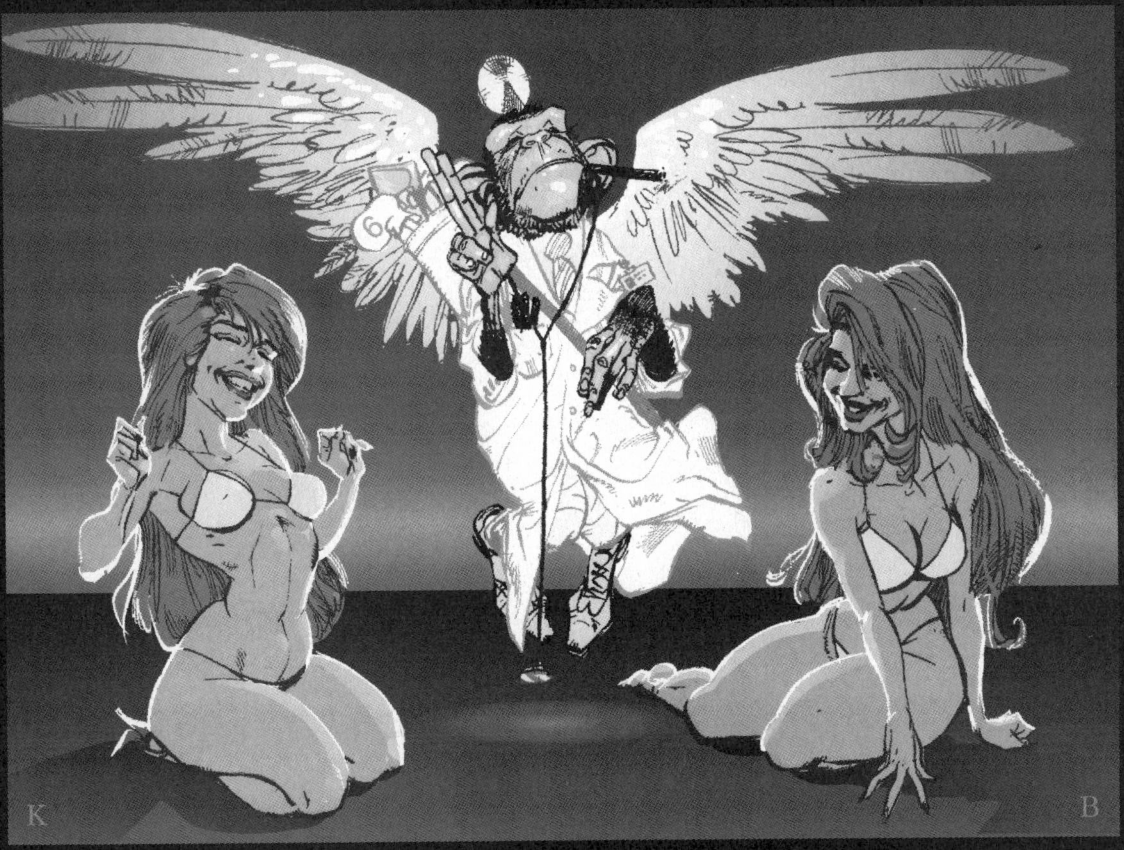

He's The Ghost Chimp,
The Ghost Chimp,
The Ghostliest Chimp In Town.

A lab coat full of cheap cigars
Conceals his vivisection scars.

He'll fill your day with merriment,
This former lab experiment.

He's colder than an icicle,
He smokes and rides a tricycle.

THE GHOSTLIEST CHIMP IN TOWN!

BOUNTY HUNTER DAD

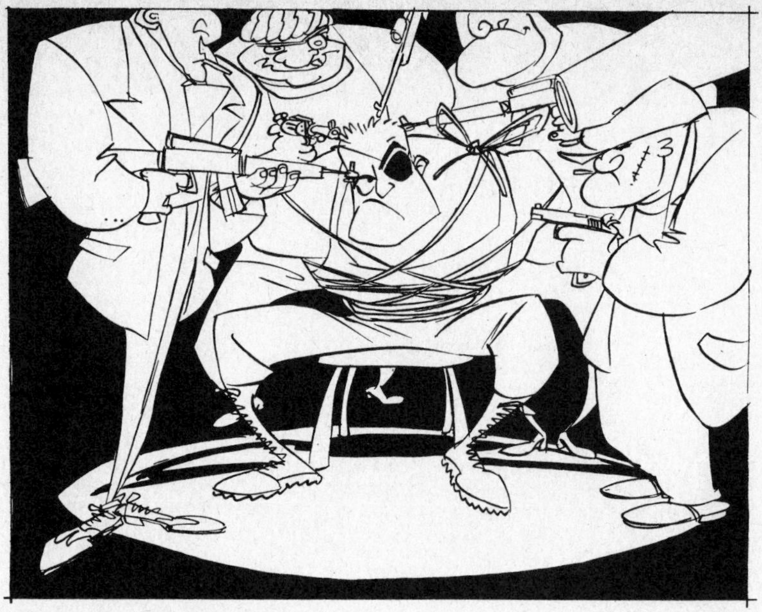

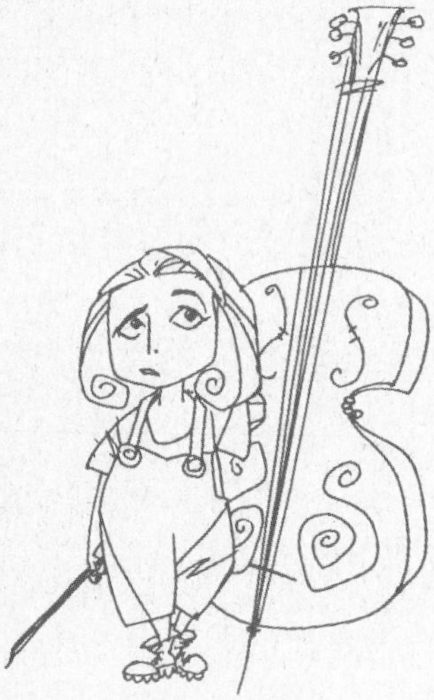

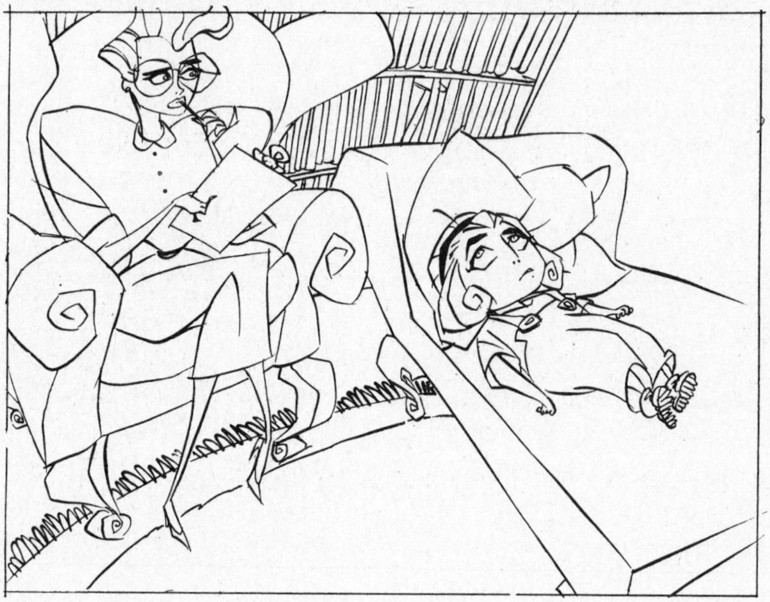

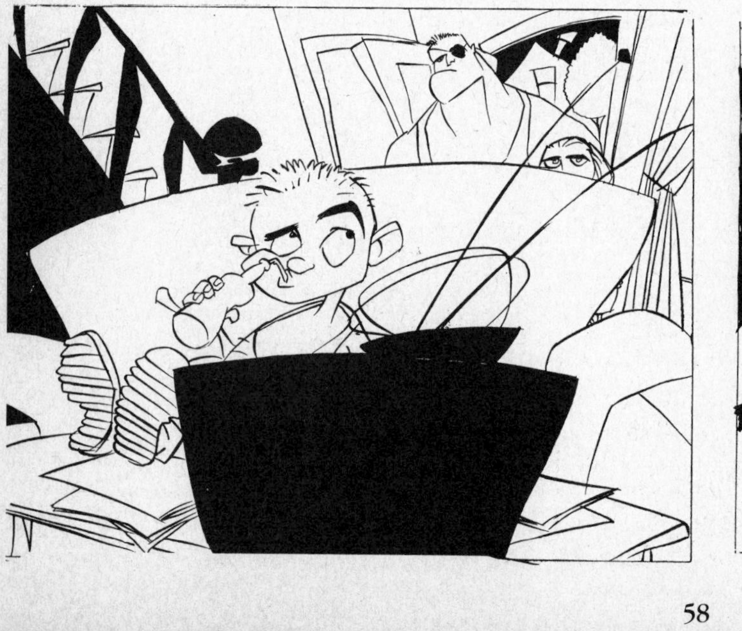

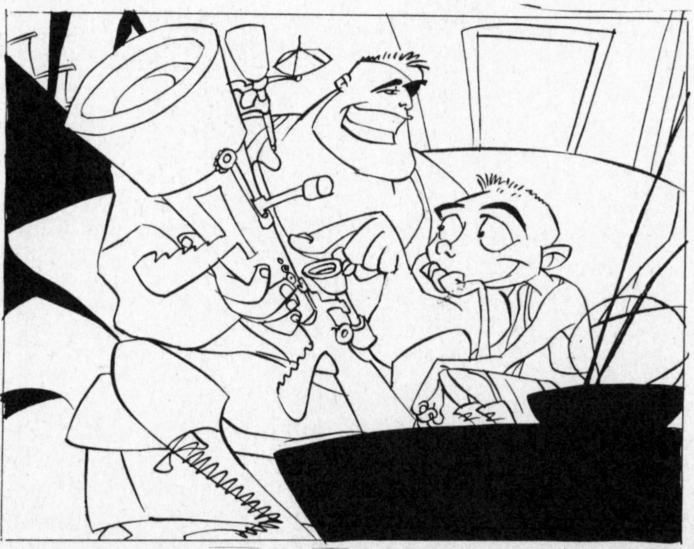

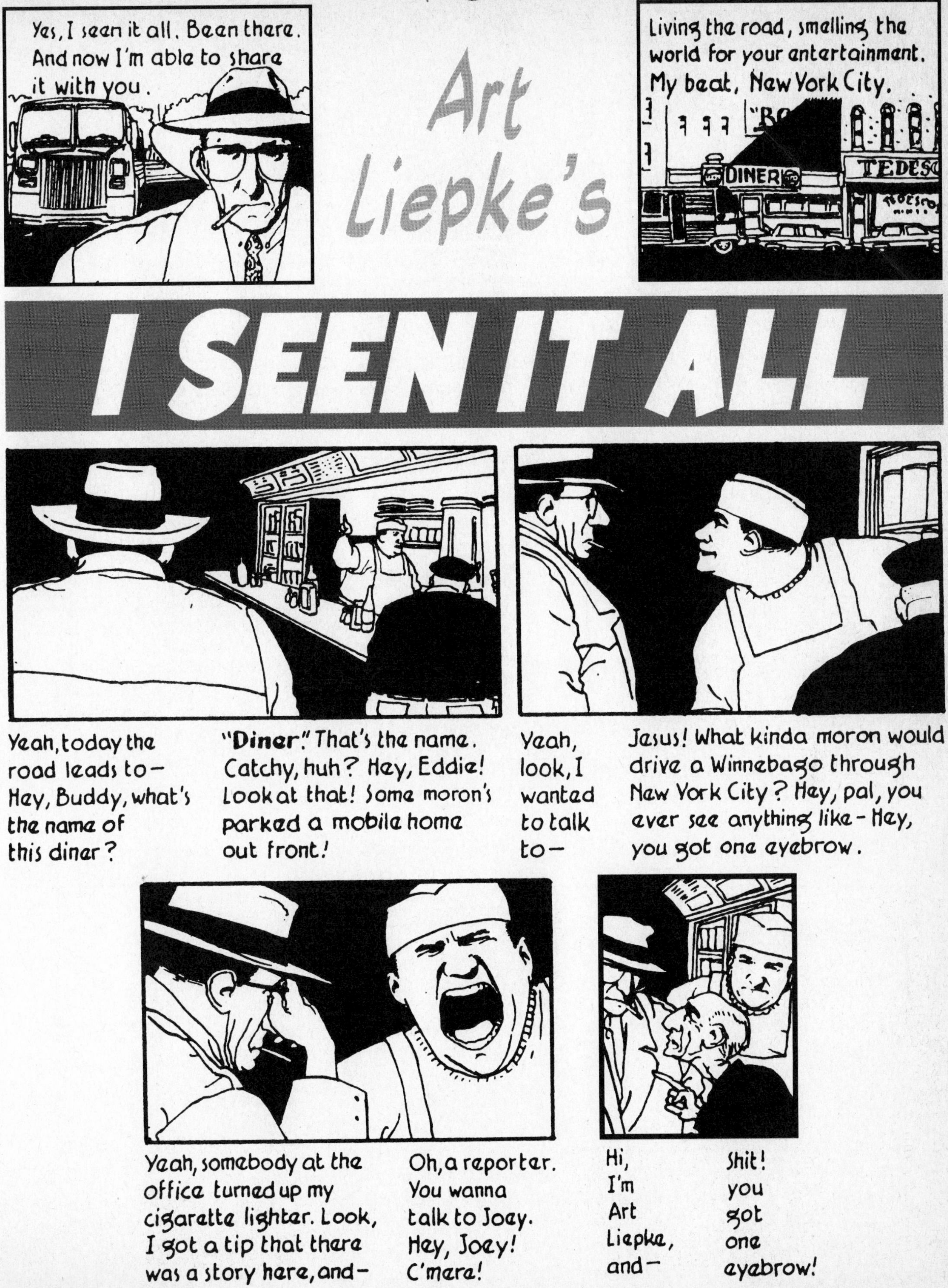
Yes, I seen it all. Been there. And now I'm able to share it with you.
Art Liepke's
Living the road, smelling the world for your entertainment. My beat, New York City.
DINER
I SEEN IT ALL
Yeah, today the road leads to— Hey, Buddy, what's the name of this diner?
"Diner." That's the name. Catchy, huh? Hey, Eddie! Look at that! Some moron's parked a mobile home out front!
Yeah, look, I wanted to talk to—
Jesus! What kinda moron would drive a Winnebago through New York City? Hey, pal, you ever see anything like— Hey, you got one eyebrow.
Yeah, somebody at the office turned up my cigarette lighter. Look, I got a tip that there was a story here, and—
Oh, a reporter. You wanna talk to Joey. Hey, Joey! C'mere!
Hi, I'm Art Liepke, and—
Shit! you got one eyebrow!

So do you.

Yeah, but mine goes all the way across. What's your excuse?

Hey, Joey, tell him your story.

Yeah, I hear you got a story.

Yeah, okay, well, you know how Mark Twain was born when Halley's comet came by, and he predicted he would die the next time it came by, and then he **did** die, and everybody was amazed?

Yeah?

Well, I was born under Halley's comet, and I predicted I would die when it came back.

But Halley's comet just left. It's not coming back for seventy something years. I think you blew it.

I know. I'll never hear the end of it. I'm a laughing stock. My life is ruined.

That's no story! Is your name Mercer?

No. It's Petrone.

I'm Mercer.

You're the guy I'm supposed to talk to! you're the one who used to be a two-headed baby!

Aw, Christ.

Where was the other head? I mean, usually two-headed babies have one on each side, but your head is right in the middle, where it's supposed to be. Did you feel guilty about being the head chosen to live while the other one died? Was the other head given a funeral or just thrown away?

Look, man, I don't know. I was a year old when they cut it off.

Oh, no. It's that pest, Murphy.

Were you close, you and the other head? I mean emotionally, not physically. Did you both have to eat, or just one?

Get out.

Hey, Charlie, Look! It's Halley's Comet!

Ooh! Ooh! I'm dyin'!

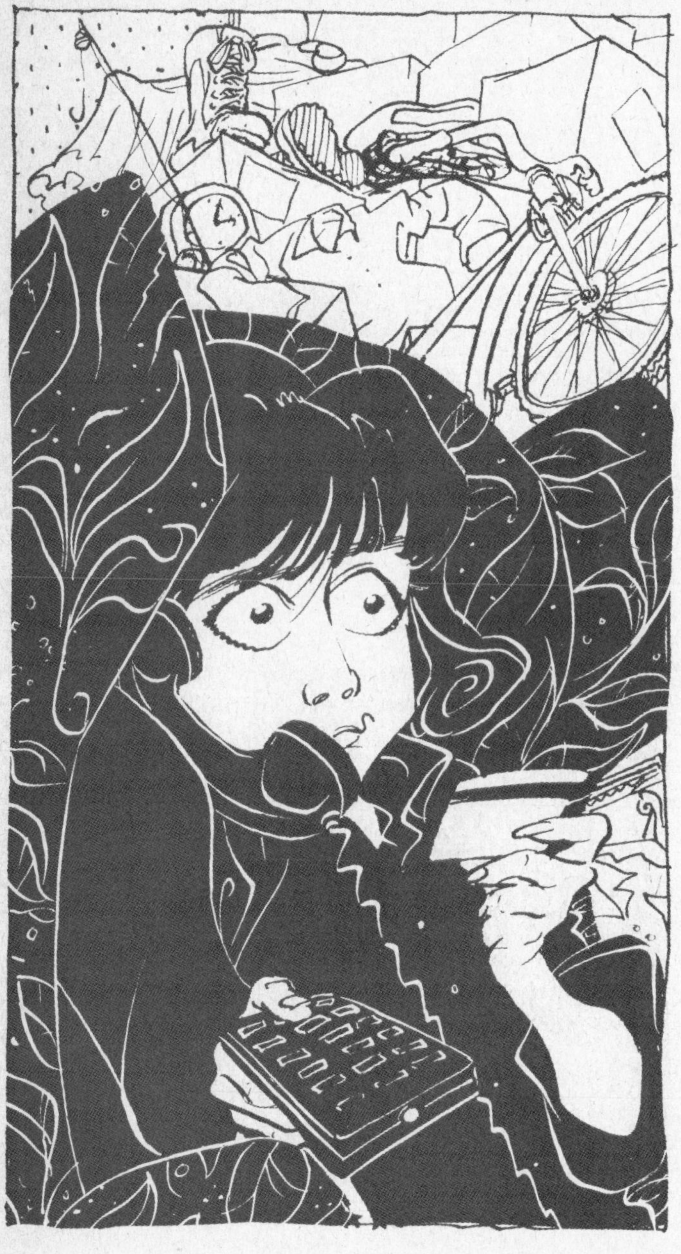

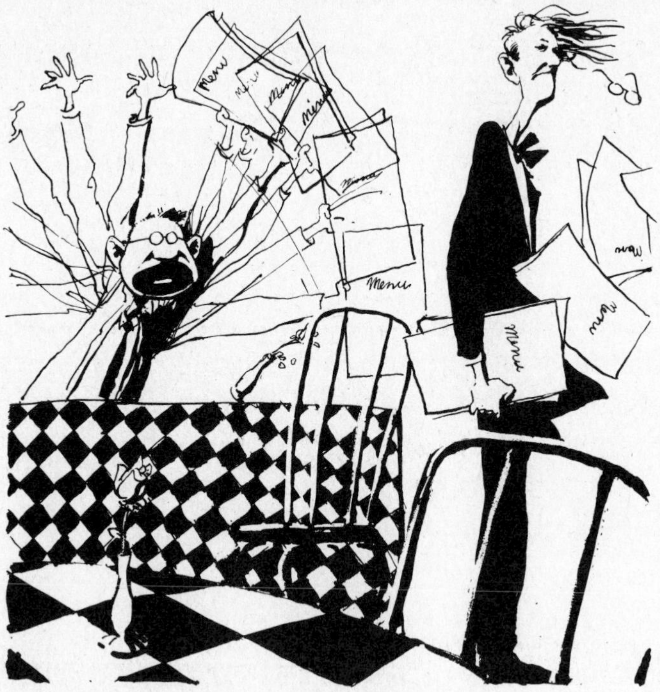

The waiter whose attention you can't get.

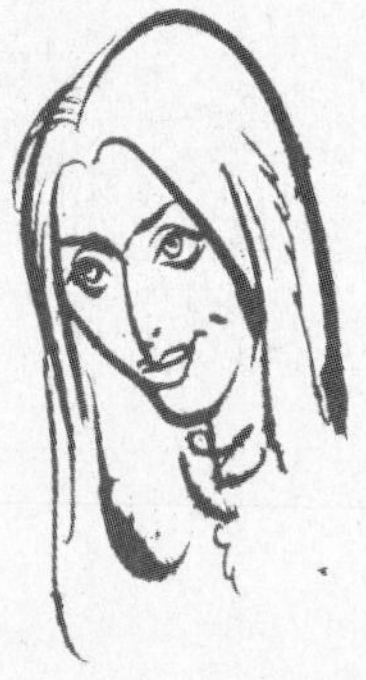

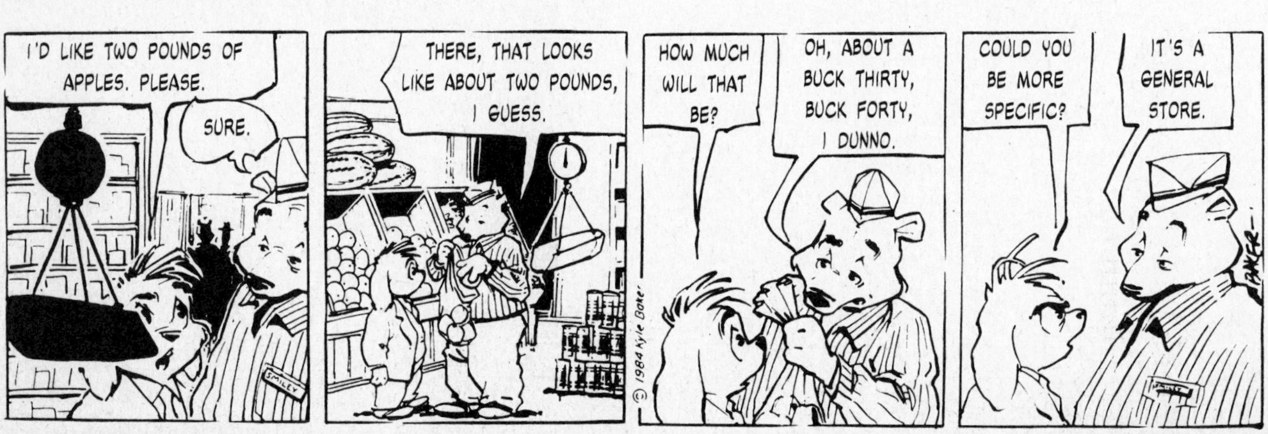
I'D LIKE TWO POUNDS OF APPLES. PLEASE.
SURE.
THERE, THAT LOOKS LIKE ABOUT TWO POUNDS, I GUESS.
© 1984 Kyle Baker
HOW MUCH WILL THAT BE?
OH, ABOUT A BUCK THIRTY, BUCK FORTY, I DUNNO.
COULD YOU BE MORE SPECIFIC?
IT'S A GENERAL STORE.
BAKER

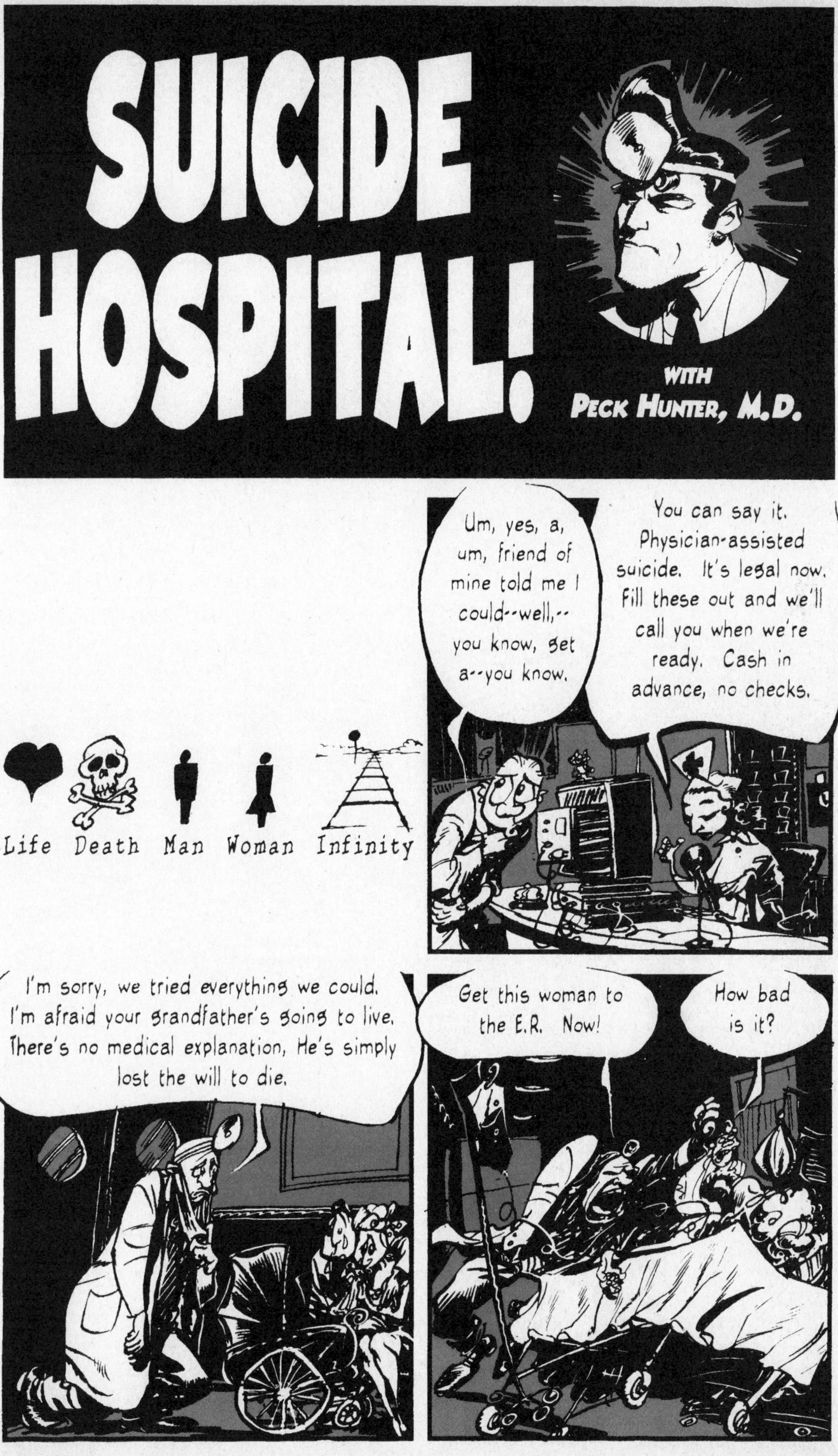
SUICIDE HOSPITAL!
WITH PECK HUNTER, M.D.
Life Death Man Woman Infinity
Um, yes, a, um, friend of mine told me I could--well,--you know, get a--you know.
You can say it. Physician-assisted suicide. It's legal now. Fill these out and we'll call you when we're ready. Cash in advance, no checks.
I'm sorry, we tried everything we could. I'm afraid your grandfather's going to live. There's no medical explanation. He's simply lost the will to die.
Get this woman to the E.R. Now!
How bad is it?

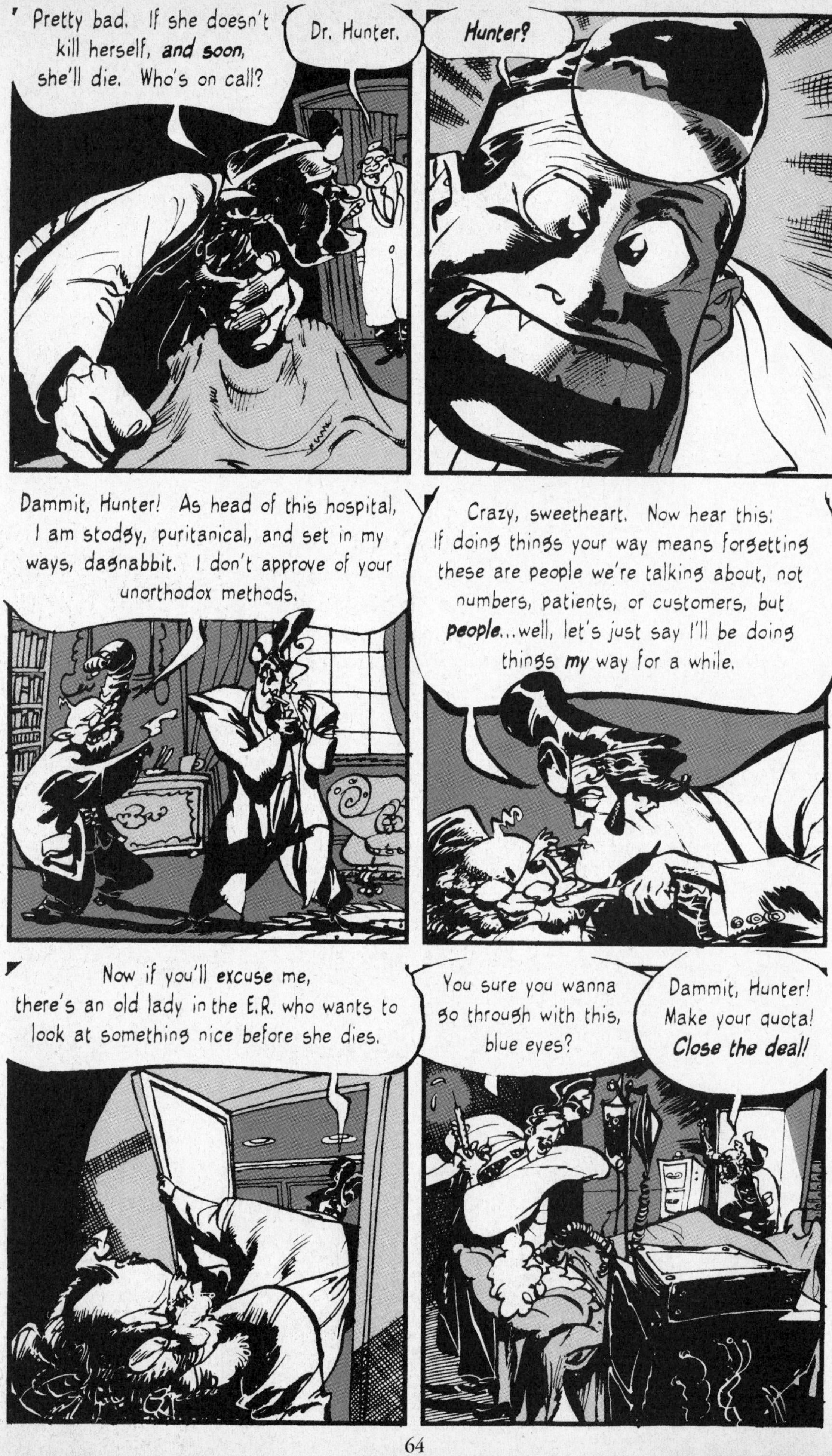
Pretty bad. If she doesn't kill herself, and soon, she'll die. Who's on call?
Dr. Hunter.
Hunter?
Dammit, Hunter! As head of this hospital, I am stodgy, puritanical, and set in my ways, dagnabbit. I don't approve of your unorthodox methods.
Crazy, sweetheart. Now hear this: If doing things your way means forgetting these are people we're talking about, not numbers, patients, or customers, but people...well, let's just say I'll be doing things my way for a while.
Now if you'll excuse me, there's an old lady in the E.R. who wants to look at something nice before she dies.
You sure you wanna go through with this, blue eyes?
Dammit, Hunter! Make your quota! Close the deal!

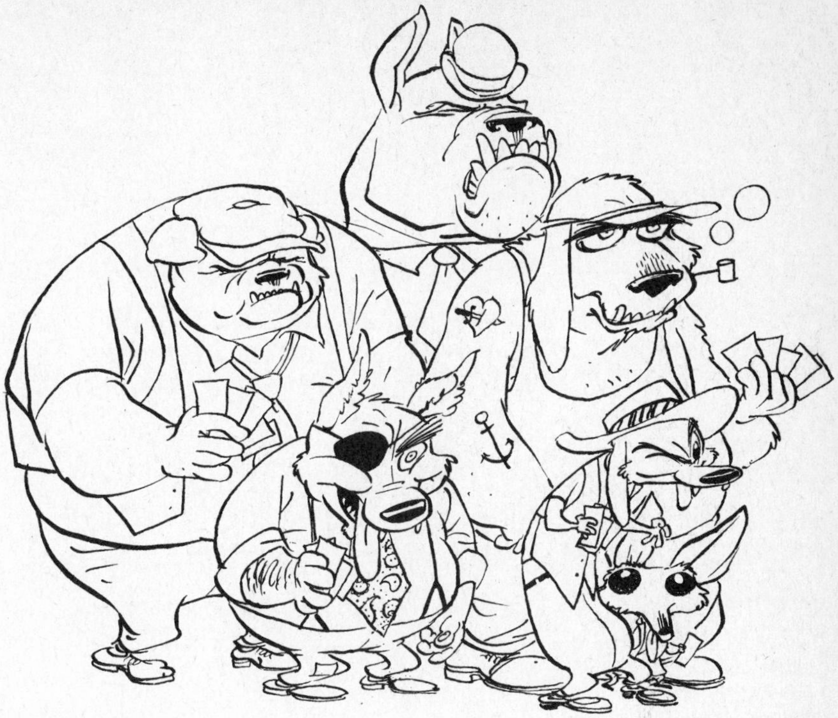

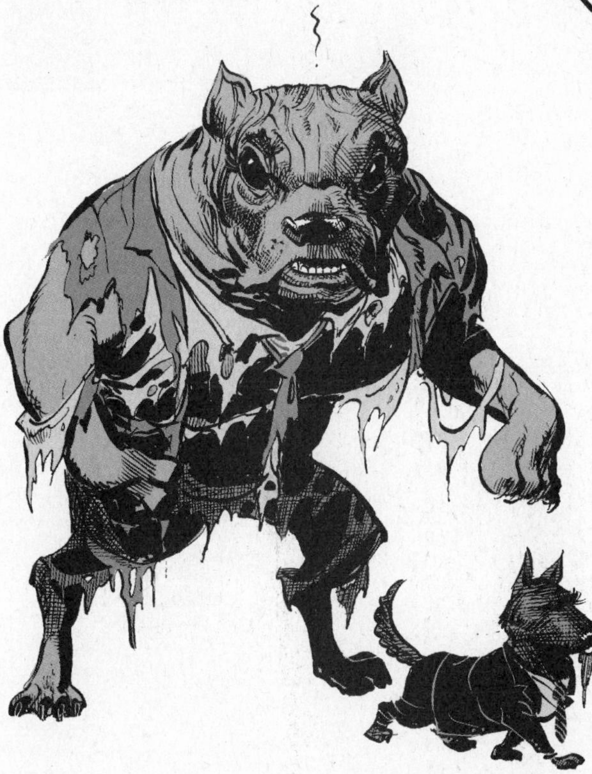

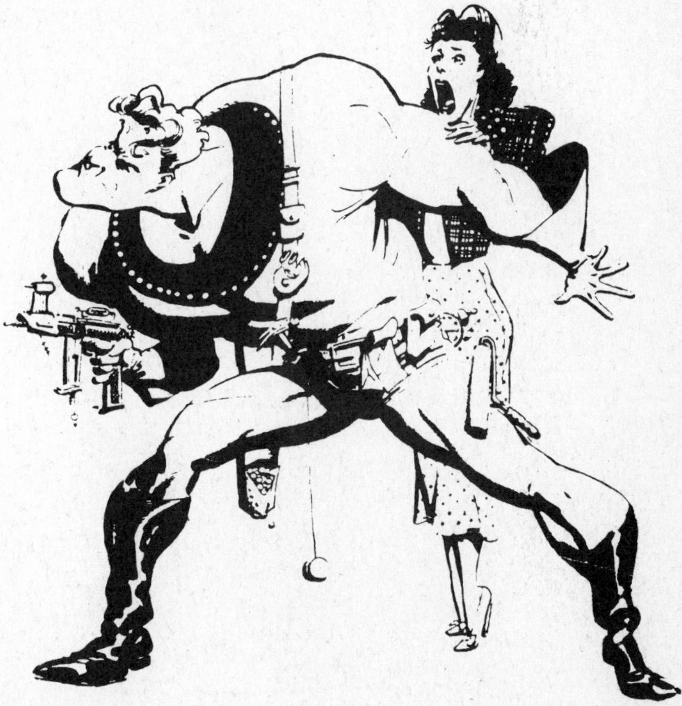

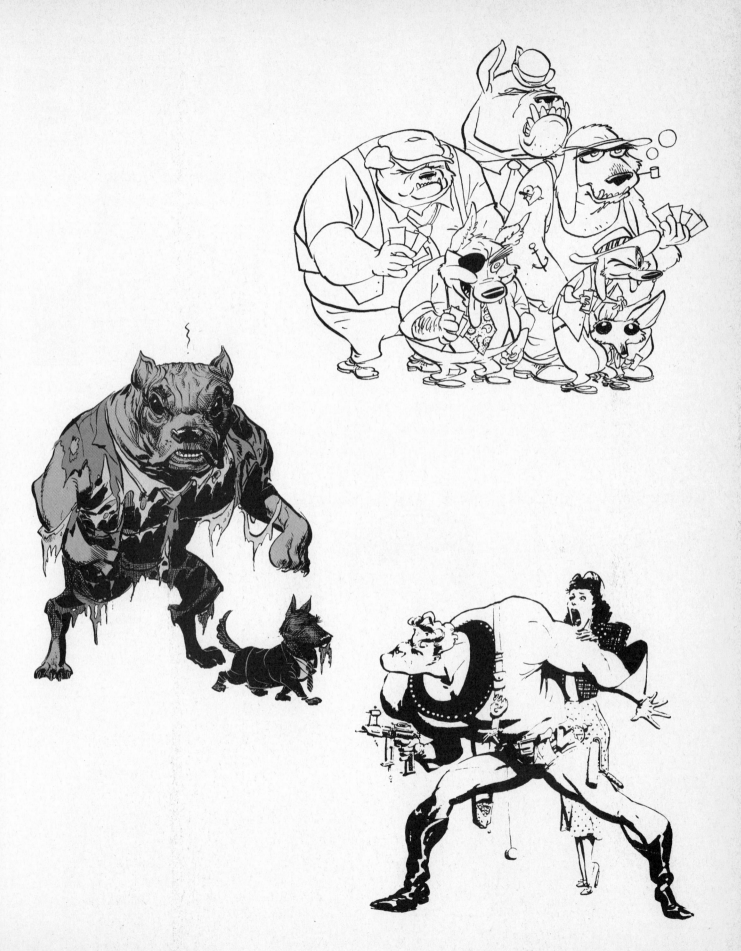

Kyle Baker

MEDIA GIANTS

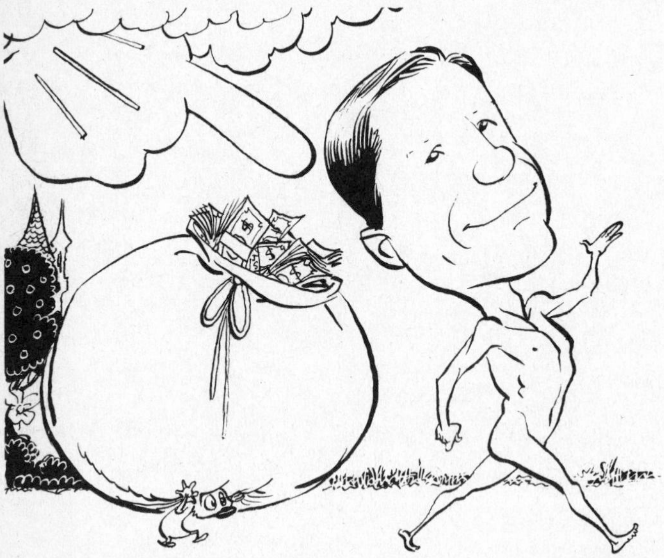

Mike Ovitz

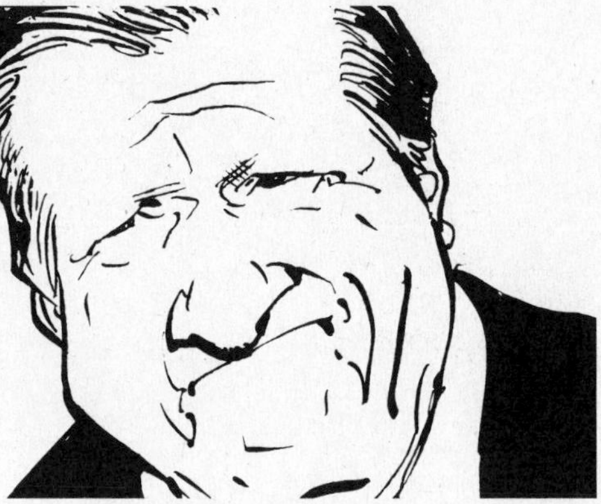

George Steinbrenner

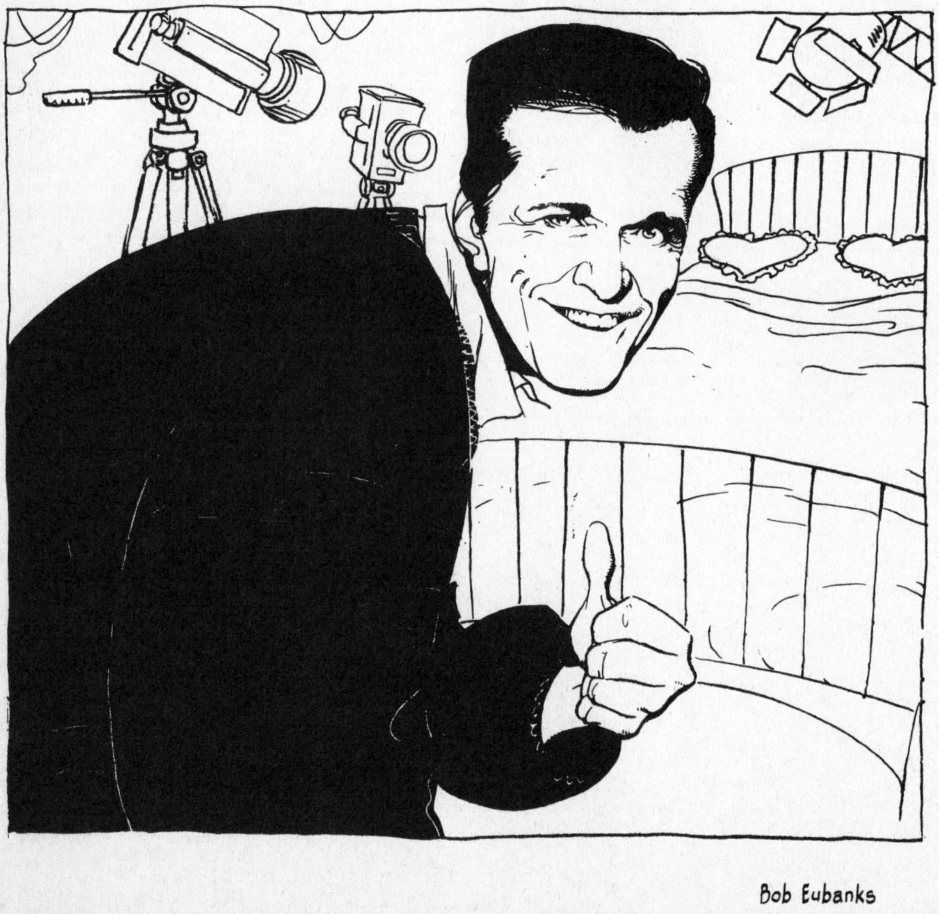

Bob Eubanks

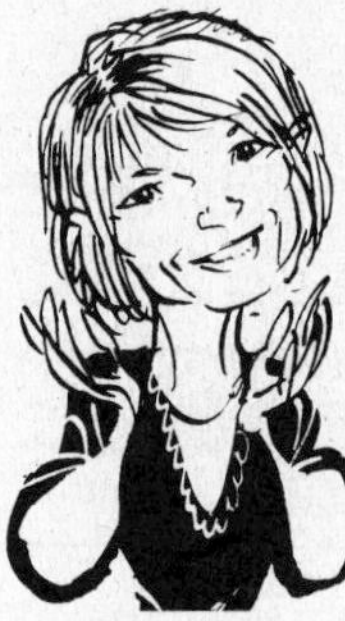

Martha Stewart

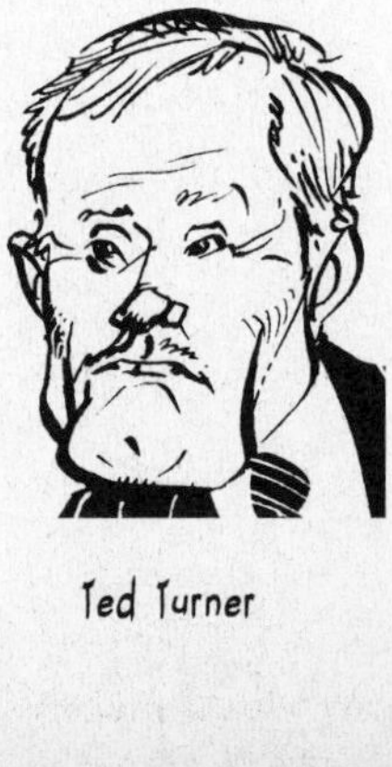

Ted Turner

KYLE BAKER

GIRLFRIEND SHIRTS!

MEN!

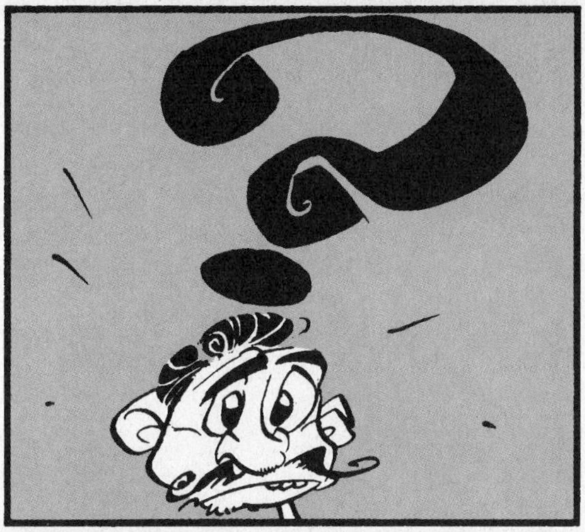

You've seen them, you've probably got one. I'm talking of course, about one of the most insidious devices of the twentieth century, although I suspect that its origins can be traced back to some arcane, pre-industrial sorcery, perhaps even back to the time when people used to paint themselves and eat roots and hallucinate for reasons other than recreational. I am talking to you men, as men, about the nefarious and infernal GIRLFRIEND SHIRT!

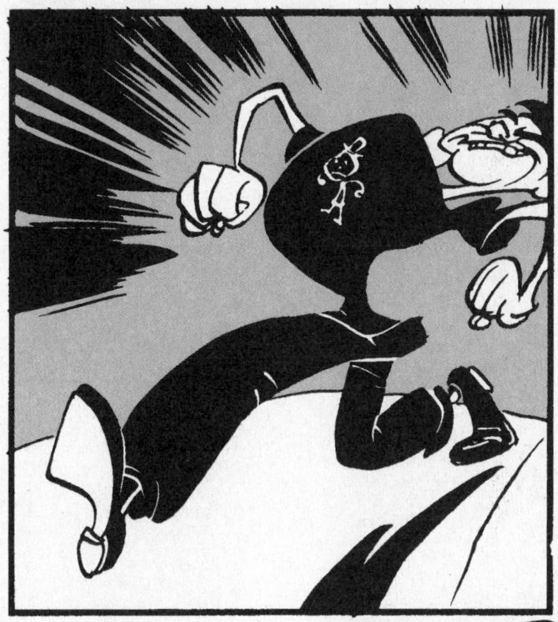

MEN! How many times has this happened to you? Your girlfriend gives you a perfectly innocent-looking shirt, so innocent, in fact, that it seems exactly the type of thing you might have purchased for yourself had you thought of it. Perhaps it is your favorite color, the color of shirts you have bought for yourself. Perhaps it goes perfectly with a pair of pants you own but rarely wear because you've never found a shirt to wear with them. Perhaps it is a T-shirt sporting the image of your favorite musician. Whatever it is, this shirt suits your taste perfectly, and you feel fortunate to be dating someone who knows you so well.

And yet, when you put it on and wear it to the office, or lunch with the guys, or when you stop into your favorite bar after work before going home, people inevitably say:

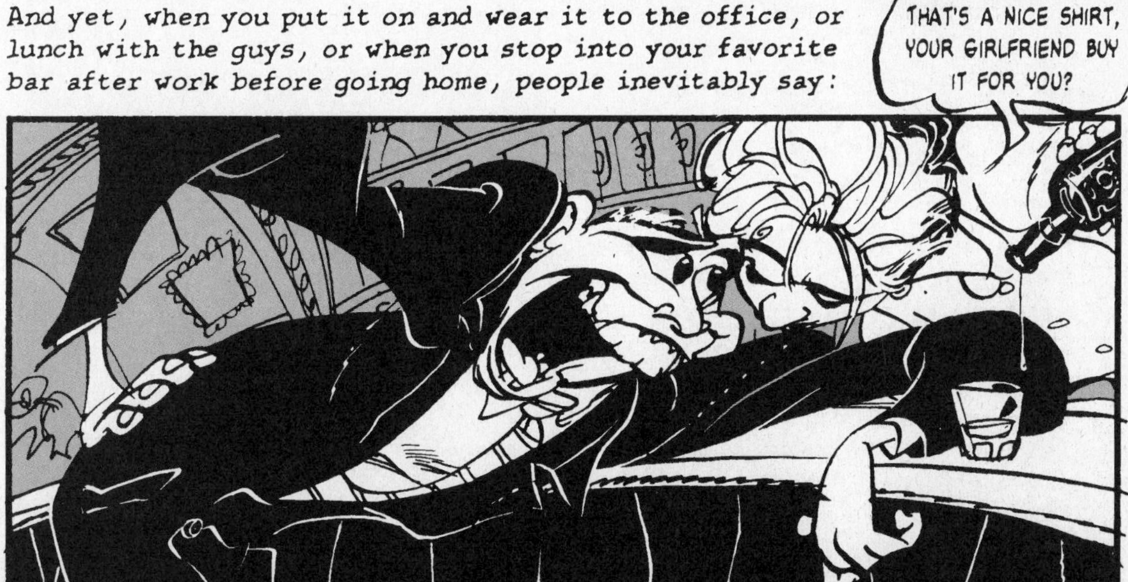
THAT'S A NICE SHIRT, YOUR GIRLFRIEND BUY IT FOR YOU?

It is then that you realize that you have been duped. You have been branded. Somehow, you have been suckered into wearing a shirt that says to the world I AM ATTACHED. You might as well be wearing a *wedding ring*, for Chrissakes! You are wearing a GIRLFRIEND SHIRT.

You can think of no good reason to stop wearing it; after all it *is* your favorite color, or favorite band or cartoon character! Anyway, she is a wonderful woman, and you would marry her if you weren't terrified that you wouldn't meet someone better immediately after you said "I do," and if you could be sure she wouldn't age as badly as her mother has.

So you're stuck. You have no choice but to wear this shirt which you are convinced has been treated with some sort of ultraviolet chemical which only women can see, but men can somehow sense. Besides, if you stop wearing it, she'll know why.

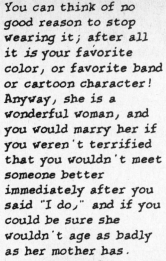

BAH, TRAPPED!

THE WARNING SIGNS OF A GIRLFRIEND SHIRT

AN ANTIQUE Men have no idea where to find a good-looking shirt for under $10.

IT LOOKS GREAT WITH YOUR GREEN SUIT, AND *ONLY* YOUR GREEN SUIT. Always a sign. Men never buy shirts that only go well with one outfit.

YOUR FAVORITE CARTOON CHARACTER
Always a sign of a girlfriend shirt. Although you may *love* Charlie Brown, you would never buy a Charlie Brown shirt for yourself. Once presented with a free one, however, you think to yourself, "How thoughtful! I *love* Charlie Brown! *How could it have never occurred to me to buy this shirt?*" How indeed, unless it is, of course, a GIRLFRIEND SHIRT!

THE CLINCHER: SHE NEVER BORROWS IT!

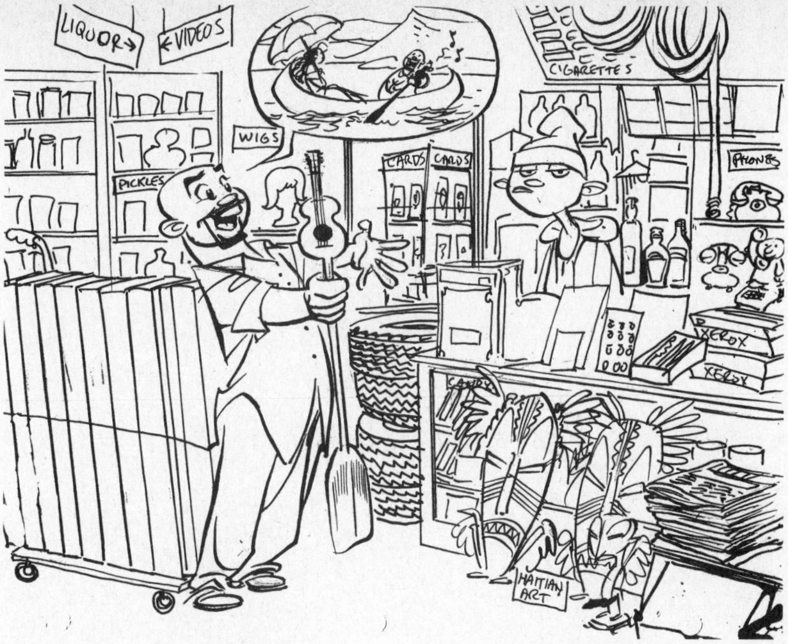
LIQUOR
VIDEOS
WIGS
PICKLES
CARDS
CARDS
CIGARETTES
PHONES
XEROX
XEROX
HAITIAN ART

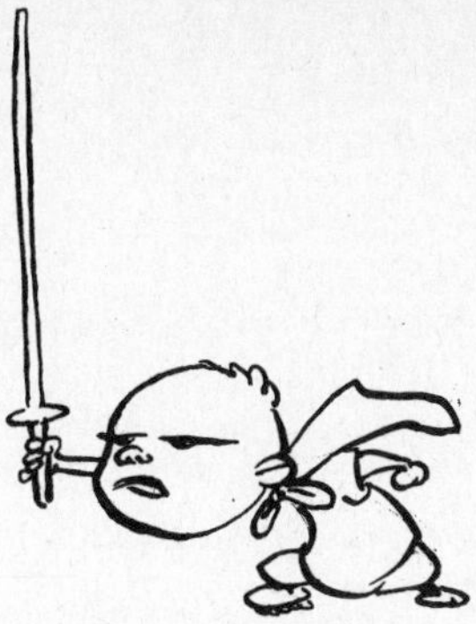

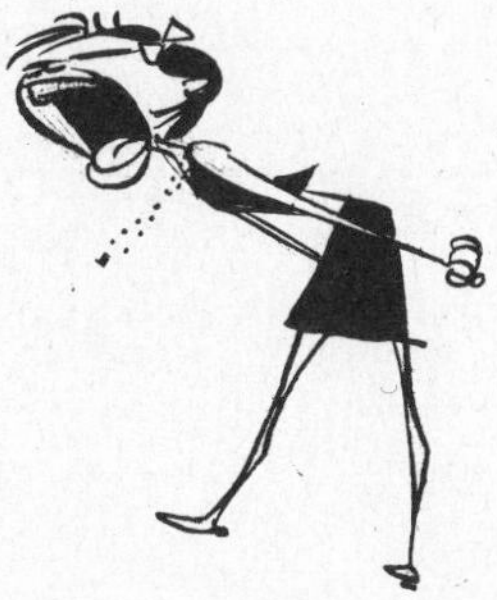

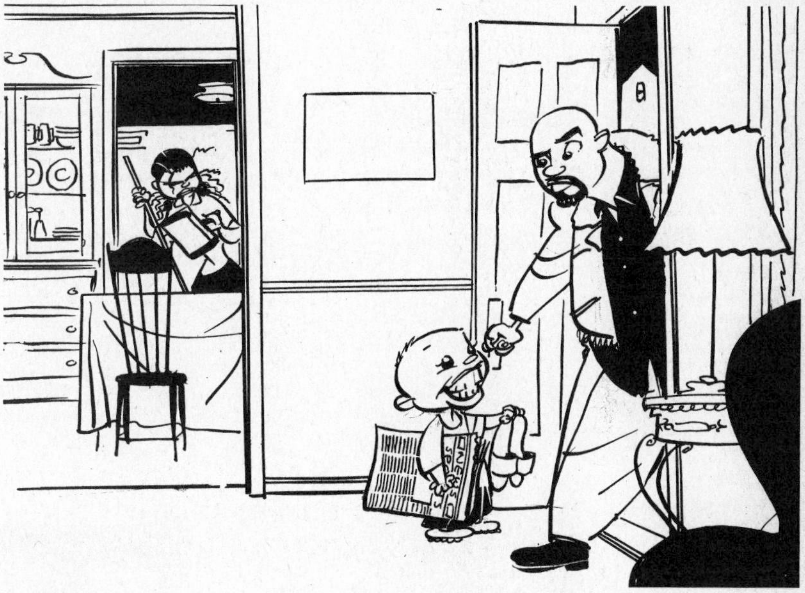

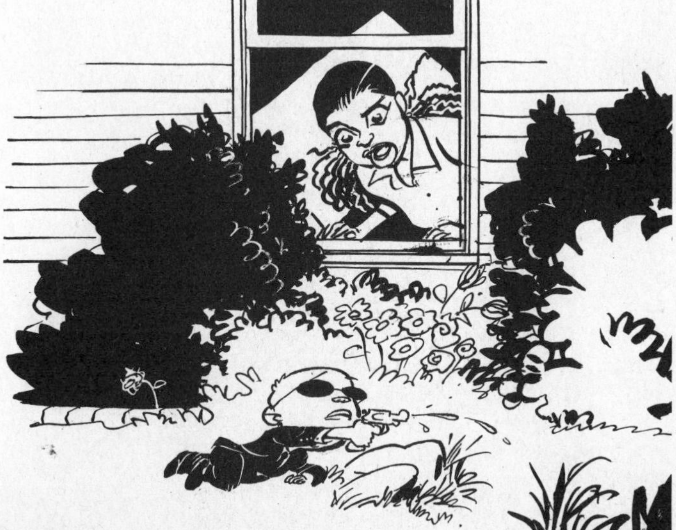

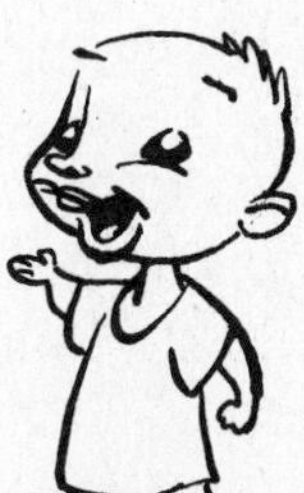

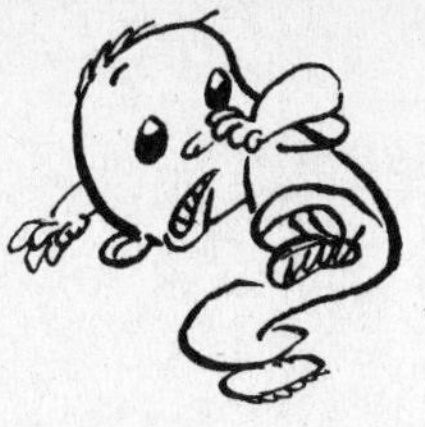

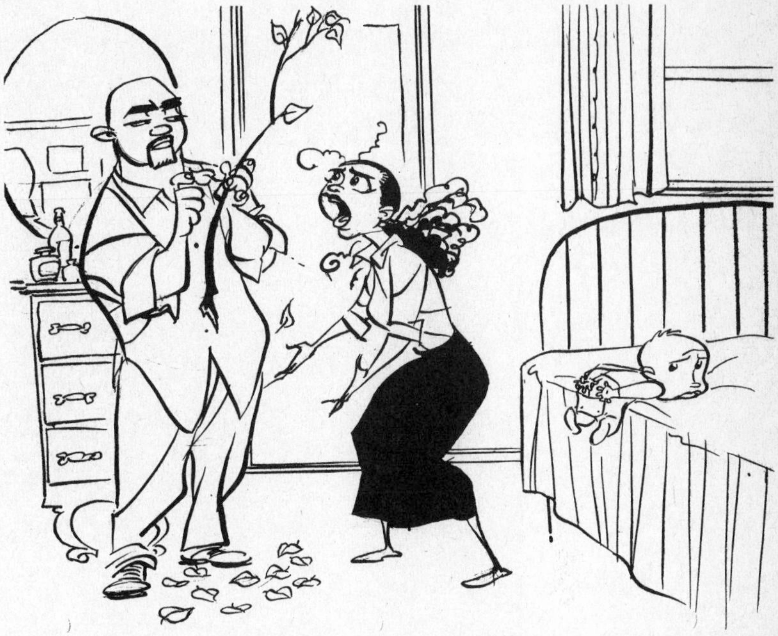

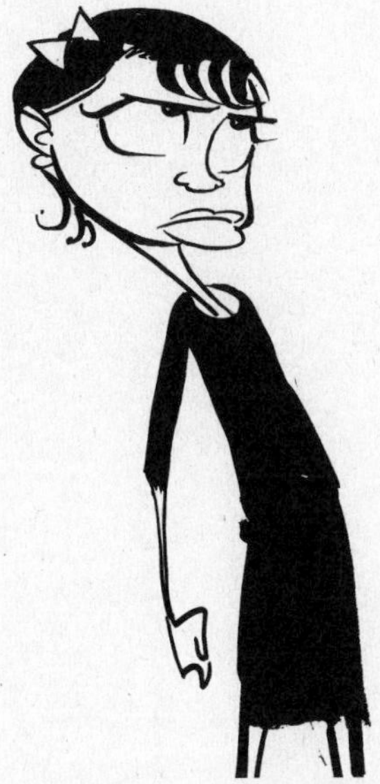

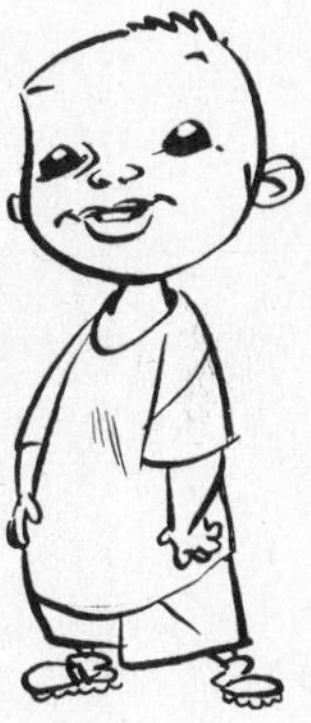

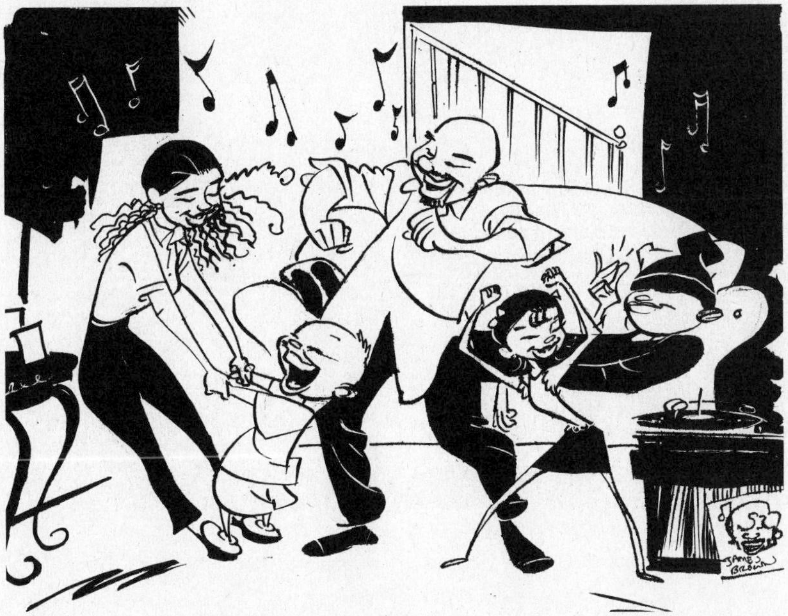
JAMES BROWN

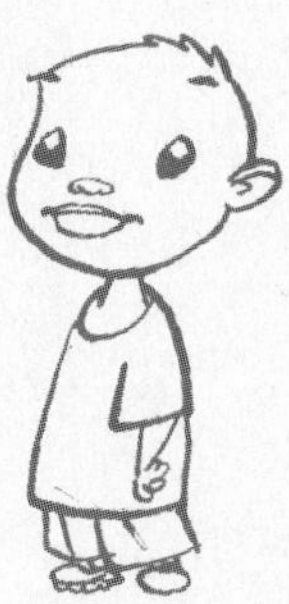

"EGREGIOUS!"

Wesley Sourapple - EAST SAUGERTIES JR. HIGH SCHOOL GAZETTE

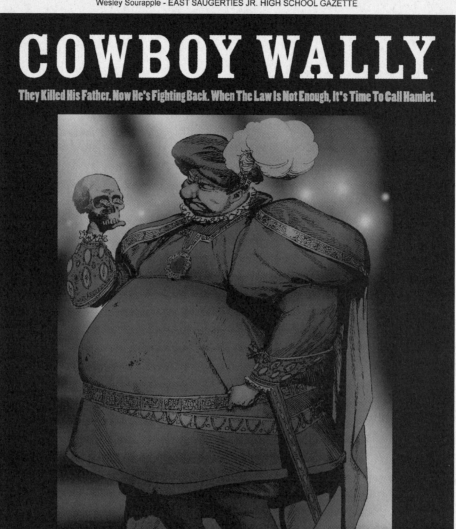

COWBOY WALLY
They Killed His Father. Now He's Fighting Back. When The Law Is Not Enough, It's Time To Call Hamlet.
KYLE BAKER
HAMLET

Now Playing

KYLE BAKER FILMS presents a COWBOY WALLY in association With WHOOSHMAN-BICARBONATE PRODUCTIONS production a COWBOY WALLY film COWBOY WALLY LEON THE KNIFE BBMSHMRT HUEY ROTTENSHANK MAXINE THE GUARD AND LENNY WALSH AS OPHELIA written and directed by COWBOY WALLY

R restricted no one will be allowed in without paying

KYLE BAKER

QUALITY JOLLITY

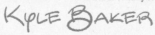

GIANTS OF COMEDY

Woody Allen

Fatty Arbuckle

William Gaines

Chevy Chase, John Belushi, Dan Akyroyd, Garret Morris

Mike Myers

Robert DeNiro

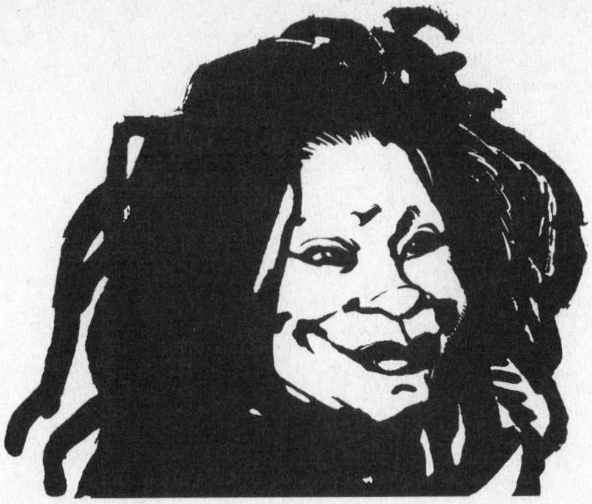

Whoopi Goldberg

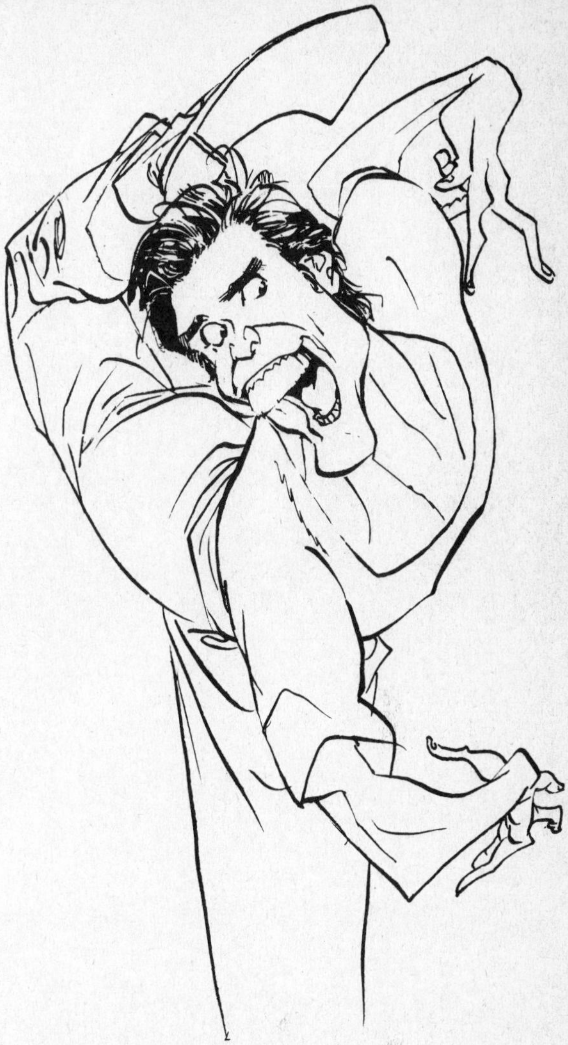

Jim Carrey

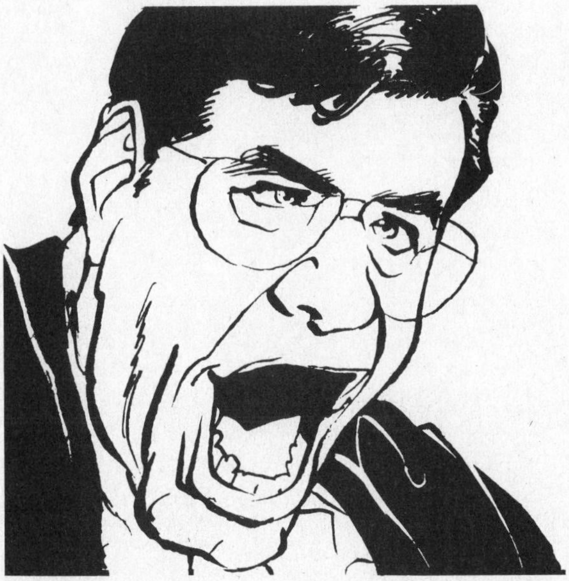

Jerry Lewis

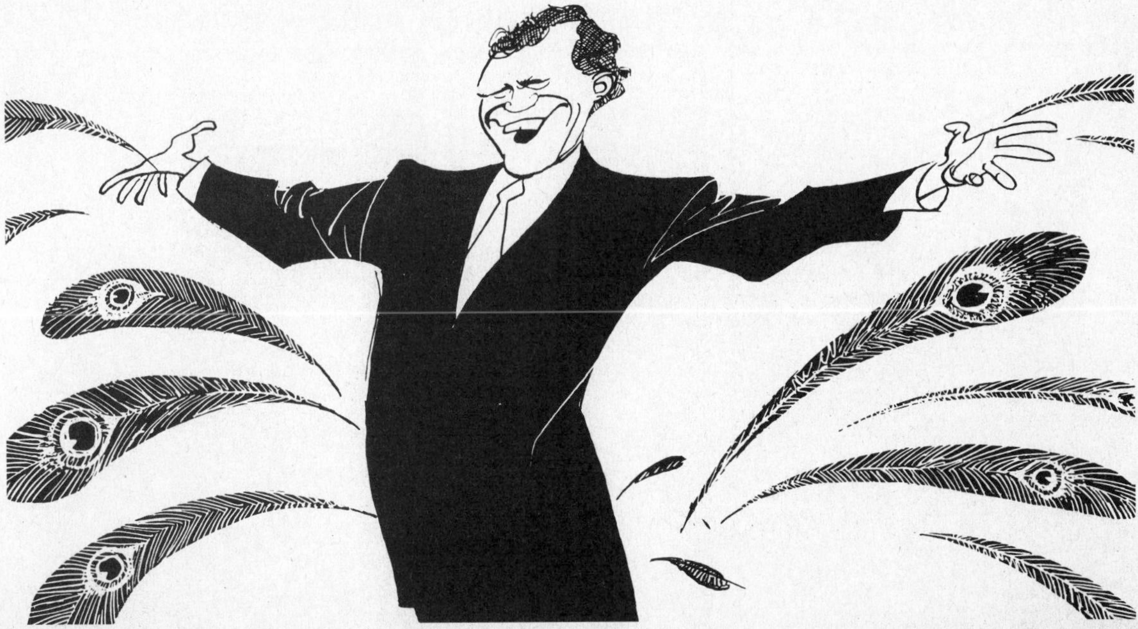

David Letterman

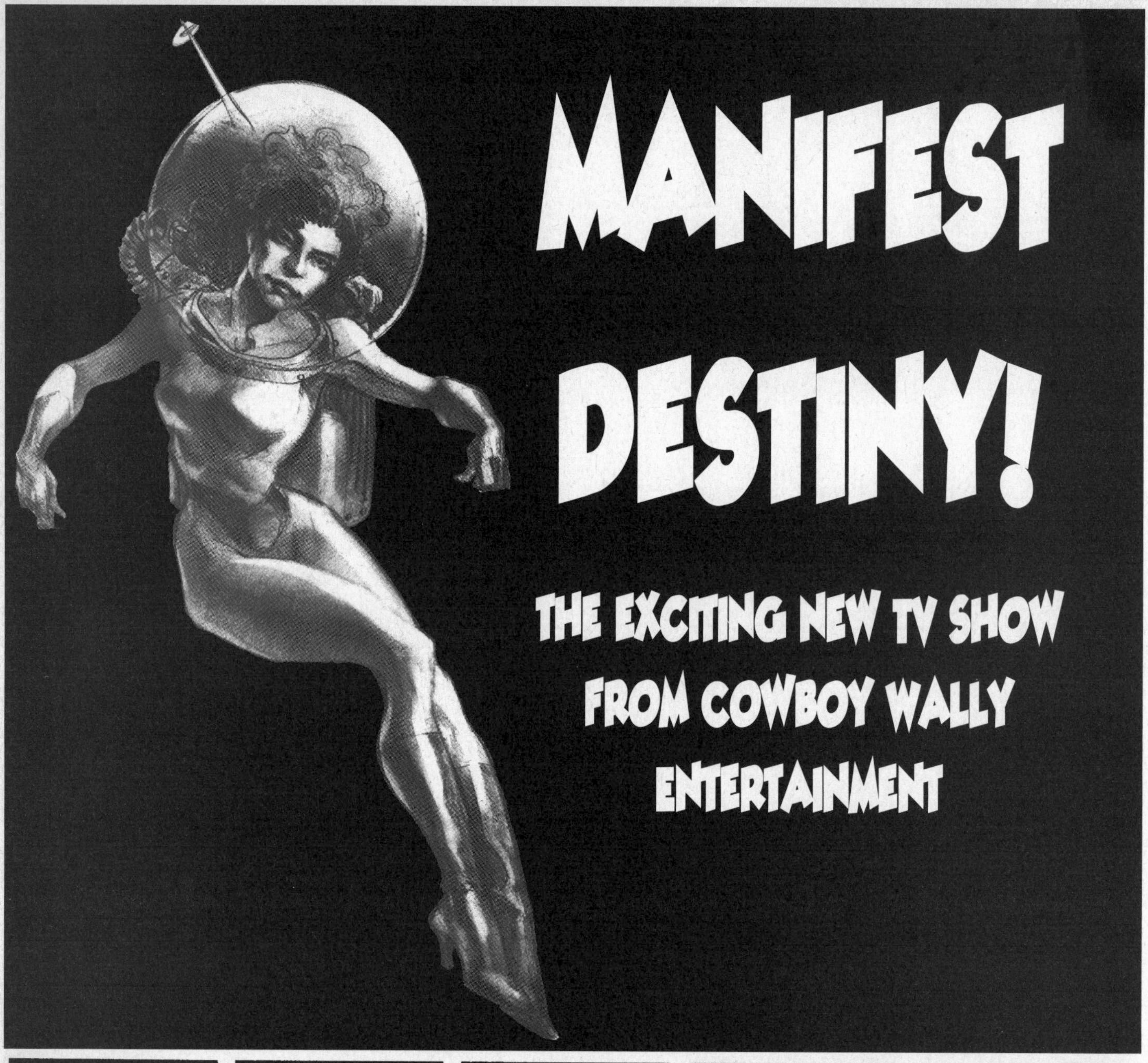
MANIFEST DESTINY!
THE EXCITING NEW TV SHOW FROM COWBOY WALLY ENTERTAINMENT

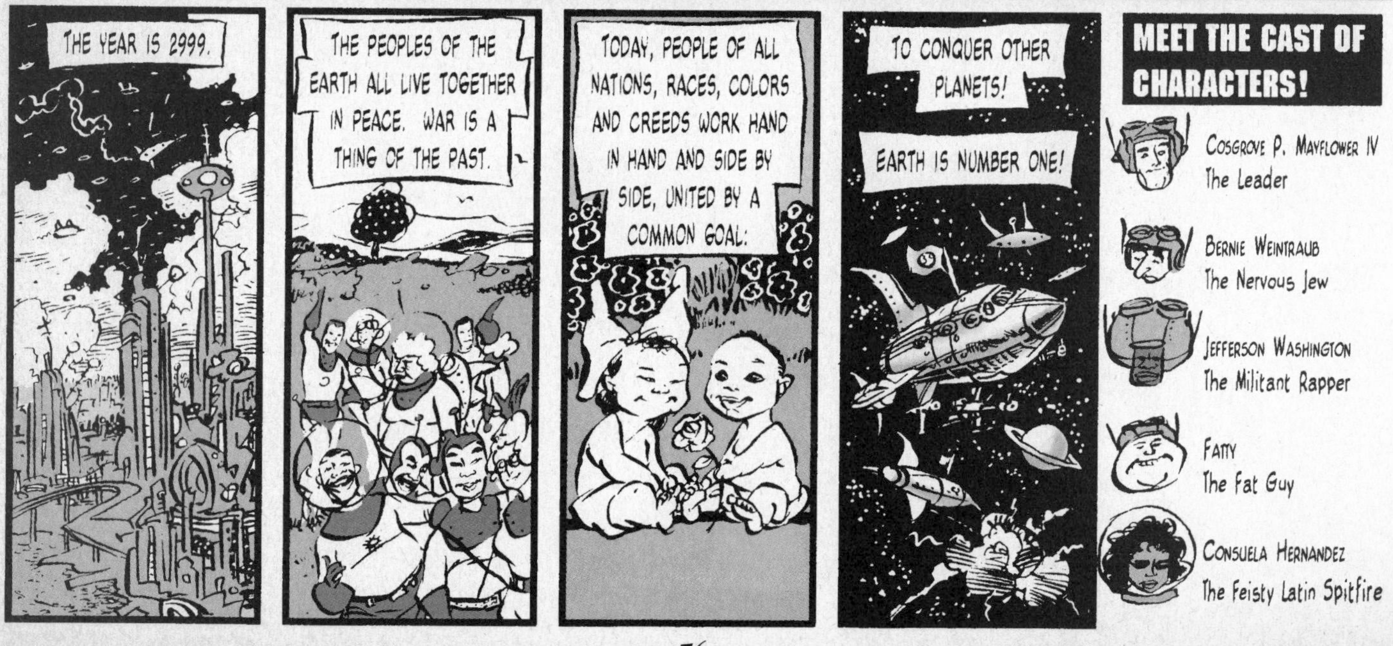
THE YEAR IS 2999.
THE PEOPLES OF THE EARTH ALL LIVE TOGETHER IN PEACE. WAR IS A THING OF THE PAST.
TODAY, PEOPLE OF ALL NATIONS, RACES, COLORS AND CREEDS WORK HAND IN HAND AND SIDE BY SIDE, UNITED BY A COMMON GOAL:
TO CONQUER OTHER PLANETS!
EARTH IS NUMBER ONE!
MEET THE CAST OF CHARACTERS!
COSGROVE P. MAYFLOWER IV
The Leader
BERNIE WEINTRAUB
The Nervous Jew
JEFFERSON WASHINGTON
The Militant Rapper
FATTY
The Fat Guy
CONSUELA HERNANDEZ
The Feisty Latin Spitfire

Flowers and pixies and rainbows for me.
Open your mind up and let it be free.
Pixies and flowers and rainbows for you.
Unicorns, banshees and popsicles, too.

Windmills and acid and phosphorous dreams.
Witches and tree-gnomes and magick moonbeams.
Faeries and mushrooms and tarot and runes,
Tie-dye and sandals and Beatles cartoons.

Wizards and hobbits, rainforests and flutes.
Native Americans, joy, love and newts.
Sandcastles, laughter, and dragons named Puff,
These are a few of my favorite stuff.

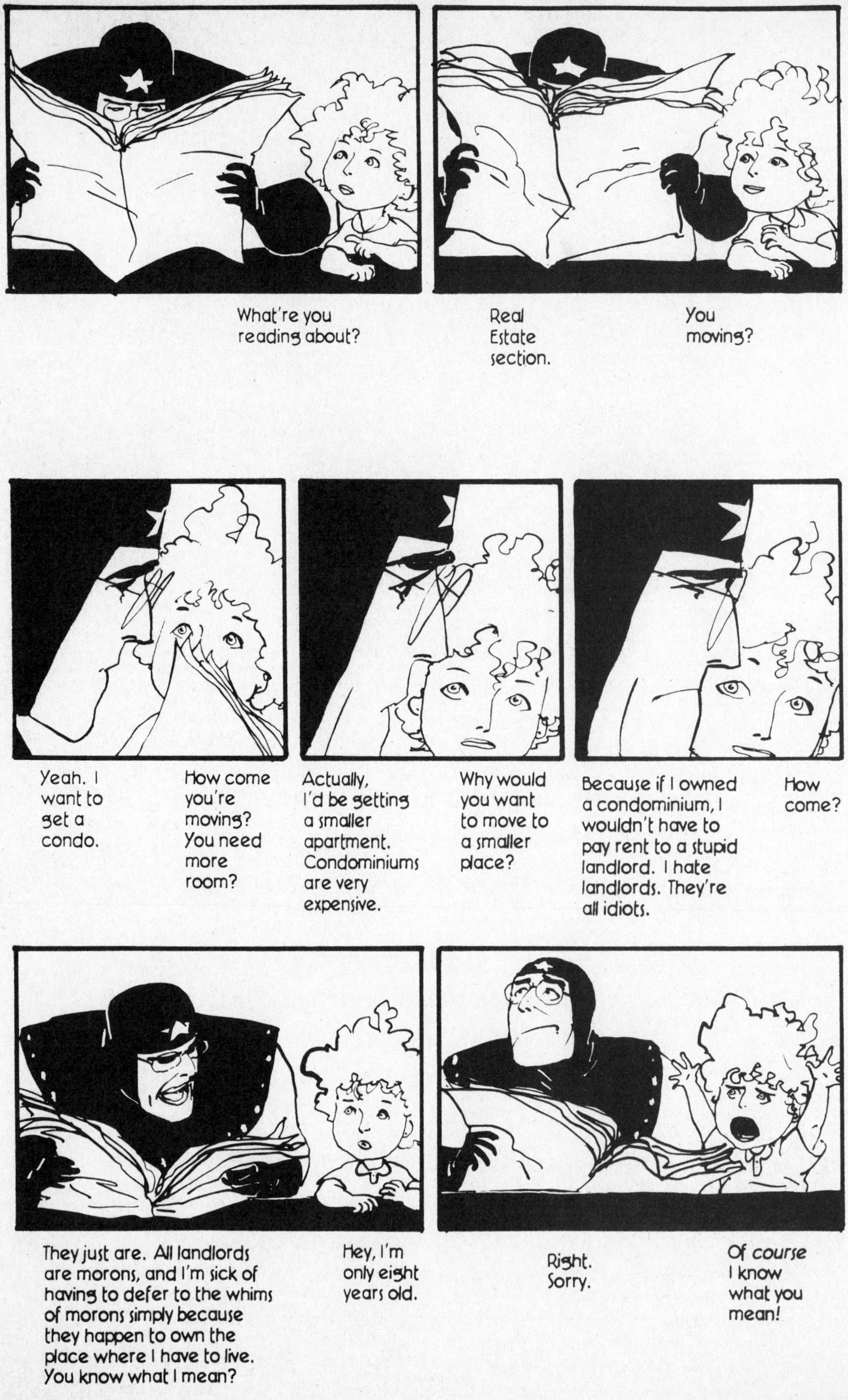
What're you reading about?
Real Estate section.
You moving?
Yeah. I want to get a condo.
How come you're moving? You need more room?
Actually, I'd be getting a smaller apartment. Condominiums are very expensive.
Why would you want to move to a smaller place?
Because if I owned a condominium, I wouldn't have to pay rent to a stupid landlord. I hate landlords. They're all idiots.
How come?
They just are. All landlords are morons, and I'm sick of having to defer to the whims of morons simply because they happen to own the place where I have to live. You know what I mean?
Hey, I'm only eight years old.
Right. Sorry.
Of *course* I know what you mean!

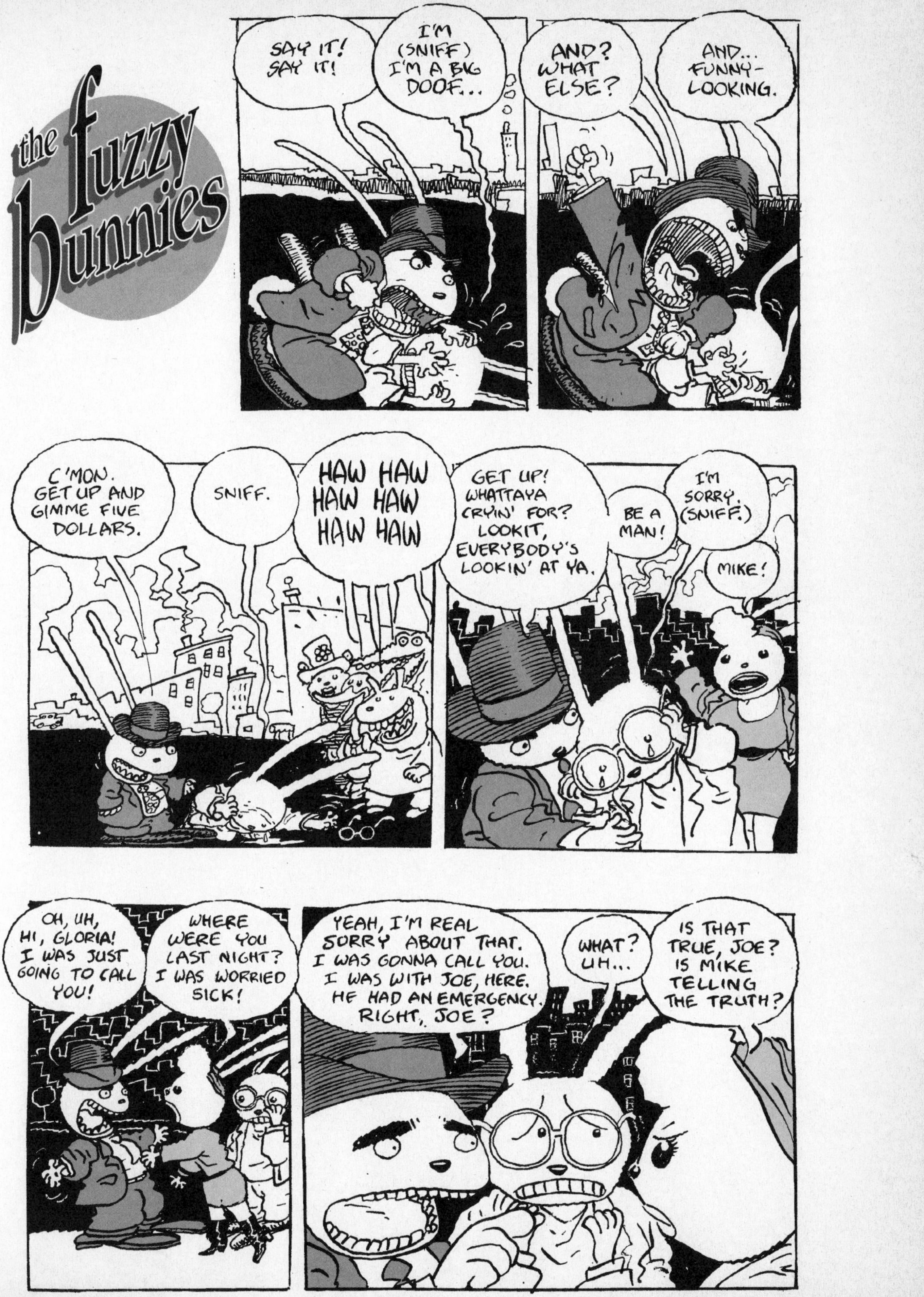
the fuzzy bunnies
SAY IT! SAY IT!
I'M (SNIFF) I'M A BIG DOOF...
AND? WHAT ELSE?
AND... FUNNY-LOOKING.
C'MON. GET UP AND GIMME FIVE DOLLARS.
SNIFF.
HAW HAW HAW HAW HAW HAW
GET UP! WHATTAYA CRYIN' FOR? LOOKIT, EVERYBODY'S LOOKIN' AT YA.
BE A MAN!
I'M SORRY. (SNIFF.)
MIKE!
OH, UH, HI, GLORIA! I WAS JUST GOING TO CALL YOU!
WHERE WERE YOU LAST NIGHT? I WAS WORRIED SICK!
YEAH, I'M REAL SORRY ABOUT THAT. I WAS GONNA CALL YOU. I WAS WITH JOE, HERE. HE HAD AN EMERGENCY. RIGHT, JOE?
WHAT? UH...
IS THAT TRUE, JOE? IS MIKE TELLING THE TRUTH?

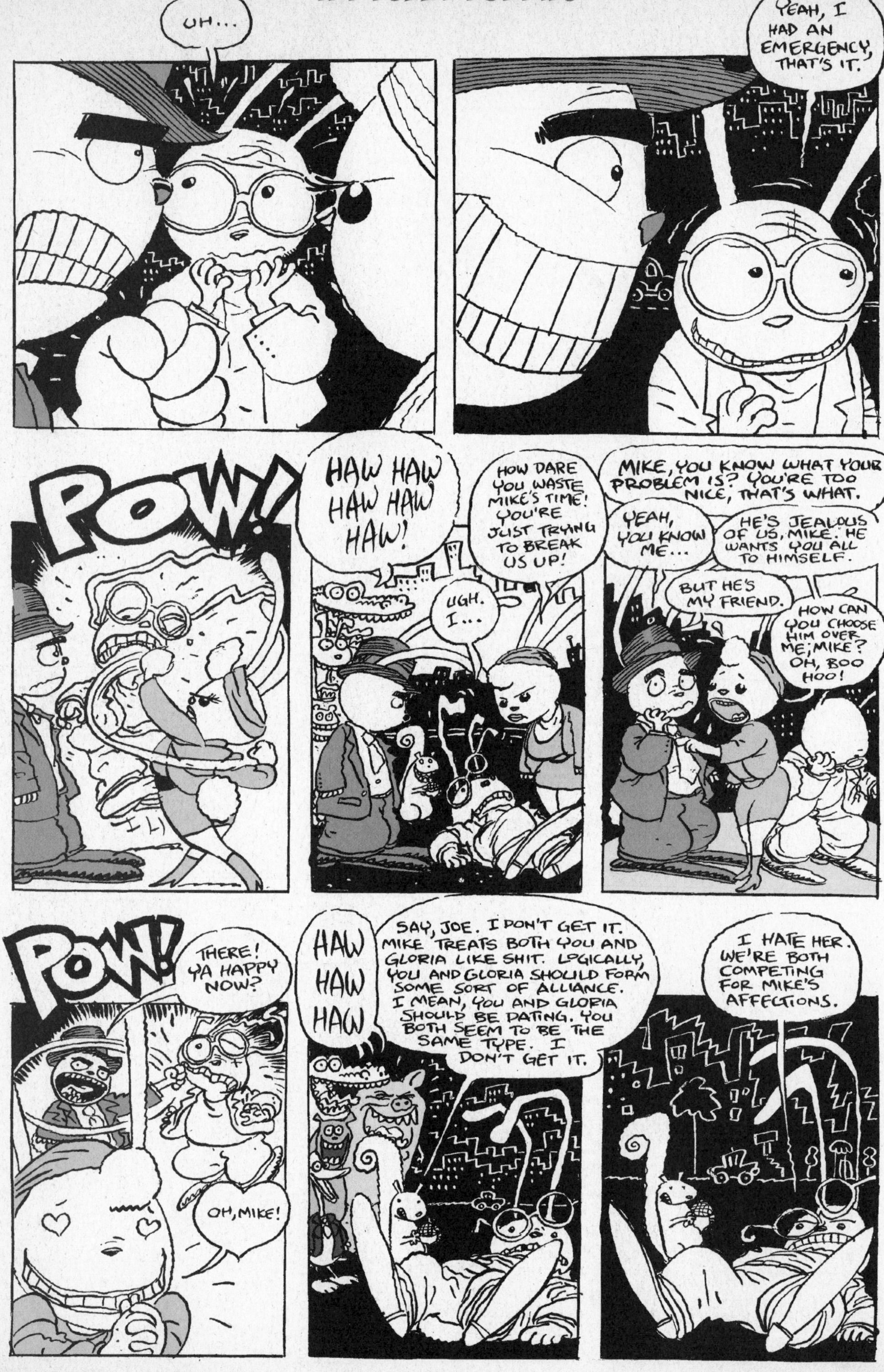
UH...
YEAH, I HAD AN EMERGENCY, THAT'S IT.
POW!
HAW HAW HAW HAW HAW!
HOW DARE YOU WASTE MIKE'S TIME! YOU'RE JUST TRYING TO BREAK US UP!
UGH. I...
MIKE, YOU KNOW WHAT YOUR PROBLEM IS? YOU'RE TOO NICE, THAT'S WHAT.
YEAH, YOU KNOW ME...
HE'S JEALOUS OF US, MIKE. HE WANTS YOU ALL TO HIMSELF.
BUT HE'S MY FRIEND.
HOW CAN YOU CHOOSE HIM OVER ME, MIKE? OH, BOO HOO!
POW!
THERE! YA HAPPY NOW?
OH, MIKE!
HAW HAW HAW
SAY, JOE. I DON'T GET IT. MIKE TREATS BOTH YOU AND GLORIA LIKE SHIT. LOGICALLY, YOU AND GLORIA SHOULD FORM SOME SORT OF ALLIANCE. I MEAN, YOU AND GLORIA SHOULD BE DATING. YOU BOTH SEEM TO BE THE SAME TYPE. I DON'T GET IT.
I HATE HER. WE'RE BOTH COMPETING FOR MIKE'S AFFECTIONS.

MOVIE STARS!

Arnold Schwarzennesser

Nicolas Cage

Will Smith

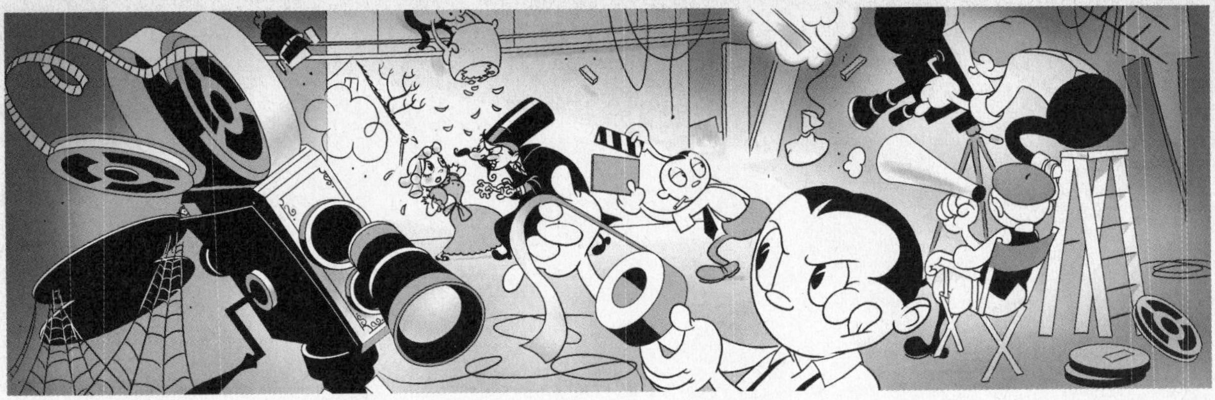

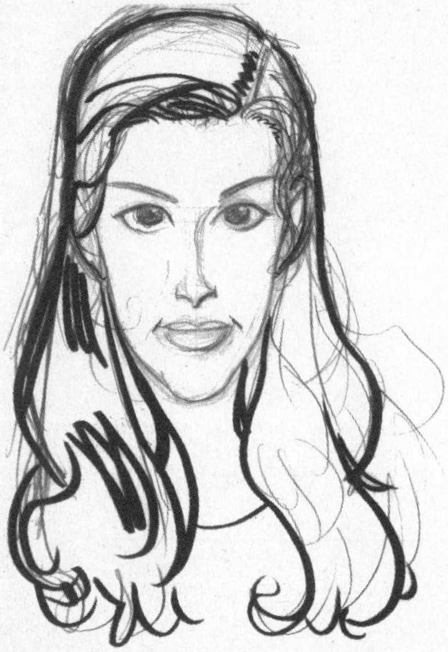

Liv Tyler

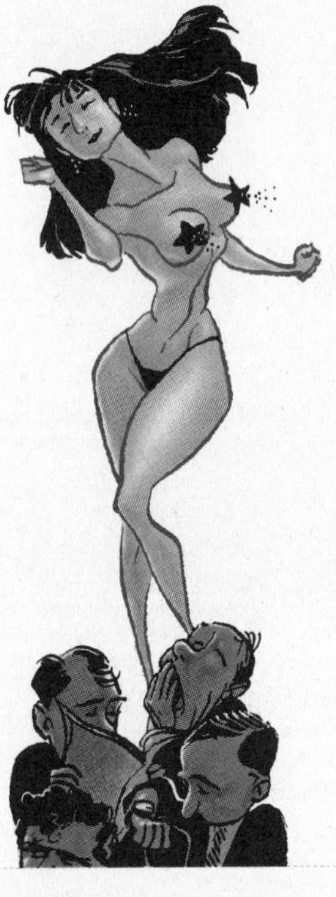

Demi Moore

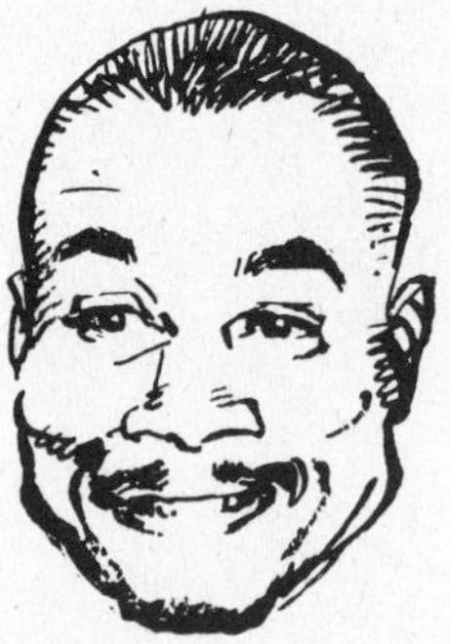

Cuba Gooding Jr.

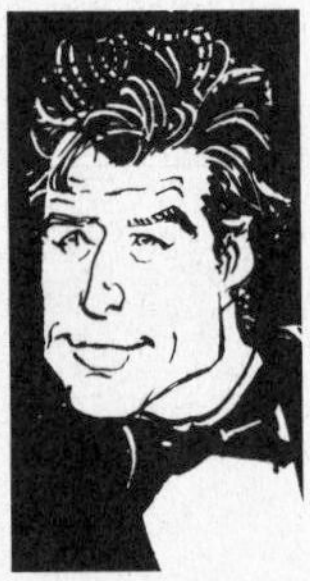

Pierce Brosnan

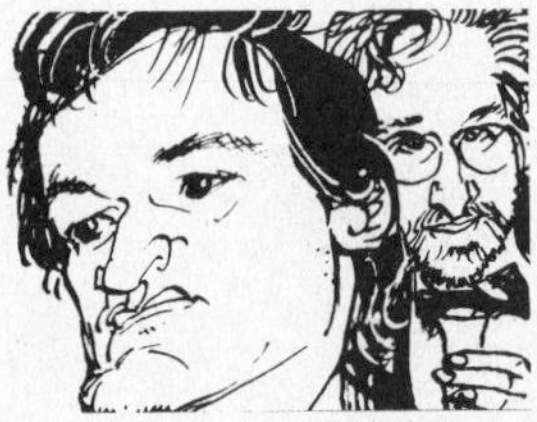

Quentin Tarantino and Steven Spielberg

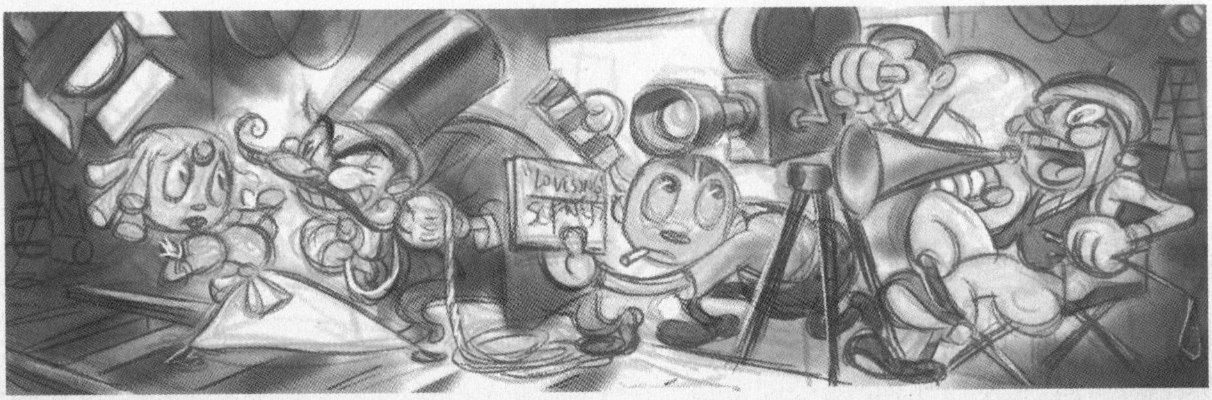

Denzel Washington

Larry Fishburne

Arnold Schwarzennegger

Forrest Whittaker

Jerry Lewis

Angela Bassett

Sam Jackson

Robert DeNiro

Morgan Freeman

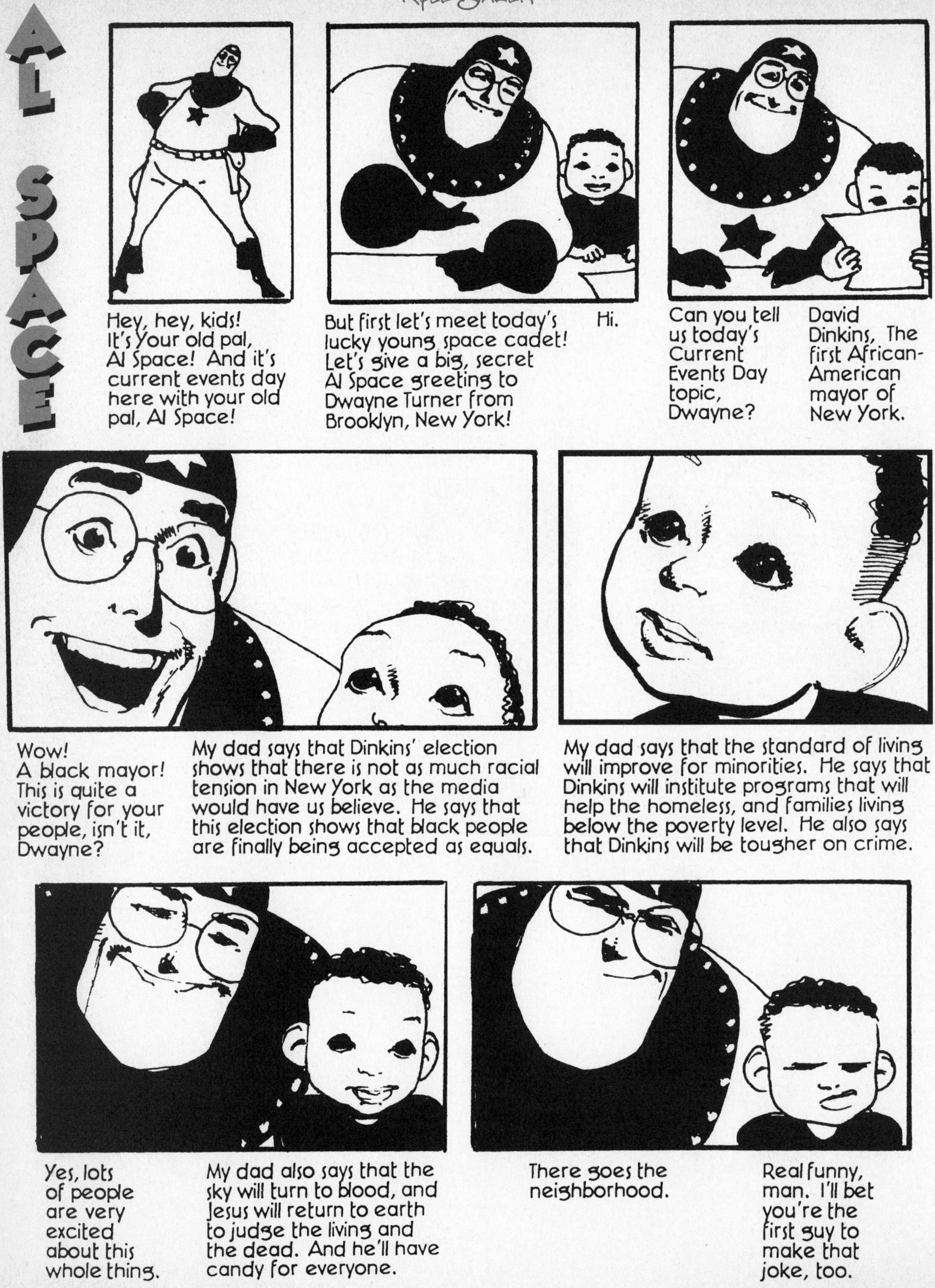
AL SPACE
Hey, hey, kids! It's your old pal, Al Space! And it's current events day here with your old pal, Al Space!
But first let's meet today's lucky young space cadet! Let's give a big, secret Al Space greeting to Dwayne Turner from Brooklyn, New York!
Hi.
Can you tell us today's Current Events Day topic, Dwayne?
David Dinkins, The first African-American mayor of New York.
Wow! A black mayor! This is quite a victory for your people, isn't it, Dwayne?
My dad says that Dinkins' election shows that there is not as much racial tension in New York as the media would have us believe. He says that this election shows that black people are finally being accepted as equals.
My dad says that the standard of living will improve for minorities. He says that Dinkins will institute programs that will help the homeless, and families living below the poverty level. He also says that Dinkins will be tougher on crime.
Yes, lots of people are very excited about this whole thing.
My dad also says that the sky will turn to blood, and Jesus will return to earth to judge the living and the dead. And he'll have candy for everyone.
There goes the neighborhood.
Real funny, man. I'll bet you're the first guy to make that joke, too.

Playing Darts
Against The Wind.

Kyle Baker

THE · COWBOY · WALLY · SHOW ·

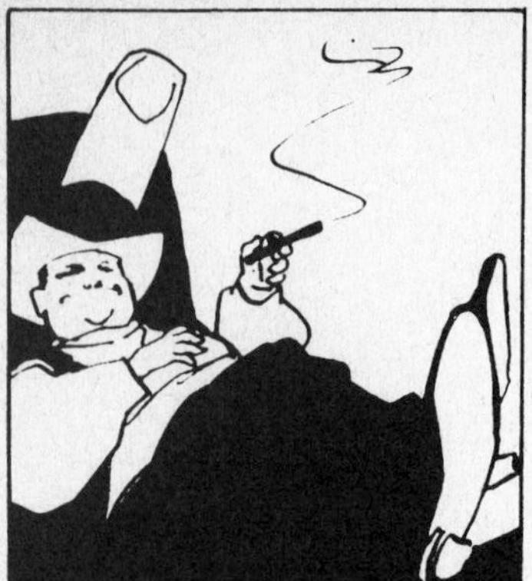

Hello, folks. You know, I'm a rich, successful kind of guy. I have a big car, big house, live the good life.

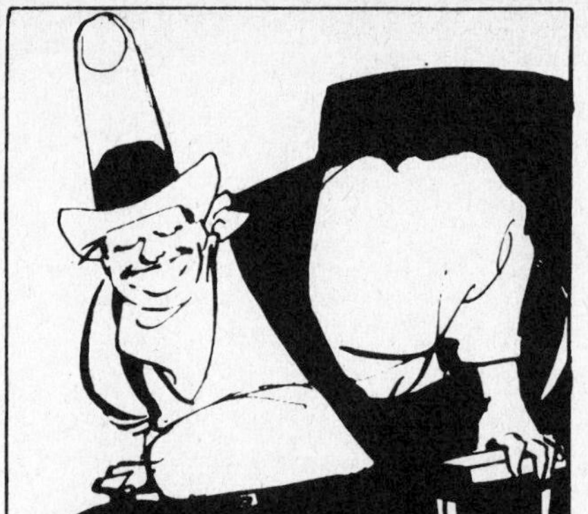

I got that way by producing what some folks call "pandering films of no artistic merit." I say "light entertainment." Some folks say I got here by indulging my greed and egotism. I say "ambition."

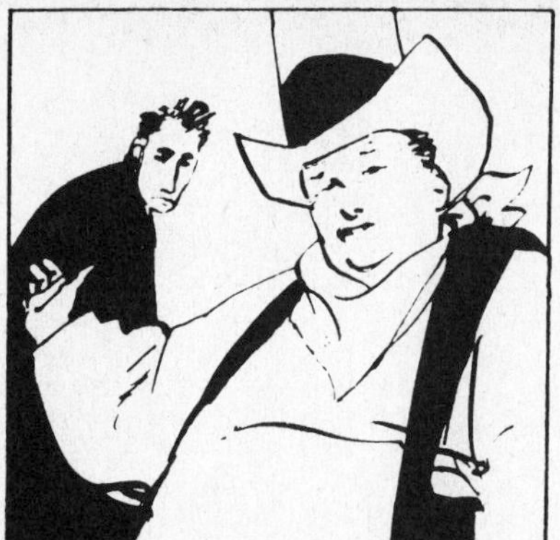

And everywhere I go, whether to the best nightclub in town, or judging a beauty contest, I hear tiny, tiny people like my assistant Lenny say the same old thing. And what is that, Lenny?

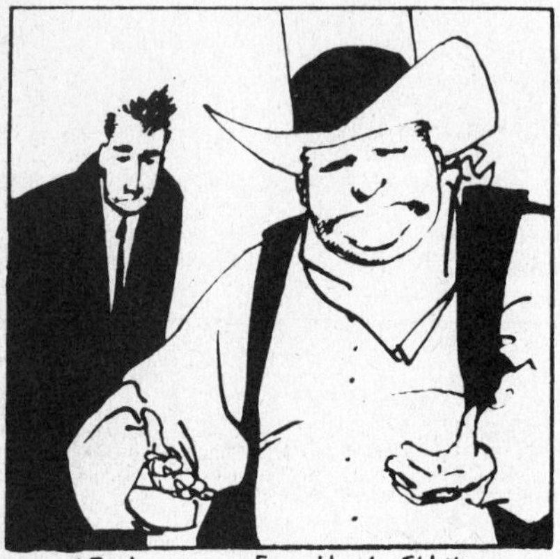

"But is he happy?"

Exactly. So I'd like to take this opportunity to address all of you tiny, tiny people. And what I want to say is this.

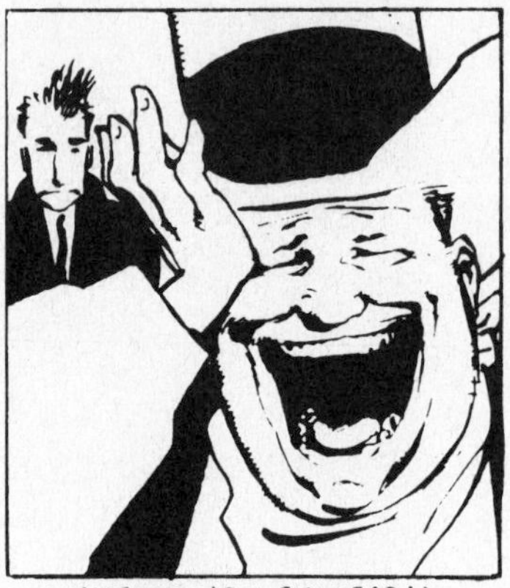

WAKE UP, YOU JUGHEADS! OF COURSE I'M HAPPY! QUIT FOOLING YOURSELVES! I'M RICH, FOR CHRISSAKES! YOU **WISH** YOU WERE ME, YOU TINY PUNKS! Hey, Vikki, c'mere!

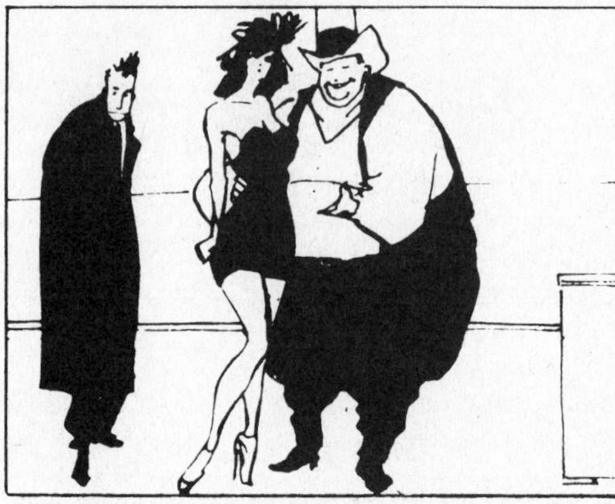

This is Vikki. She spells it V-I-K-K-I, the kind of misspelling which is the mark of a quality babe. Look at her. As if you could help it. Check out her fabulous body. Look at those heels. Look at all that makeup. And I get babes like this all the time.

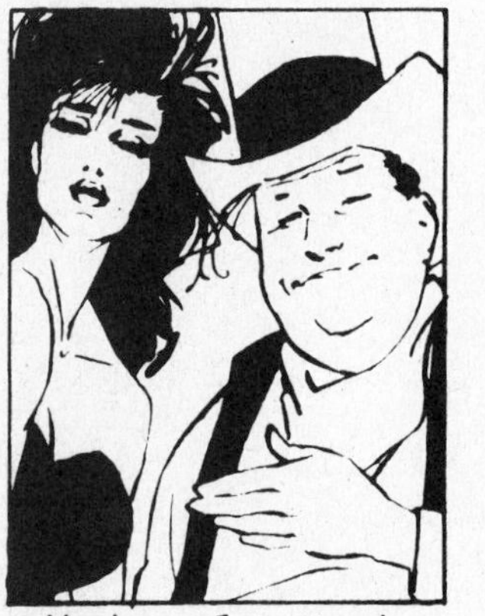

You know, I see great chicks like this walking down the street, and hear tiny, tiny, women mutter to each other, and what do they mutter, Lenny?

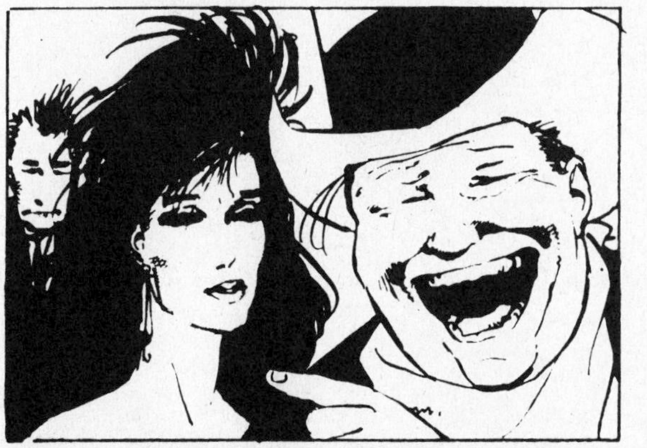

"Who's she kidding?"

HAH! WHO'S SHE KIDDING? SHE'S NOT KIDDING ANYONE! SHE'S SIX FEET TALL, WEIGHS 110 POUNDS, AND HAS GIGANTIC BREASTS! SHE'S DUMB AS A POST AND HAPPY ABOUT IT! GIVE UP, YOU PATHETIC TINY RODENT PEOPLE! WE'RE HAPPY, YOU'RE SAD! IT'S THAT SIMPLE! WHAT D'YOU SAY TO THAT?

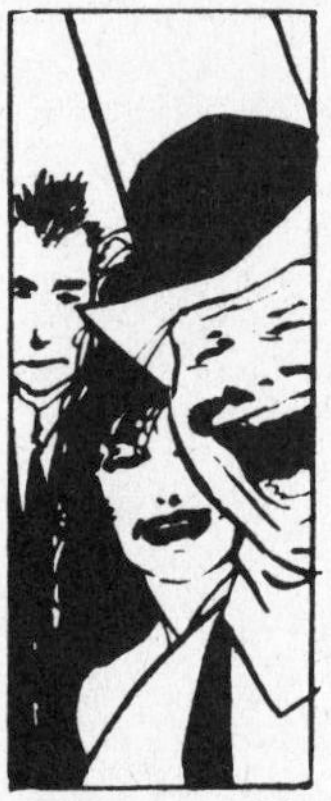

"You'll never get to heaven."

HA
HA
HA
HA
HA
HA

PEACE ON EARTH

Once upon a time, there was a man named Lou, and one day, he found a magic bottle, and when he opened it, a genie appeared.

The genie said,"I will grant you one wish."

"I thought it was three wishes."

"I don't really feel like it today, what're you gonna do about it, get another genie? Ha! Look, you want this wish or not?"

"Okay, I'll take it."

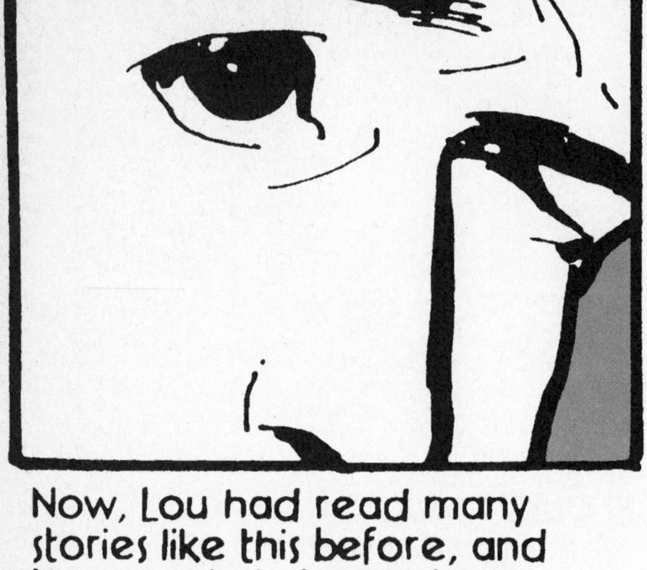

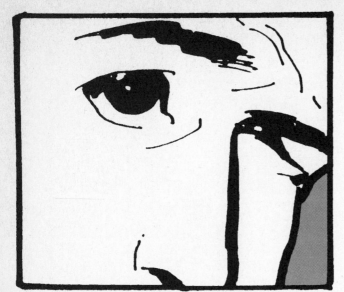

Now, Lou had read many stories like this before, and the people in these stories were usually outdone by their greed. Lou decided he would try a different tactic.

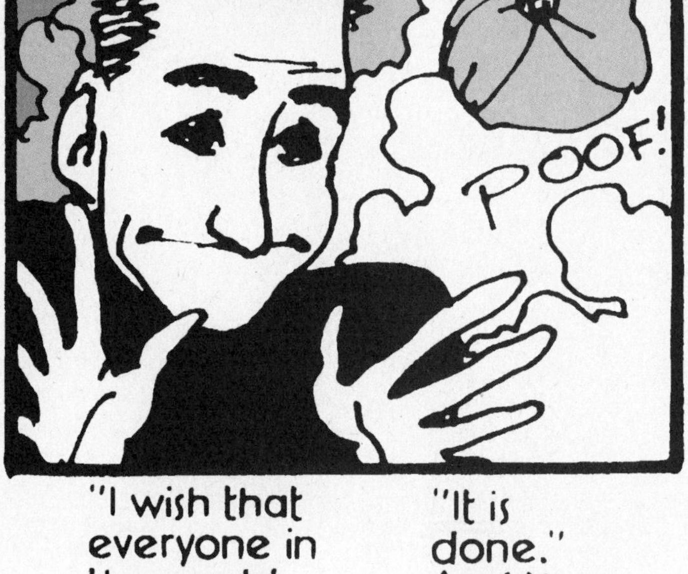
POOF!

"I wish that everyone in the world would love each other."

"It is done." And the genie vanished.

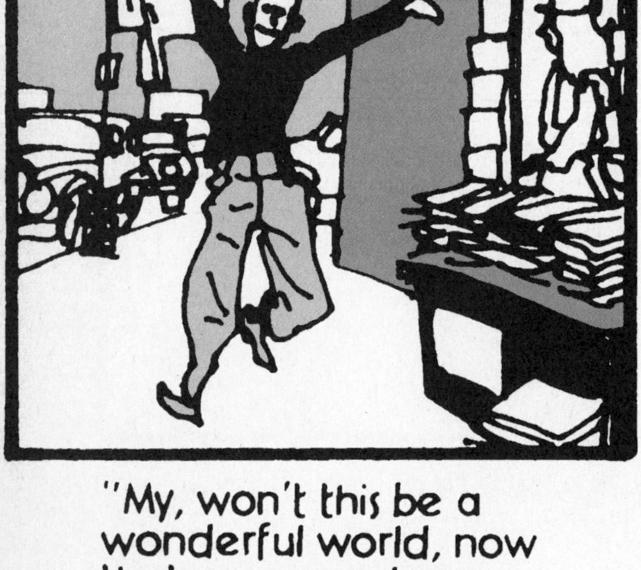

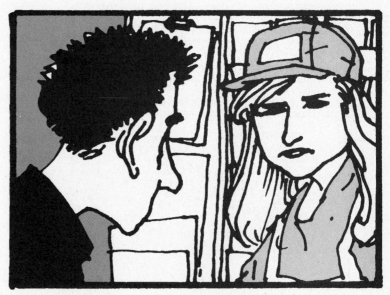

"My, won't this be a wonderful world, now that everyone loves each other," thought Lou, as he went out to get his newspaper.

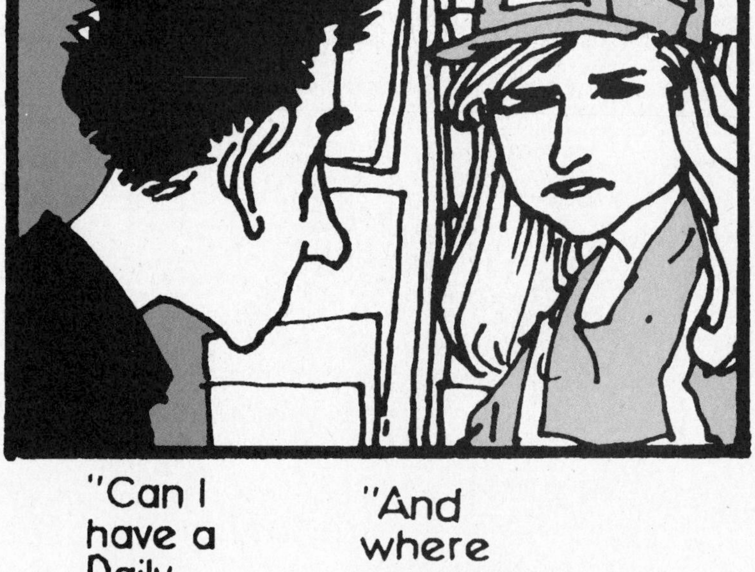

"Can I have a Daily News, please?

"And where were *you* yesterday?"

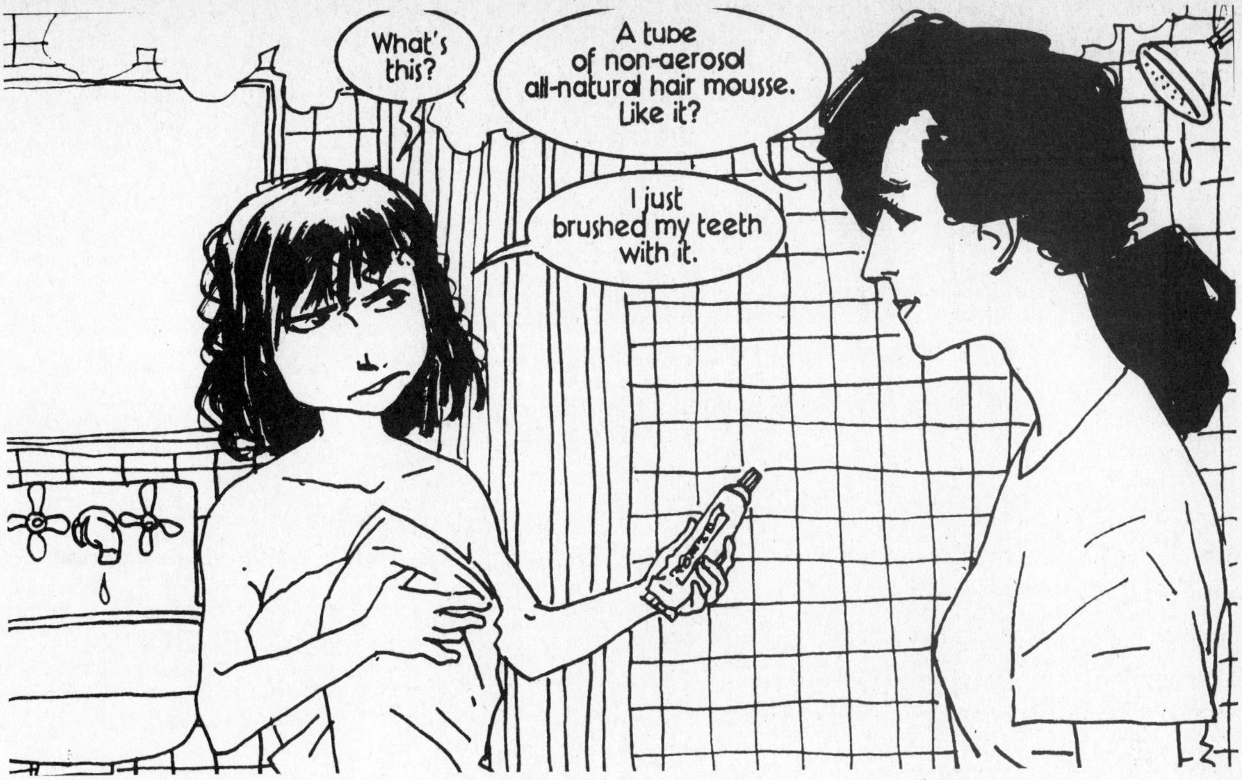
What's this?
A tube of non-aerosol all-natural hair mousse. Like it?
I just brushed my teeth with it.

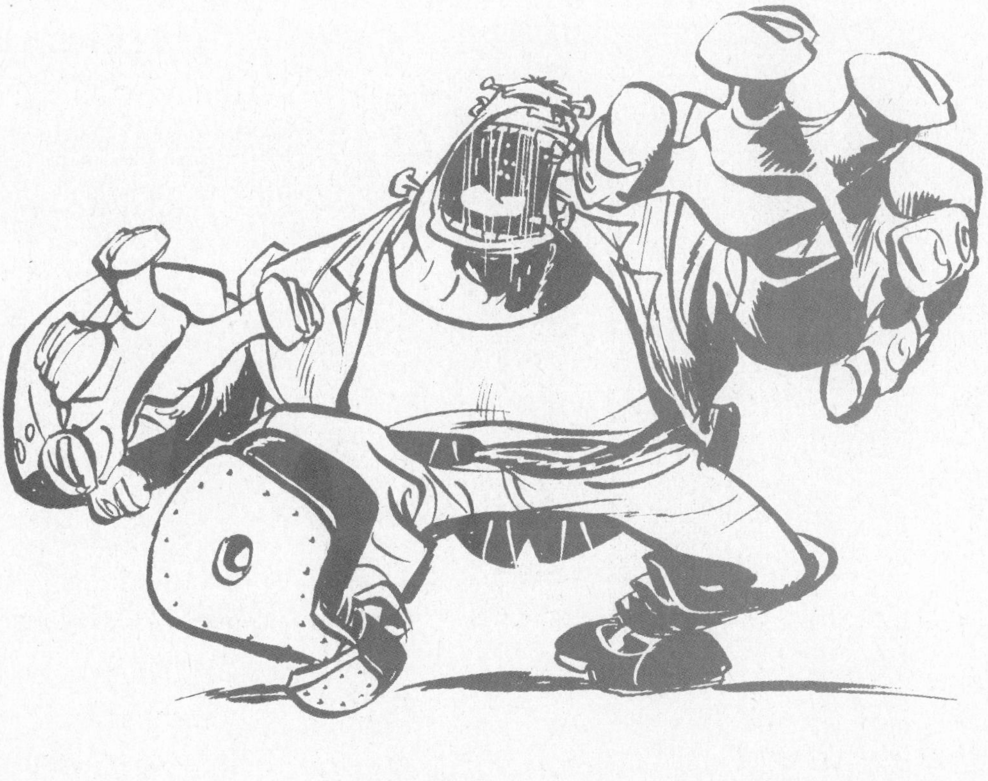

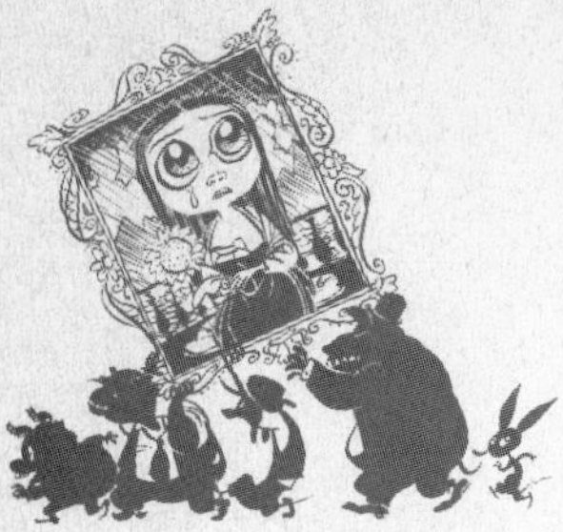

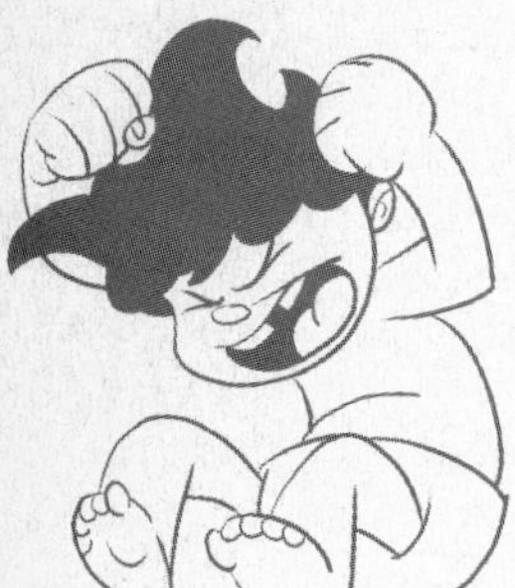

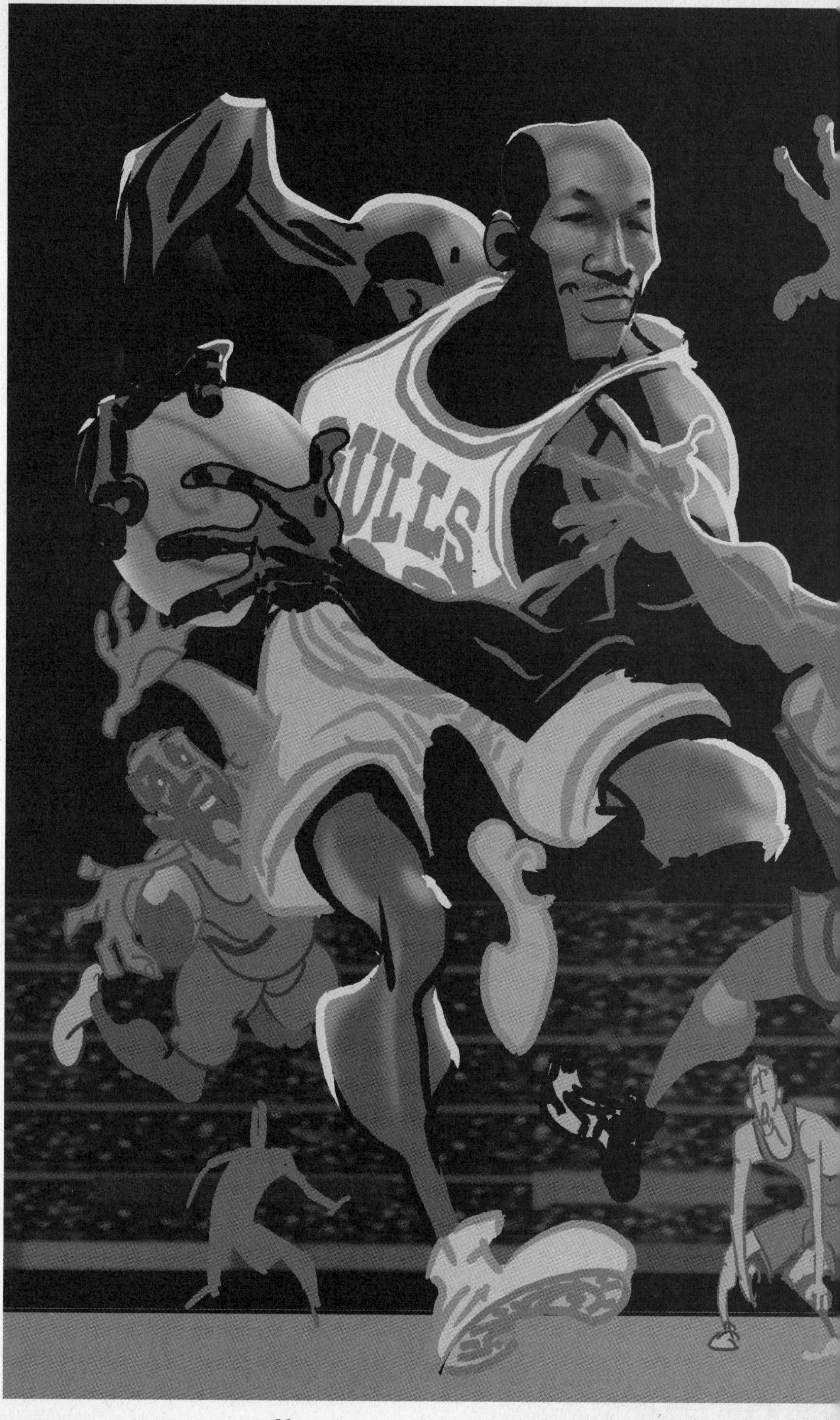
ULLS

SURE, WE'VE ALL HEARD ABOUT THE ENDORSEMENTS, THE COLOGNE, THE BIG-SCREEN ANTICS WITH BUGS BUNNY, AND THE SHOES, BUT DID YOU ALSO KNOW THAT MICHAEL JORDAN WAS ONCE A PROFESSIONAL BASKETBALL PLAYER? TEST YOUR MJ KNOWLEDGE WITH THIS—

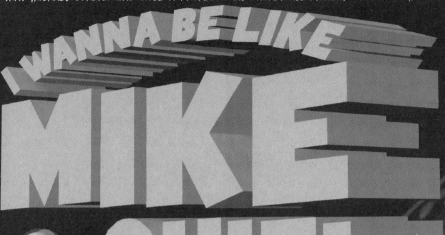

I WANNA BE LIKE MIKE QUIZ!

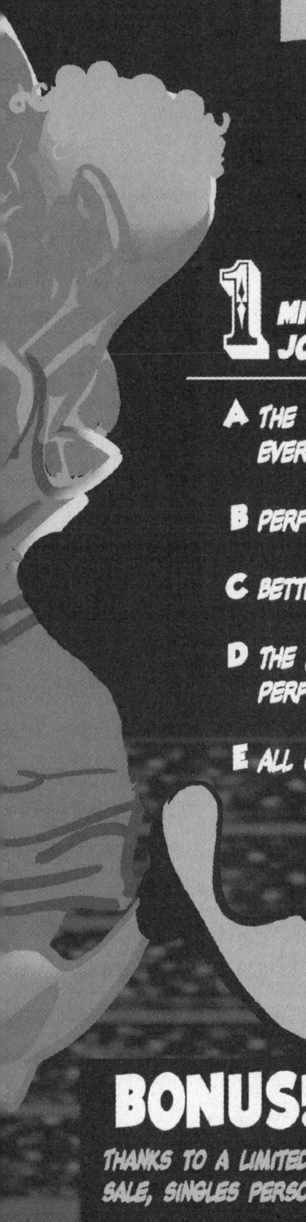

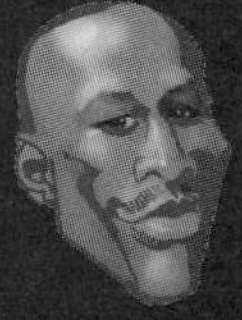

1 MICHAEL JORDAN IS:

A THE LIVING EMBODIMENT OF EVERY HUMAN IDEAL.

B PERFECT.

C BETTER THAN PERFECT.

D THE MICHAEL JORDAN OF PERFECTION.

E ALL OF THE ABOVE.

2 MICHAEL JORDAN CAN:

A LIFT A CAR OVER HIS HEAD.

B SHOOT LASER BEAMS FROM HIS EYES.

C BEND A REINFORCED STEEL I-BEAM WITH MENTAL TELEPATHY.

D MAKE YOU FORGET RODMAN'S IN THE SHOT.

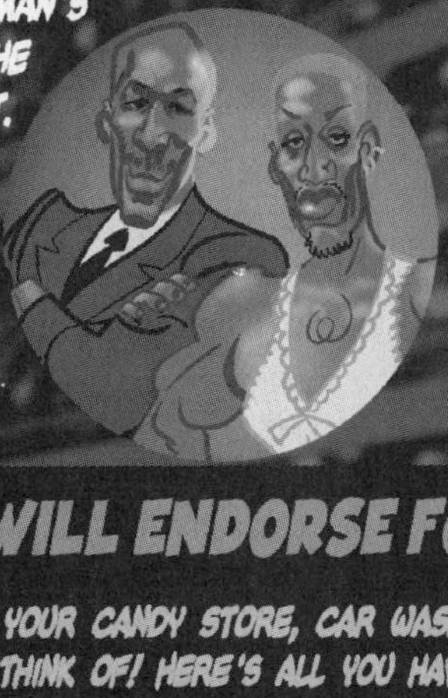

3 MICHAEL JORDAN'S NEXT VENTURE WILL BE:

A 114 NEW VARIETIES OF THE "AIR JORDAN MEGAPLATINUM HYPER-DELUXE LIMITED EDITION 3-D SIGNED AND NUMBERED BLASTMASTER SHOE".

B HEALING INCURABLE DISEASE AND BRINGING SIGHT TO THE BLIND MERELY BY LAYING HIS HANDS UPON THE AFFLICTED.

C SPENDING MORE TIME WITH HIS KIDS.

D ALL OF THE ABOVE.

BONUS! MICHAEL JORDAN WILL ENDORSE FOR YOU!

THANKS TO A LIMITED-TIME OFFER, MICHAEL WILL ENDORSE YOUR CANDY STORE, CAR WASH, CHURCH BAKE SALE, SINGLES PERSONAL AD OR WHATEVER ELSE YOU CAN THINK OF! HERE'S ALL YOU HAVE TO DO:

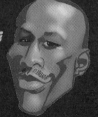

STEP ONE: CUT OUT THE HANDY MJ TRADEMARK (FIG. 1, AT RIGHT), AND AFFIX IT TO WHATEVER YOU WANT MICHAEL TO ENDORSE.

STEP TWO: SEND MICHAEL A CERTIFIED CHECK FOR TWO HUNDRED MILLION DOLLARS.

IT'S THAT SIMPLE!

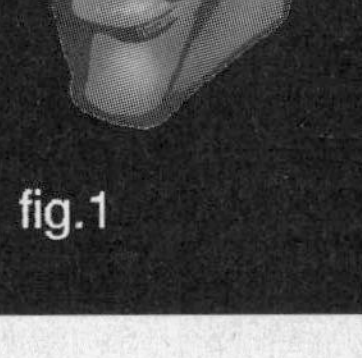

fig.1

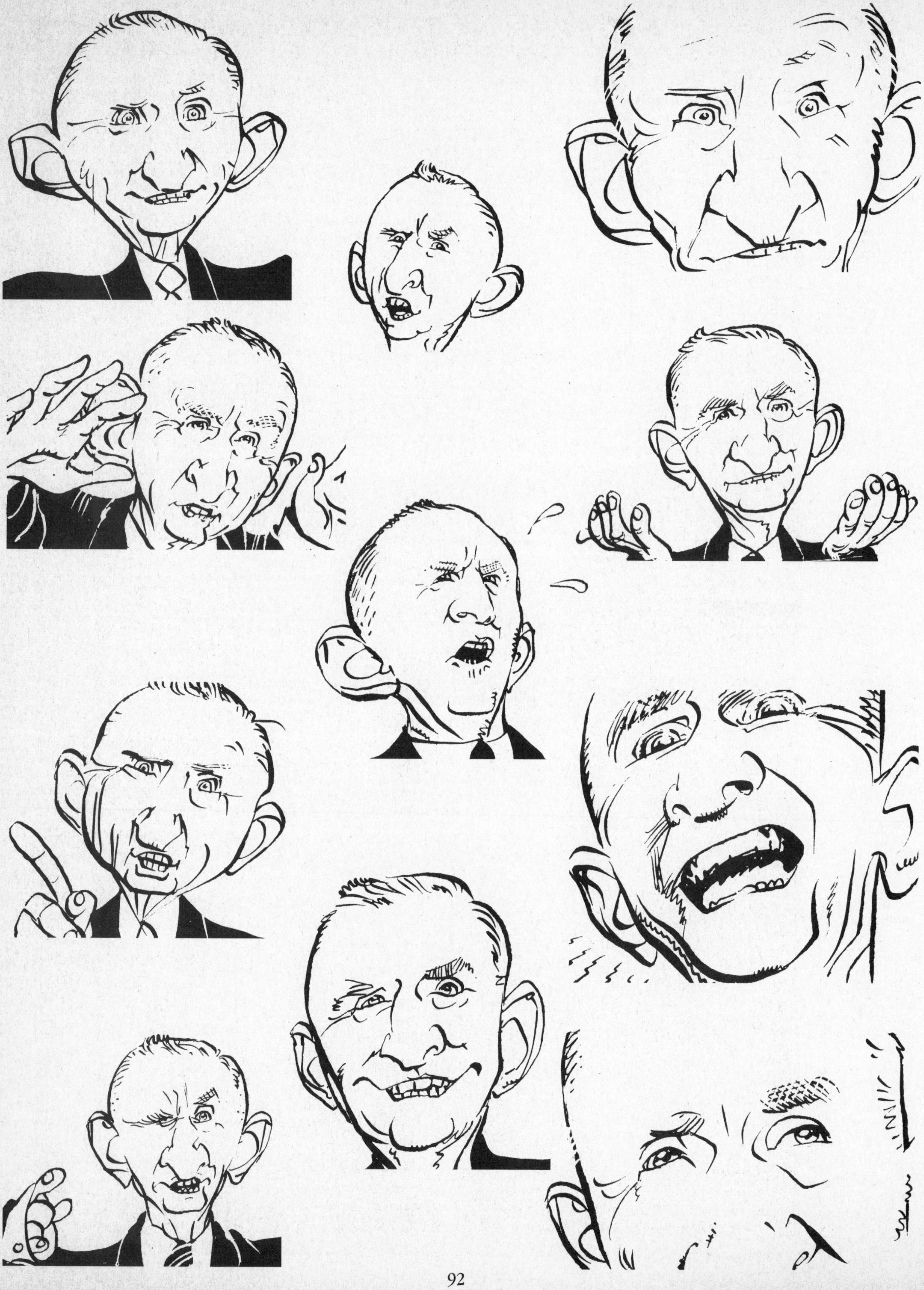

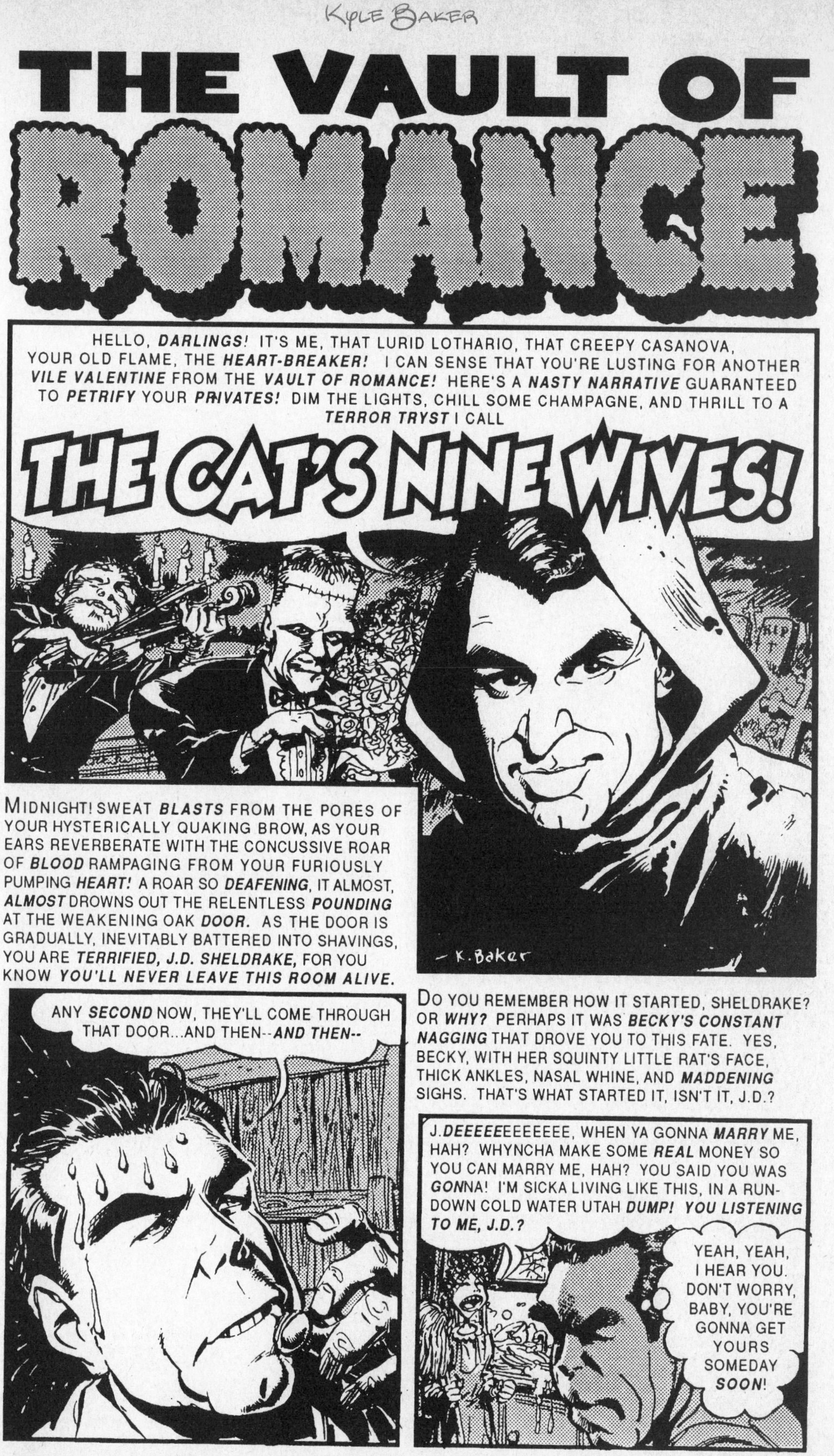
KYLE BAKER
THE VAULT OF
ROMANCE
HELLO, DARLINGS! IT'S ME, THAT LURID LOTHARIO, THAT CREEPY CASANOVA, YOUR OLD FLAME, THE HEART-BREAKER! I CAN SENSE THAT YOU'RE LUSTING FOR ANOTHER VILE VALENTINE FROM THE VAULT OF ROMANCE! HERE'S A NASTY NARRATIVE GUARANTEED TO PETRIFY YOUR PRIVATES! DIM THE LIGHTS, CHILL SOME CHAMPAGNE, AND THRILL TO A TERROR TRYST I CALL
THE CAT'S NINE WIVES!
— K. Baker
MIDNIGHT! SWEAT BLASTS FROM THE PORES OF YOUR HYSTERICALLY QUAKING BROW, AS YOUR EARS REVERBERATE WITH THE CONCUSSIVE ROAR OF BLOOD RAMPAGING FROM YOUR FURIOUSLY PUMPING HEART! A ROAR SO DEAFENING, IT ALMOST, ALMOST DROWNS OUT THE RELENTLESS POUNDING AT THE WEAKENING OAK DOOR. AS THE DOOR IS GRADUALLY, INEVITABLY BATTERED INTO SHAVINGS, YOU ARE TERRIFIED, J.D. SHELDRAKE, FOR YOU KNOW YOU'LL NEVER LEAVE THIS ROOM ALIVE.
ANY SECOND NOW, THEY'LL COME THROUGH THAT DOOR...AND THEN--AND THEN--
DO YOU REMEMBER HOW IT STARTED, SHELDRAKE? OR WHY? PERHAPS IT WAS BECKY'S CONSTANT NAGGING THAT DROVE YOU TO THIS FATE. YES, BECKY, WITH HER SQUINTY LITTLE RAT'S FACE, THICK ANKLES, NASAL WHINE, AND MADDENING SIGHS. THAT'S WHAT STARTED IT, ISN'T IT, J.D.?
J.DEEEEEEEEEEE, WHEN YA GONNA MARRY ME, HAH? WHYNCHA MAKE SOME REAL MONEY SO YOU CAN MARRY ME, HAH? YOU SAID YOU WAS GONNA! I'M SICKA LIVING LIKE THIS, IN A RUN-DOWN COLD WATER UTAH DUMP! YOU LISTENING TO ME, J.D.?
YEAH, YEAH, I HEAR YOU. DON'T WORRY, BABY, YOU'RE GONNA GET YOURS SOMEDAY SOON!

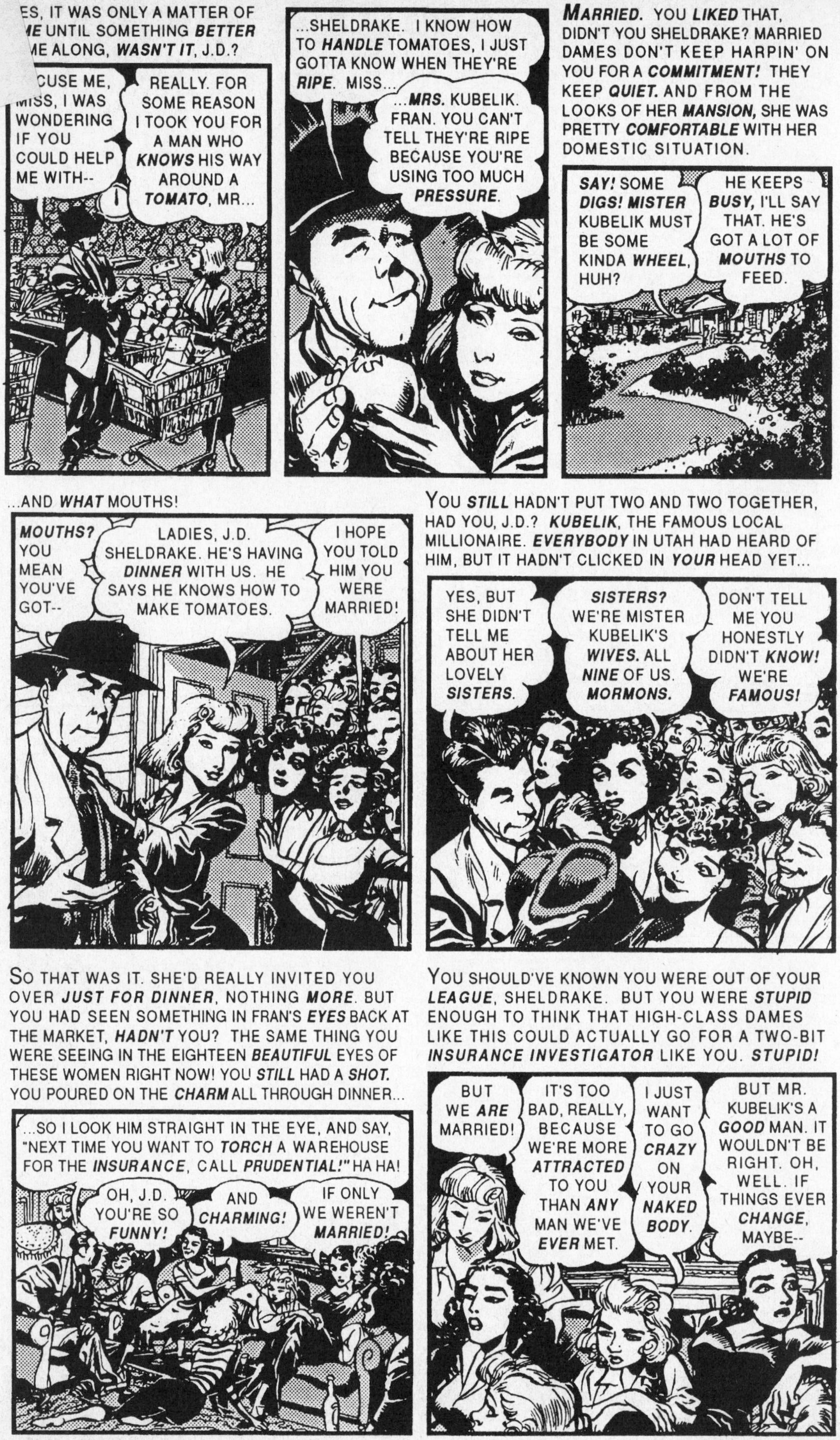
ES, IT WAS ONLY A MATTER OF
ME UNTIL SOMETHING BETTER
ME ALONG, WASN'T IT, J.D.?
CUSE ME, MISS, I WAS WONDERING IF YOU COULD HELP ME WITH--
REALLY. FOR SOME REASON I TOOK YOU FOR A MAN WHO KNOWS HIS WAY AROUND A TOMATO, MR...
...SHELDRAKE. I KNOW HOW TO HANDLE TOMATOES, I JUST GOTTA KNOW WHEN THEY'RE RIPE. MISS...
...MRS. KUBELIK. FRAN. YOU CAN'T TELL THEY'RE RIPE BECAUSE YOU'RE USING TOO MUCH PRESSURE.
MARRIED. YOU LIKED THAT, DIDN'T YOU SHELDRAKE? MARRIED DAMES DON'T KEEP HARPIN' ON YOU FOR A COMMITMENT! THEY KEEP QUIET. AND FROM THE LOOKS OF HER MANSION, SHE WAS PRETTY COMFORTABLE WITH HER DOMESTIC SITUATION.
SAY! SOME DIGS! MISTER KUBELIK MUST BE SOME KINDA WHEEL, HUH?
HE KEEPS BUSY, I'LL SAY THAT. HE'S GOT A LOT OF MOUTHS TO FEED.
...AND WHAT MOUTHS!
MOUTHS? YOU MEAN YOU'VE GOT--
LADIES, J.D. SHELDRAKE. HE'S HAVING DINNER WITH US. HE SAYS HE KNOWS HOW TO MAKE TOMATOES.
I HOPE YOU TOLD HIM YOU WERE MARRIED!
YOU STILL HADN'T PUT TWO AND TWO TOGETHER, HAD YOU, J.D.? KUBELIK, THE FAMOUS LOCAL MILLIONAIRE. EVERYBODY IN UTAH HAD HEARD OF HIM, BUT IT HADN'T CLICKED IN YOUR HEAD YET...
YES, BUT SHE DIDN'T TELL ME ABOUT HER LOVELY SISTERS.
SISTERS? WE'RE MISTER KUBELIK'S WIVES. ALL NINE OF US. MORMONS.
DON'T TELL ME YOU HONESTLY DIDN'T KNOW! WE'RE FAMOUS!
SO THAT WAS IT. SHE'D REALLY INVITED YOU OVER JUST FOR DINNER, NOTHING MORE. BUT YOU HAD SEEN SOMETHING IN FRAN'S EYES BACK AT THE MARKET, HADN'T YOU? THE SAME THING YOU WERE SEEING IN THE EIGHTEEN BEAUTIFUL EYES OF THESE WOMEN RIGHT NOW! YOU STILL HAD A SHOT. YOU POURED ON THE CHARM ALL THROUGH DINNER...
...SO I LOOK HIM STRAIGHT IN THE EYE, AND SAY, "NEXT TIME YOU WANT TO TORCH A WAREHOUSE FOR THE INSURANCE, CALL PRUDENTIAL!" HA HA!
OH, J.D. YOU'RE SO FUNNY!
AND CHARMING!
IF ONLY WE WEREN'T MARRIED!
YOU SHOULD'VE KNOWN YOU WERE OUT OF YOUR LEAGUE, SHELDRAKE. BUT YOU WERE STUPID ENOUGH TO THINK THAT HIGH-CLASS DAMES LIKE THIS COULD ACTUALLY GO FOR A TWO-BIT INSURANCE INVESTIGATOR LIKE YOU. STUPID!
BUT WE ARE MARRIED!
IT'S TOO BAD, REALLY, BECAUSE WE'RE MORE ATTRACTED TO YOU THAN ANY MAN WE'VE EVER MET.
I JUST WANT TO GO CRAZY ON YOUR NAKED BODY.
BUT MR. KUBELIK'S A GOOD MAN. IT WOULDN'T BE RIGHT. OH, WELL. IF THINGS EVER CHANGE, MAYBE--

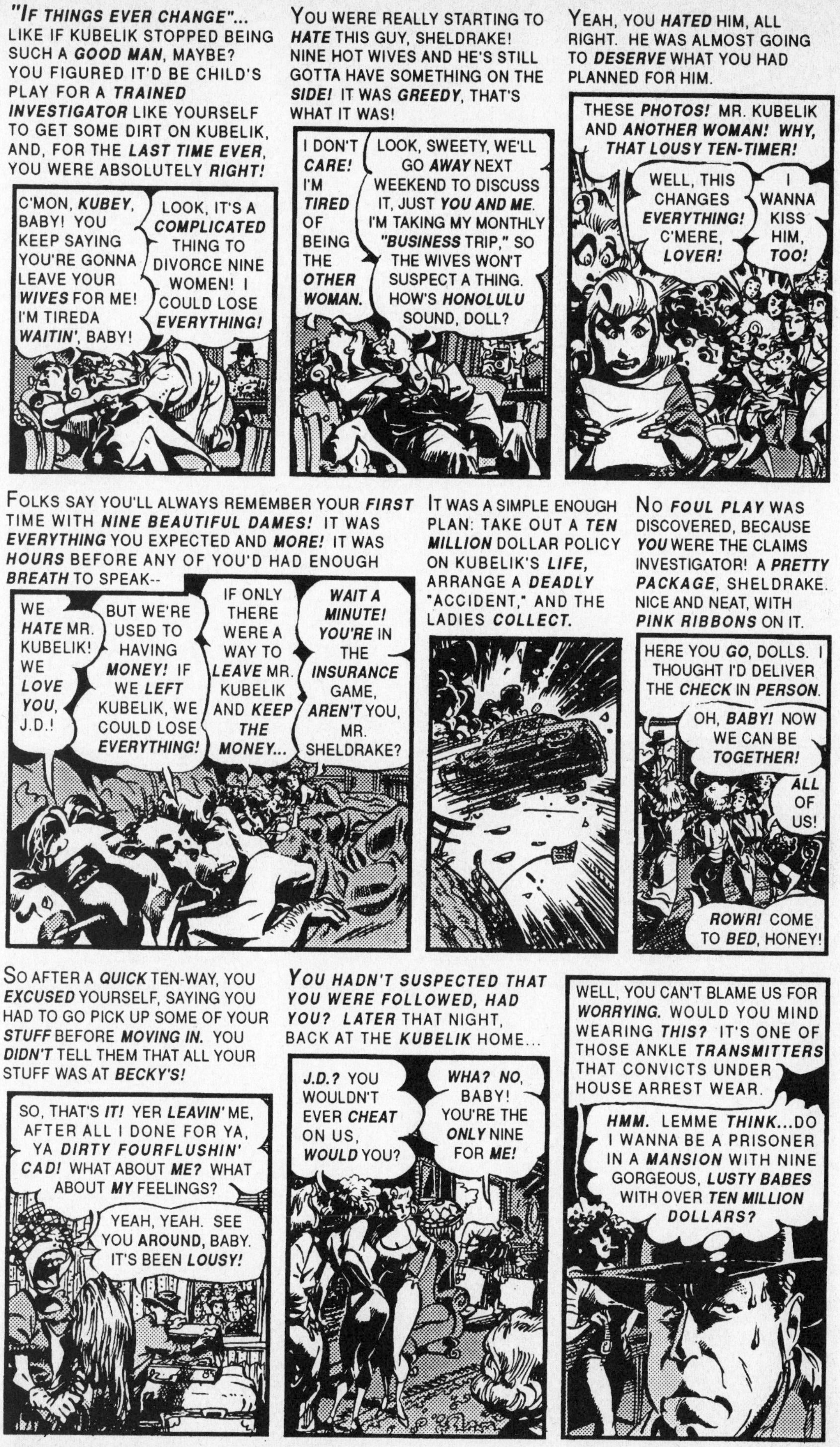
"IF THINGS EVER CHANGE"... LIKE IF KUBELIK STOPPED BEING SUCH A GOOD MAN, MAYBE? YOU FIGURED IT'D BE CHILD'S PLAY FOR A TRAINED INVESTIGATOR LIKE YOURSELF TO GET SOME DIRT ON KUBELIK, AND, FOR THE LAST TIME EVER, YOU WERE ABSOLUTELY RIGHT!
C'MON, KUBEY, BABY! YOU KEEP SAYING YOU'RE GONNA LEAVE YOUR WIVES FOR ME! I'M TIREDA WAITIN', BABY!
LOOK, IT'S A COMPLICATED THING TO DIVORCE NINE WOMEN! I COULD LOSE EVERYTHING!
YOU WERE REALLY STARTING TO HATE THIS GUY, SHELDRAKE! NINE HOT WIVES AND HE'S STILL GOTTA HAVE SOMETHING ON THE SIDE! IT WAS GREEDY, THAT'S WHAT IT WAS!
I DON'T CARE! I'M TIRED OF BEING THE OTHER WOMAN.
LOOK, SWEETY, WE'LL GO AWAY NEXT WEEKEND TO DISCUSS IT, JUST YOU AND ME. I'M TAKING MY MONTHLY "BUSINESS TRIP," SO THE WIVES WON'T SUSPECT A THING. HOW'S HONOLULU SOUND, DOLL?
YEAH, YOU HATED HIM, ALL RIGHT. HE WAS ALMOST GOING TO DESERVE WHAT YOU HAD PLANNED FOR HIM.
THESE PHOTOS! MR. KUBELIK AND ANOTHER WOMAN! WHY, THAT LOUSY TEN-TIMER!
WELL, THIS CHANGES EVERYTHING! C'MERE, LOVER!
I WANNA KISS HIM, TOO!
FOLKS SAY YOU'LL ALWAYS REMEMBER YOUR FIRST TIME WITH NINE BEAUTIFUL DAMES! IT WAS EVERYTHING YOU EXPECTED AND MORE! IT WAS HOURS BEFORE ANY OF YOU'D HAD ENOUGH BREATH TO SPEAK--
WE HATE MR. KUBELIK! WE LOVE YOU, J.D.!
BUT WE'RE USED TO HAVING MONEY! IF WE LEFT KUBELIK, WE COULD LOSE EVERYTHING!
IF ONLY THERE WERE A WAY TO LEAVE MR. KUBELIK AND KEEP THE MONEY...
WAIT A MINUTE! YOU'RE IN THE INSURANCE GAME, AREN'T YOU, MR. SHELDRAKE?
IT WAS A SIMPLE ENOUGH PLAN: TAKE OUT A TEN MILLION DOLLAR POLICY ON KUBELIK'S LIFE, ARRANGE A DEADLY "ACCIDENT," AND THE LADIES COLLECT.
NO FOUL PLAY WAS DISCOVERED, BECAUSE YOU WERE THE CLAIMS INVESTIGATOR! A PRETTY PACKAGE, SHELDRAKE. NICE AND NEAT, WITH PINK RIBBONS ON IT.
HERE YOU GO, DOLLS. I THOUGHT I'D DELIVER THE CHECK IN PERSON.
OH, BABY! NOW WE CAN BE TOGETHER!
ALL OF US!
ROWR! COME TO BED, HONEY!
SO AFTER A QUICK TEN-WAY, YOU EXCUSED YOURSELF, SAYING YOU HAD TO GO PICK UP SOME OF YOUR STUFF BEFORE MOVING IN. YOU DIDN'T TELL THEM THAT ALL YOUR STUFF WAS AT BECKY'S!
SO, THAT'S IT! YER LEAVIN' ME, AFTER ALL I DONE FOR YA, YA DIRTY FOURFLUSHIN' CAD! WHAT ABOUT ME? WHAT ABOUT MY FEELINGS?
YEAH, YEAH. SEE YOU AROUND, BABY. IT'S BEEN LOUSY!
YOU HADN'T SUSPECTED THAT YOU WERE FOLLOWED, HAD YOU? LATER THAT NIGHT, BACK AT THE KUBELIK HOME...
J.D.? YOU WOULDN'T EVER CHEAT ON US, WOULD YOU?
WHA? NO, BABY! YOU'RE THE ONLY NINE FOR ME!
WELL, YOU CAN'T BLAME US FOR WORRYING. WOULD YOU MIND WEARING THIS? IT'S ONE OF THOSE ANKLE TRANSMITTERS THAT CONVICTS UNDER HOUSE ARREST WEAR.
HMM. LEMME THINK...DO I WANNA BE A PRISONER IN A MANSION WITH NINE GORGEOUS, LUSTY BABES WITH OVER TEN MILLION DOLLARS?

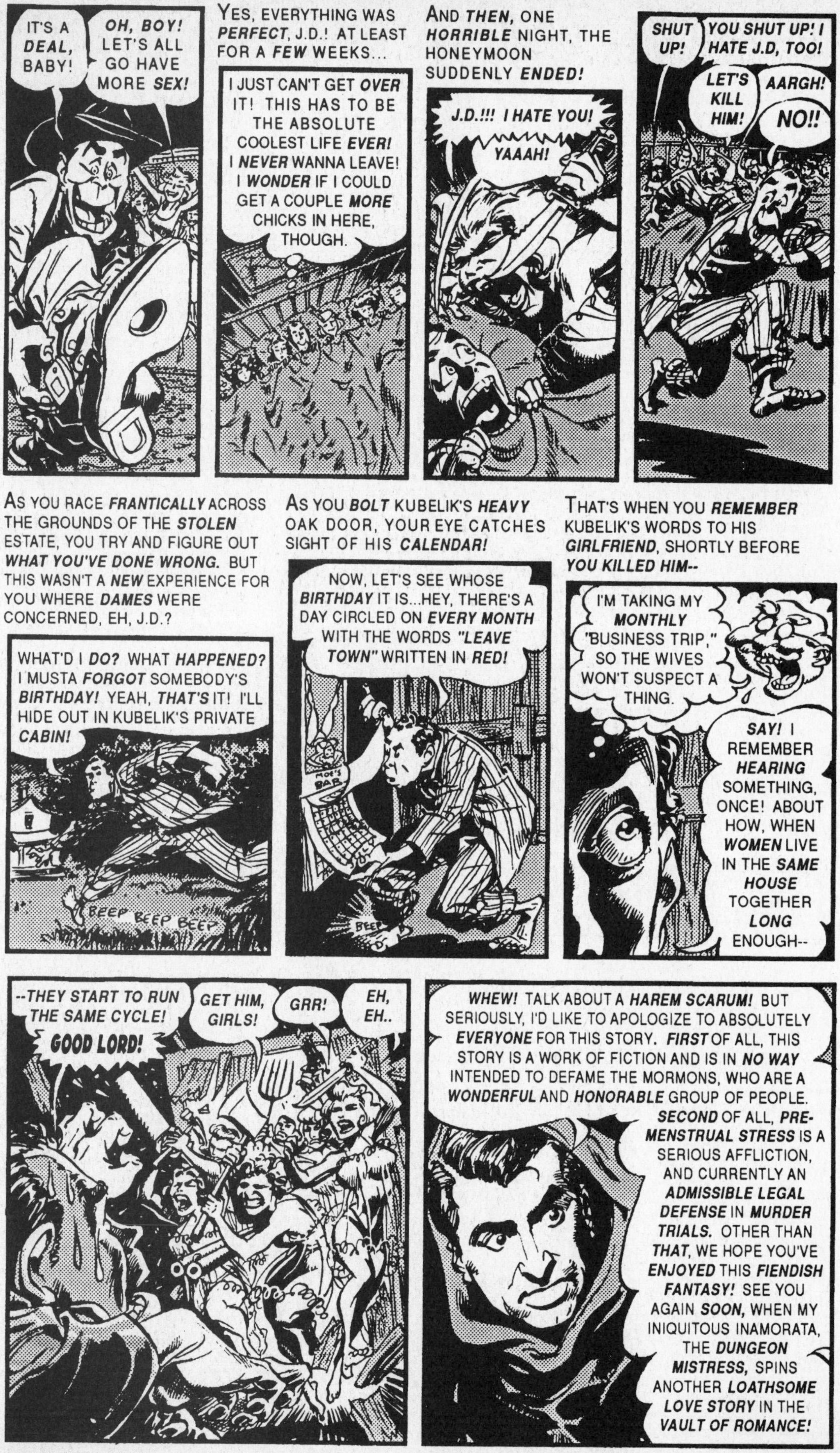
IT'S A DEAL, BABY!
OH, BOY! LET'S ALL GO HAVE MORE SEX!
YES, EVERYTHING WAS PERFECT, J.D.! AT LEAST FOR A FEW WEEKS...
I JUST CAN'T GET OVER IT! THIS HAS TO BE THE ABSOLUTE COOLEST LIFE EVER! I NEVER WANNA LEAVE! I WONDER IF I COULD GET A COUPLE MORE CHICKS IN HERE, THOUGH.
AND THEN, ONE HORRIBLE NIGHT, THE HONEYMOON SUDDENLY ENDED!
J.D.!!! I HATE YOU!
YAAAH!
SHUT UP!
YOU SHUT UP! I HATE J.D, TOO!
LET'S KILL HIM!
AARGH!
NO!!
AS YOU RACE FRANTICALLY ACROSS THE GROUNDS OF THE STOLEN ESTATE, YOU TRY AND FIGURE OUT WHAT YOU'VE DONE WRONG. BUT THIS WASN'T A NEW EXPERIENCE FOR YOU WHERE DAMES WERE CONCERNED, EH, J.D.?
WHAT'D I DO? WHAT HAPPENED? I MUSTA FORGOT SOMEBODY'S BIRTHDAY! YEAH, THAT'S IT! I'LL HIDE OUT IN KUBELIK'S PRIVATE CABIN!
BEEP BEEP BEEP
AS YOU BOLT KUBELIK'S HEAVY OAK DOOR, YOUR EYE CATCHES SIGHT OF HIS CALENDAR!
NOW, LET'S SEE WHOSE BIRTHDAY IT IS...HEY, THERE'S A DAY CIRCLED ON EVERY MONTH WITH THE WORDS "LEAVE TOWN" WRITTEN IN RED!
MOE'S BAR
BEEP
THAT'S WHEN YOU REMEMBER KUBELIK'S WORDS TO HIS GIRLFRIEND, SHORTLY BEFORE YOU KILLED HIM--
I'M TAKING MY MONTHLY "BUSINESS TRIP," SO THE WIVES WON'T SUSPECT A THING.
SAY! I REMEMBER HEARING SOMETHING, ONCE! ABOUT HOW, WHEN WOMEN LIVE IN THE SAME HOUSE TOGETHER LONG ENOUGH--
--THEY START TO RUN THE SAME CYCLE!
GOOD LORD!
GET HIM, GIRLS!
GRR!
EH, EH..
WHEW! TALK ABOUT A HAREM SCARUM! BUT SERIOUSLY, I'D LIKE TO APOLOGIZE TO ABSOLUTELY EVERYONE FOR THIS STORY. FIRST OF ALL, THIS STORY IS A WORK OF FICTION AND IS IN NO WAY INTENDED TO DEFAME THE MORMONS, WHO ARE A WONDERFUL AND HONORABLE GROUP OF PEOPLE. SECOND OF ALL, PRE-MENSTRUAL STRESS IS A SERIOUS AFFLICTION, AND CURRENTLY AN ADMISSIBLE LEGAL DEFENSE IN MURDER TRIALS. OTHER THAN THAT, WE HOPE YOU'VE ENJOYED THIS FIENDISH FANTASY! SEE YOU AGAIN SOON, WHEN MY INIQUITOUS INAMORATA, THE DUNGEON MISTRESS, SPINS ANOTHER LOATHSOME LOVE STORY IN THE VAULT OF ROMANCE!

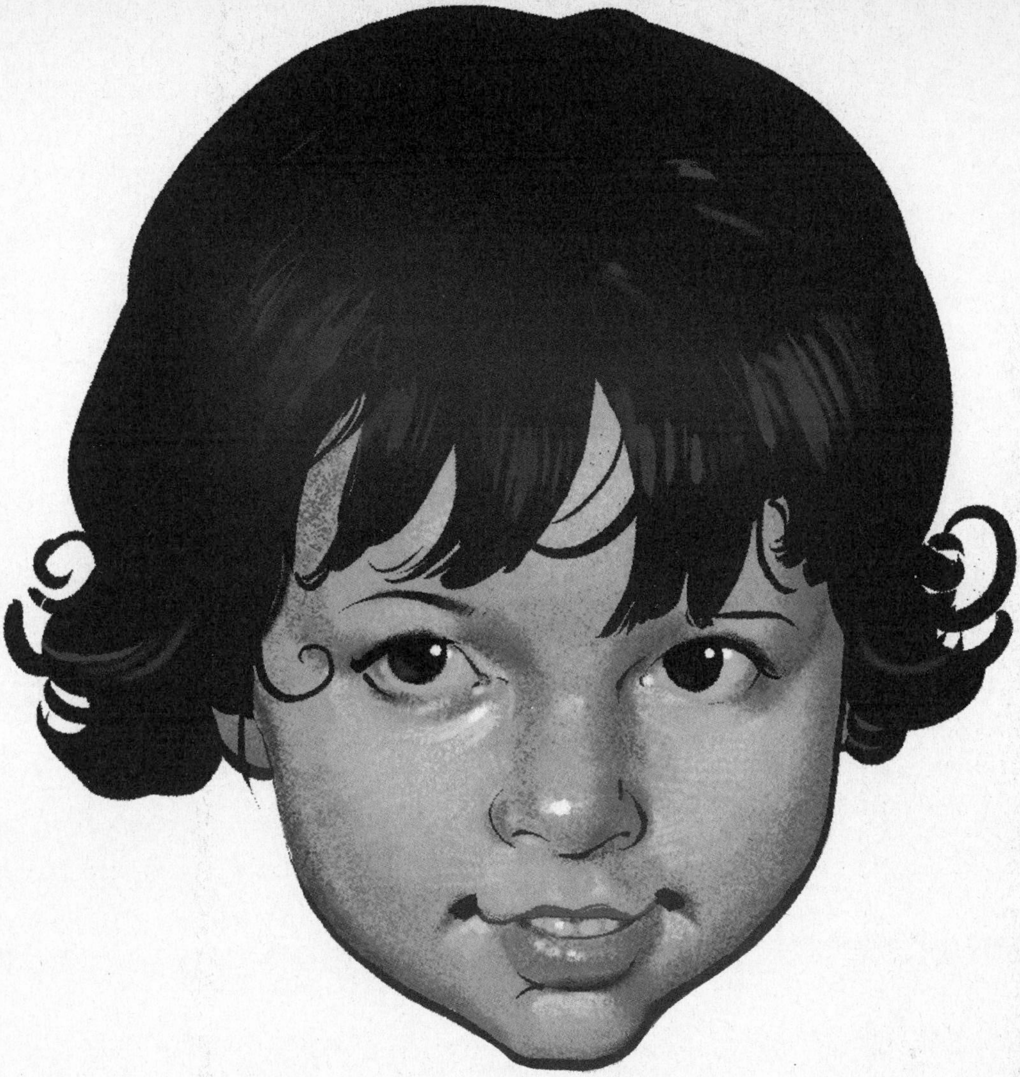

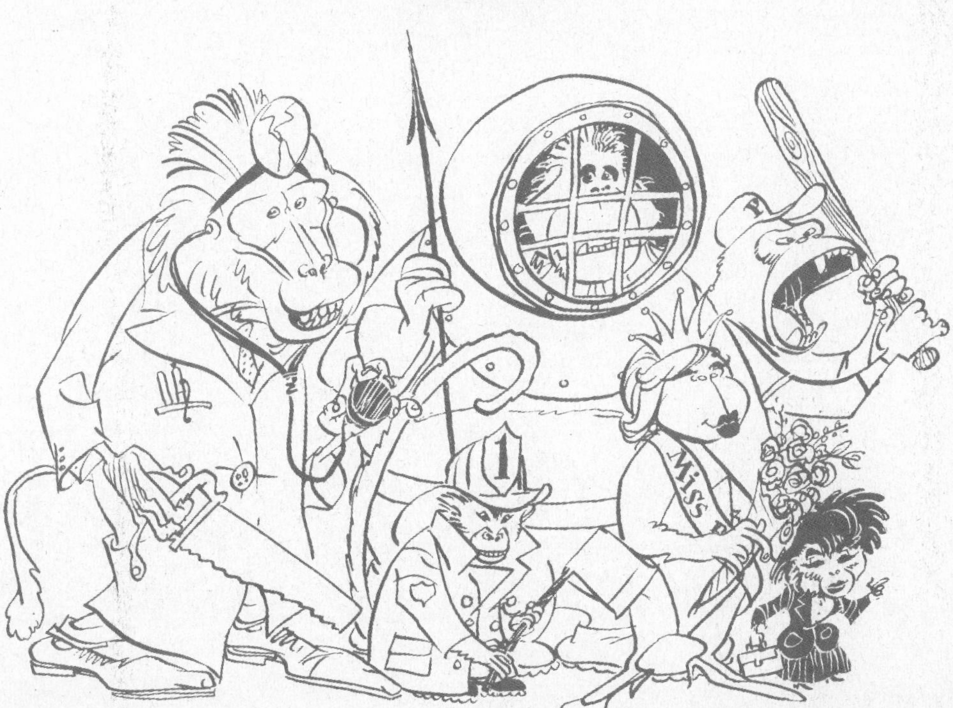
1
Miss

BAKER

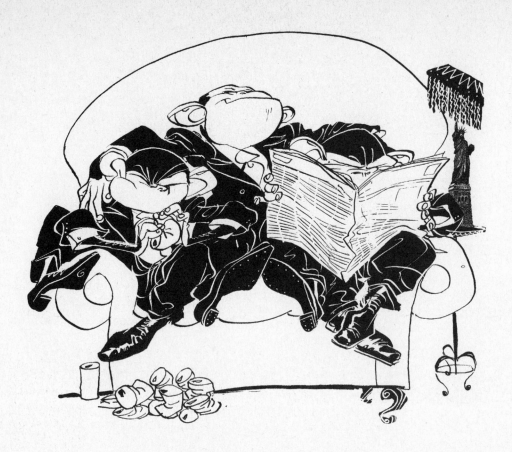

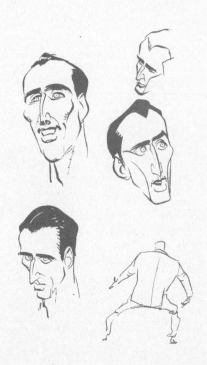

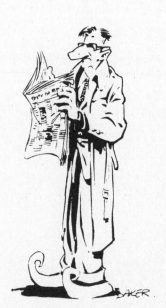

Undercover Genie.

GOD BLESS ALTERNATIVE ROCK!

by Kyle Baker, 1992

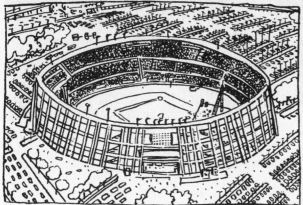

Oh, Glory Hallelujah! I just have to tell you kids out there that I'm so darn glad that Alternative Rock is finally getting the recognition it deserves.

It's about time somebody came up with the idea of featuring bands of long-haired white guys with no shirts and big muscles! It's so alternative!

And how about *Under the Bridge!* I still can't believe anything as heavy and progressive as *Under the Bridge* would actually get on **MTV**, let alone top 40 radio!

And that guy from *Pearl Jam!* Is he out of control or what? Who ever heard of a lead singer jumping off the stage! *Into the mosh pit!* Can you believe it? It's so alternative!

And the styles! The new bands and all the hip kids wear (get this!) *Plaid Flannel Shirts and Doc Martens!* Or just plain old white T-shirts and sneakers! That is so progressive, so alternative!

I tell you, I can't believe that these things are finally catching on! It gives me hope for the future, yes it does. It's good to see the kids rocking out.

Say, Judy, what's wrong?

It's Valentine's day tomorrow, and I never get any valentines.

Yeah, that's rough.

Amy Miller always gets plenty of Valentines. She's prettier than me.

Don't worry, sweetheart. Girls who are accepted at an early age for their looks learn to get by on just their looks, but the less beautiful girls develop personalities instead.

So?

So, in twenty years, Amy won't be so pretty, but you'll still have a personality. You'll be in demand.

Then I'll be happy?

Probably not. The next twenty years will be hard for you. Especially when you want to start dating. Teenage boys usually ask out the prettiest girls. You'll probably either stay a virgin for a long time, or you'll become promiscuous and eventually grow to hate men.

Wow.

Or maybe you'll meet a nice guy who's been turned down by all the prettier girls, and he'll settle for you, until he can find a prettier girl with a low self-image.

Good lord.

Of course, these are all worst-case scenarios. You're only nine. Maybe you'll have big breasts.

Or get hit by a truck.

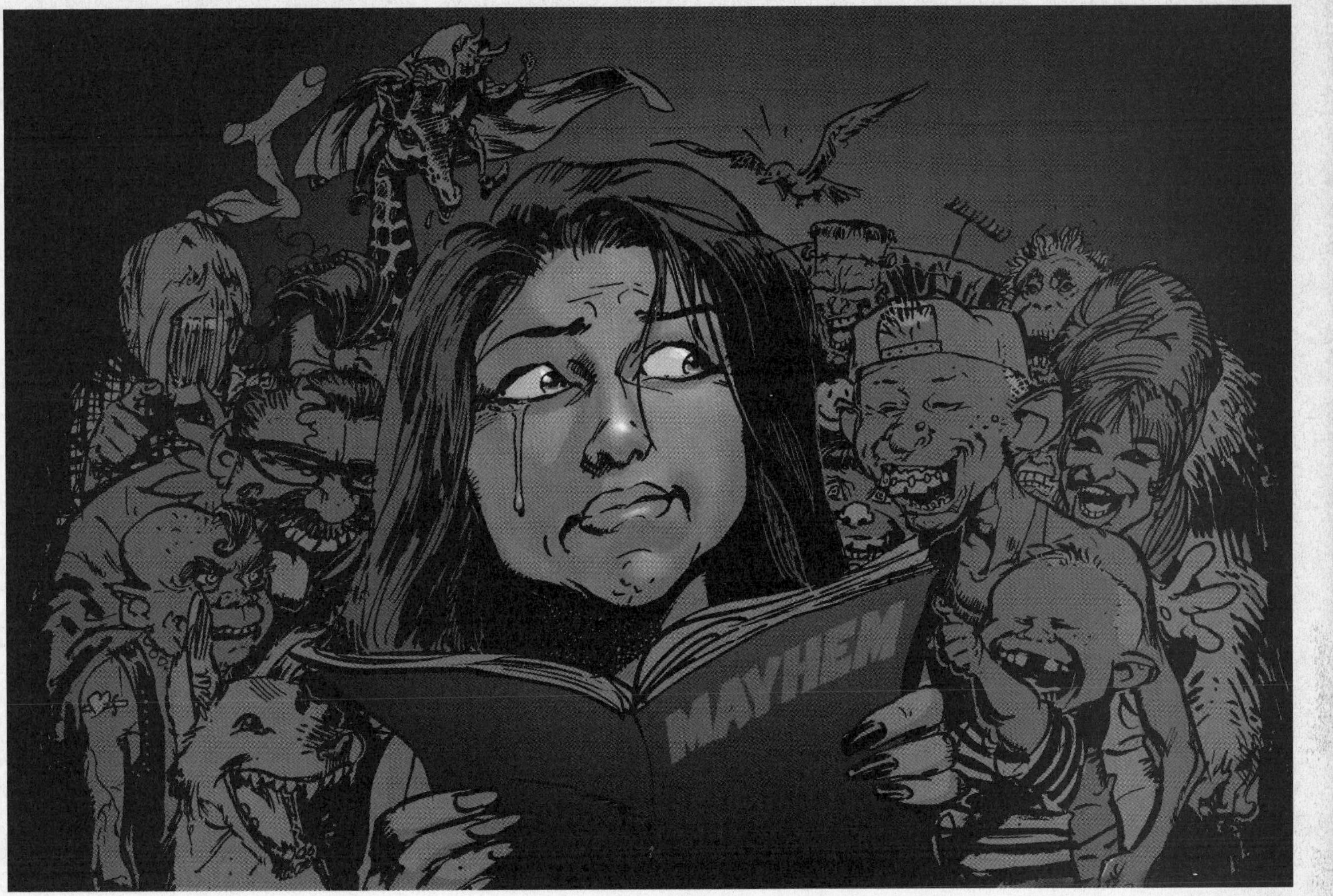
MAYHEM

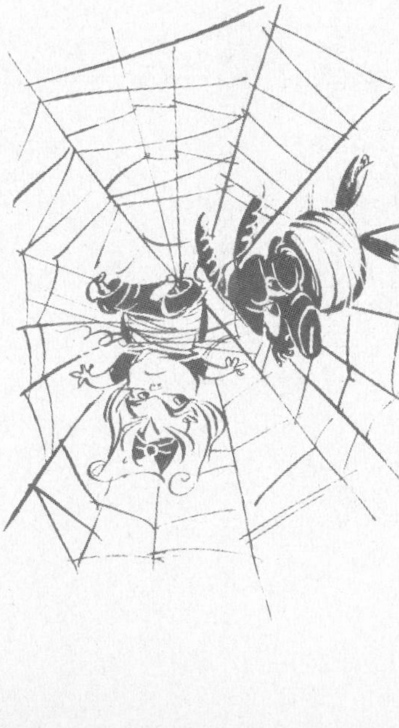

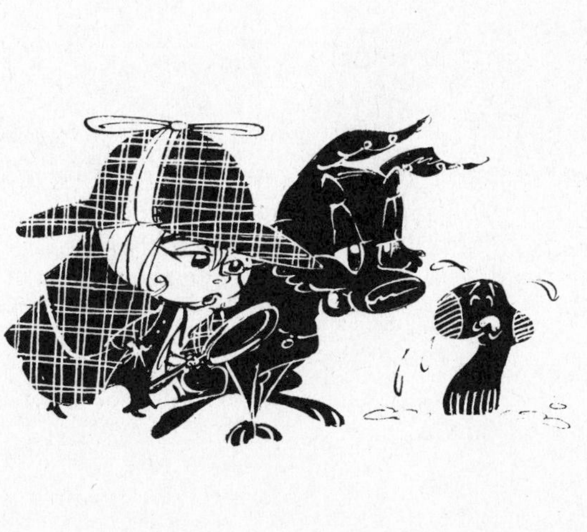

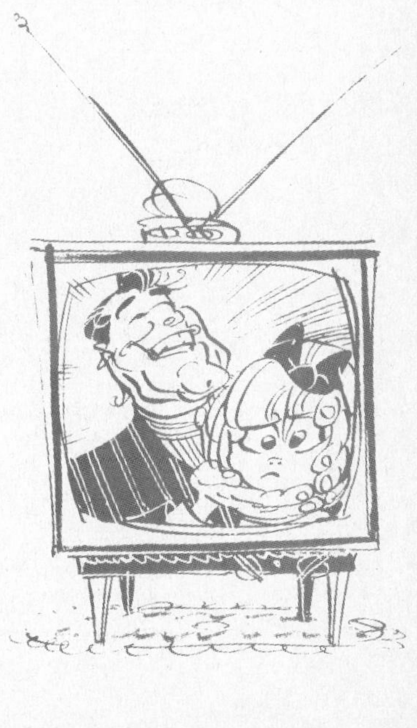

ED SMITH, LIZARD OF DOOM!

Oh, no one's sure exactly when
   the lizard came to town.
It all depends on who you ask,
   and who else is aroun'.

Ev'ryone claims they were there,
   although accounts all vary
as far as when and where and how,
   and whether it was scary.

A barmaid says she saw it all
   the night the air went "Boom!"
and dropped upon this hapless earth
   Ed Smith, Lizard of Doom.

She swears that she will ne'er forget
   how her soul shook with dread
when first she saw a toenail twice
   the size of her own head.

"Oh, bullshit", say some tie-dyed girls
   who stop their game of pool
to tell me they were into Ed
   before Ed Smith was cool.

"Ed Smith's been here for quite some time,"
   one girl says, chewing gum.
"He used to squat with friends of ours
   in an abandoned slum.

"He taught them all of peace and love,
   and the pitfalls of greed.
He taught them how to feel and share
   and how to write and read.

"One day, he simply disappeared.
   He only left a note.
'Thank you,' it said, and underneath
   he'd left a Bible quote.

"But just the number, not the quote,
   and there's no way to look
up 'Matthew, page 122',
   'cause Ed left with the book.

"Oh, sometimes, when I'm all alone
   in twilight's anxious gloom,
I feel the mystic presence of
   Ed Smith, Lizard of Doom.

"I know that some day he'll return
   and I'll know how to treat him.
I've practiced what I'm gonna say
   The day I finally meet him."

ED SMITH, LIZARD OF DOOM!

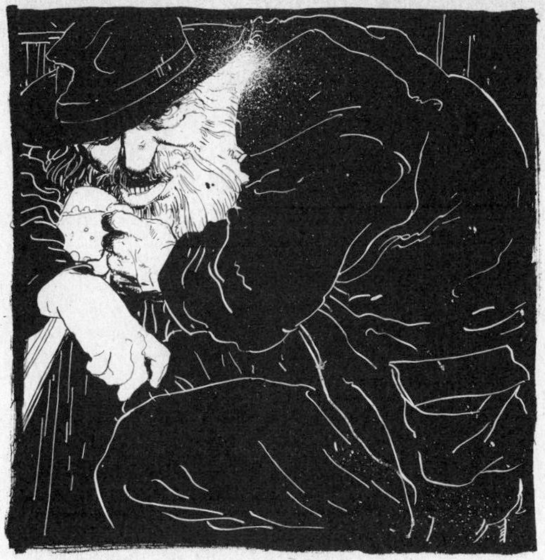

"You never met the Lizard, eh?
  You're better off, sweetheart!"
says a deep voice from down the bar,
  which gives the girls a start.

The voice belongs to an old man
  with fingers short and thick,
with eyes as cold as death itself
  that seem to see through brick.

A hush descends upon the bar.
  A chill runs through the room.
The old man says," I'll tell you all
  of Smith, Lizard of Doom."

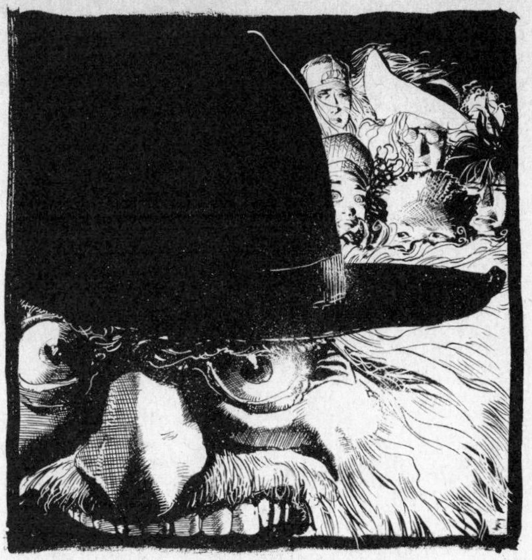

The crowd leans in to hear him speak.
  This old man, hunched and pale.
He clears his throat and downs his shot
  before he starts his tale.

He clears his throat again and sighs.
  He knits his brow and leers.
He coughs, he farts, he blows his nose
  and fiddles with his ears.

He opens up his mouth and then
  emits a high-pitched whine;
"That asshole's owed me fifty bucks
  since 1989!"

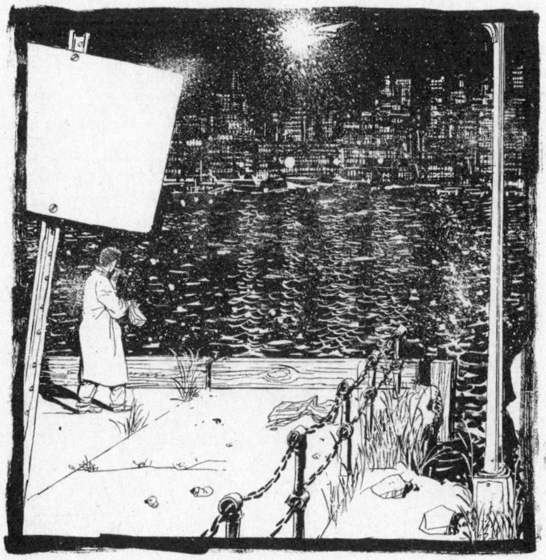

They all talk at once. "He ate
  my dog." "He saved my life."
"A messenger of God, he was."
  "The lizard stole my wife!"

I pay the bartender and leave
  this screaming bullshit bunch.
I walk down to the riverside
  and eat my bag of lunch.

I'll never figure out the truth.
  I guess I'd best forget thee,
great Mister Smith of myth, Oh, well. . .

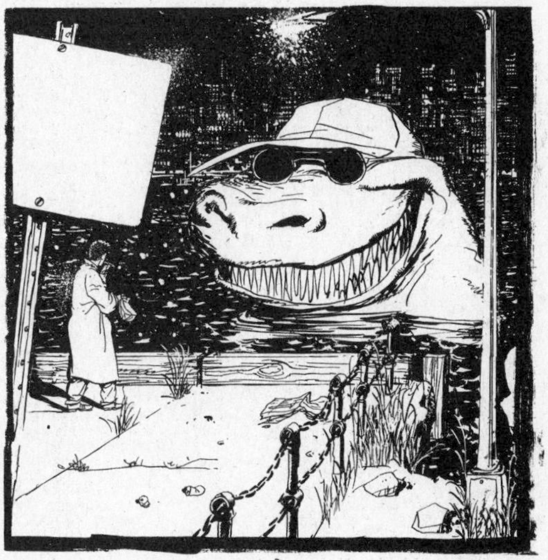

"Hey man, is that spaghetti?"

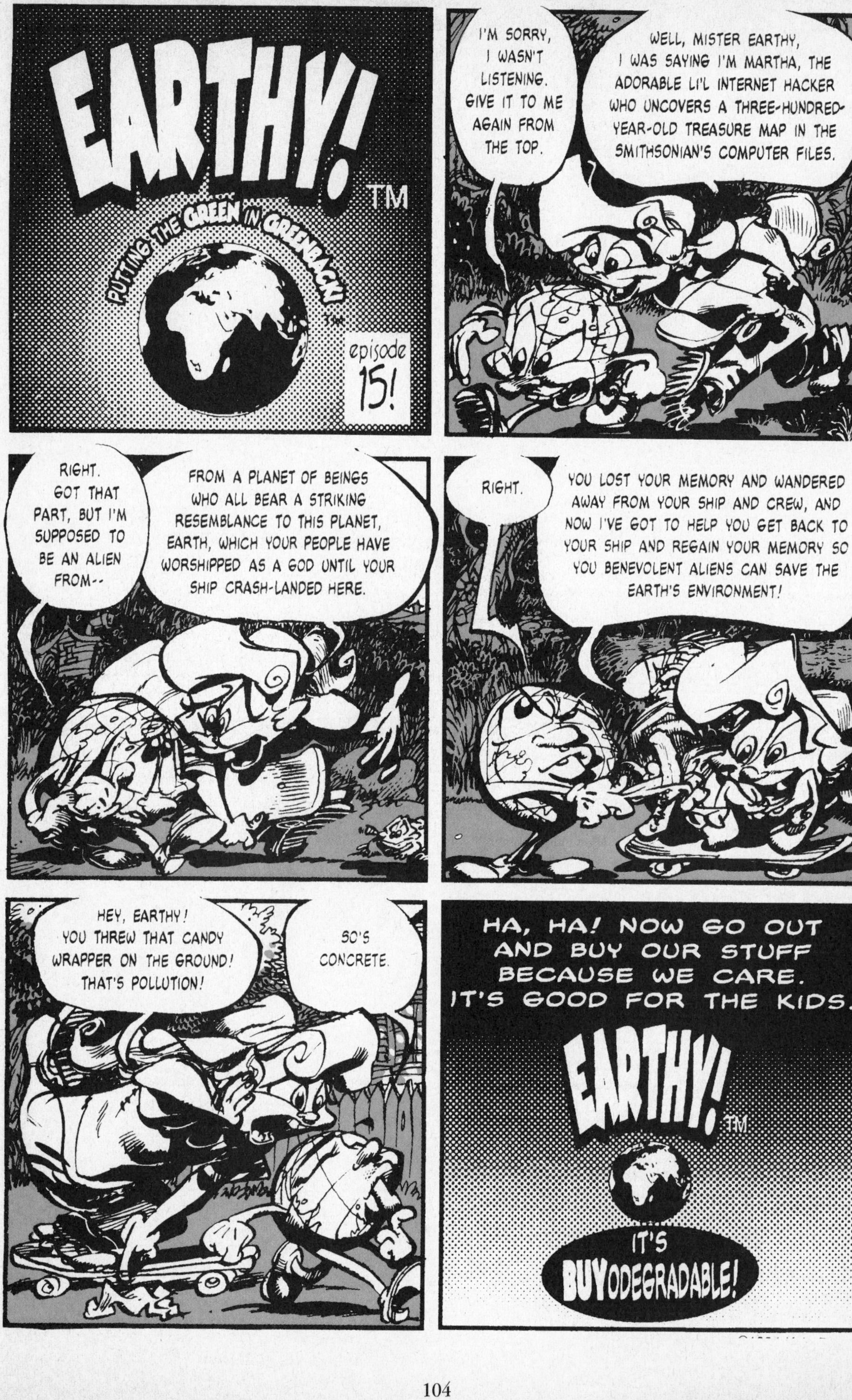
EARTHY!™
PUTTING THE GREEN IN GREENBACK!
episode 15!
I'M SORRY, I WASN'T LISTENING. GIVE IT TO ME AGAIN FROM THE TOP.
WELL, MISTER EARTHY, I WAS SAYING I'M MARTHA, THE ADORABLE LI'L INTERNET HACKER WHO UNCOVERS A THREE-HUNDRED-YEAR-OLD TREASURE MAP IN THE SMITHSONIAN'S COMPUTER FILES.
RIGHT. GOT THAT PART, BUT I'M SUPPOSED TO BE AN ALIEN FROM--
FROM A PLANET OF BEINGS WHO ALL BEAR A STRIKING RESEMBLANCE TO THIS PLANET, EARTH, WHICH YOUR PEOPLE HAVE WORSHIPPED AS A GOD UNTIL YOUR SHIP CRASH-LANDED HERE.
RIGHT.
YOU LOST YOUR MEMORY AND WANDERED AWAY FROM YOUR SHIP AND CREW, AND NOW I'VE GOT TO HELP YOU GET BACK TO YOUR SHIP AND REGAIN YOUR MEMORY SO YOU BENEVOLENT ALIENS CAN SAVE THE EARTH'S ENVIRONMENT!
HEY, EARTHY! YOU THREW THAT CANDY WRAPPER ON THE GROUND! THAT'S POLLUTION!
SO'S CONCRETE.
HA, HA! NOW GO OUT AND BUY OUR STUFF BECAUSE WE CARE. IT'S GOOD FOR THE KIDS.
EARTHY!™
IT'S BUYODEGRADABLE!

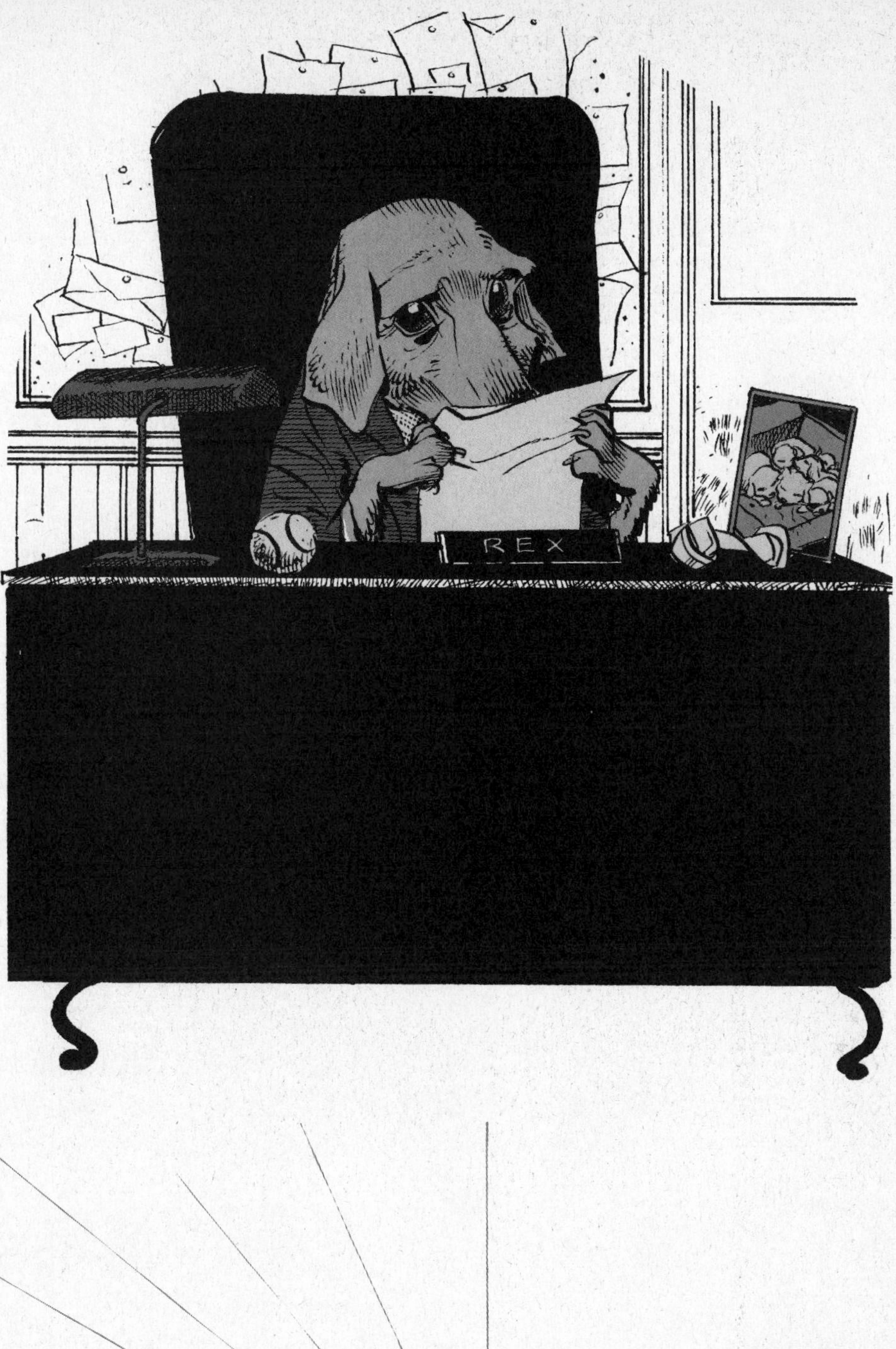
REX

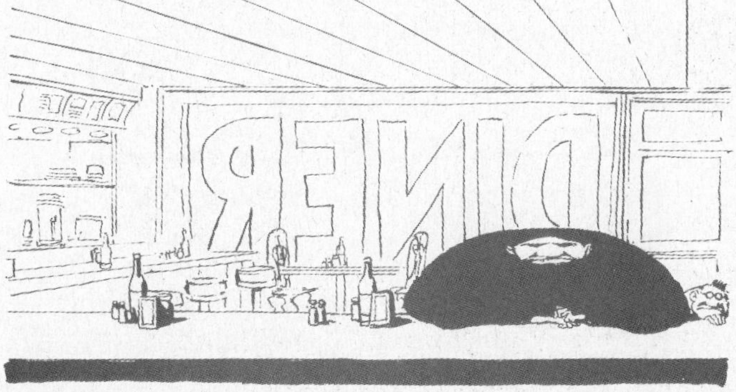
DINER

Even though the place is empty, he sits down next to you.

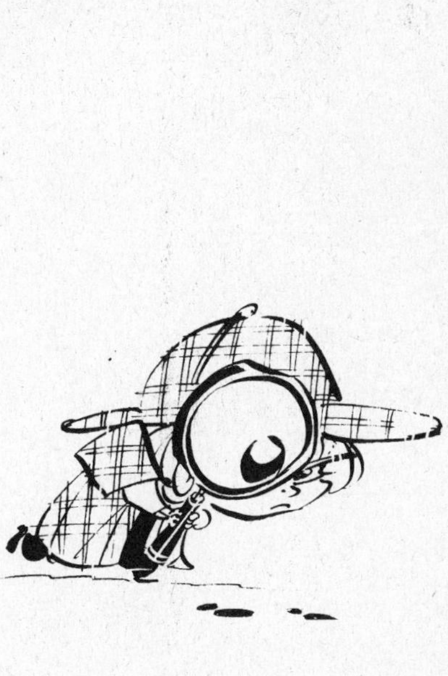

What
was
that?

What
was
what?

You know
what. *That!*
You just tried
to pick up
the waitress!

What are
you talking
about? I was
just ordering
some food!

Where does
it say on the
menu, "You
have nice
eyes"?

What're
you,
jealous?

Yes I am. I've
already turned
you down.
She's still got it
to look forward
to. Why don't
you grow up?

I have! A
year ago, I
would have
ordered the
tongue!

I don't want to talk about this. Change the subject while I still have an appetite.

Did you see that guy on the news last night? The one who got crushed under a ton of concrete?

Oh, *that's* better. Did I *see* him? They must've showed the tape fifty times now. Every channel. If he weren't dead, he could probably get his own series.

I hope that when I die, there's no cameras around. If you die on film, people want to see it over and over.

Just my luck, I'll die on vacation. My kids'll sell slides of me exploding in a giant teacup with Goofy.

Last year, I saw this woman on the news, threw her baby out the ninth-floor window, then jumped herself. Nine stories.

That must've irritated the media. "Damn, should the camera follow the baby all the way down? We might miss the mother!"

The networks must've shown it a hundred times in two hours. But you know what the most disturbing thing was?

What?

I couldn't stop watching it! They showed it a hundred times, I watched it a hundred times. The first time I saw it, I was wondering what it would sound like when she landed.

The baby or the mother?

See? We're all sick.

You started it, with your concrete guy. You brought it up.

Now *he* was a nut. I mean, he chains himself up, strait-jackets himself, gets in a plexiglass coffin, has it lowered into a grave, and has wet cement poured over him, and says he's gonna escape in three minutes.

And the people just sat around and watched him *do* it! Like nobody could figure out what six feet of wet cement weighs!

He didn't stand a chance, even if the plexiglass *hadn't* collapsed!

KYLE BAKER

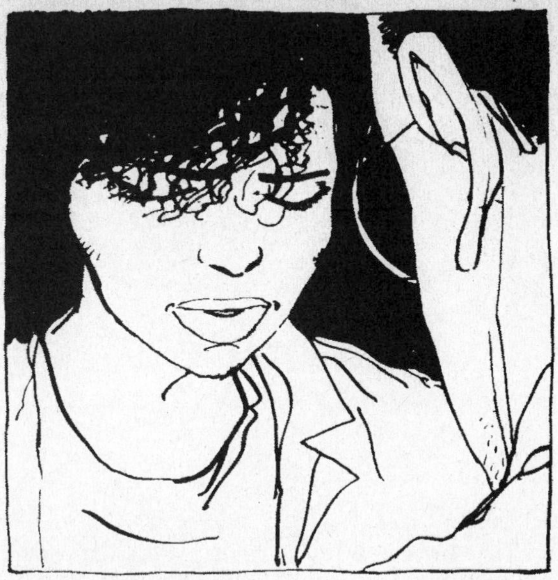

Why do people do that stuff? Why do people catch bullets in their mouths, and let people break cinderblocks on their stomachs with sledgehammers?

They want to get famous.

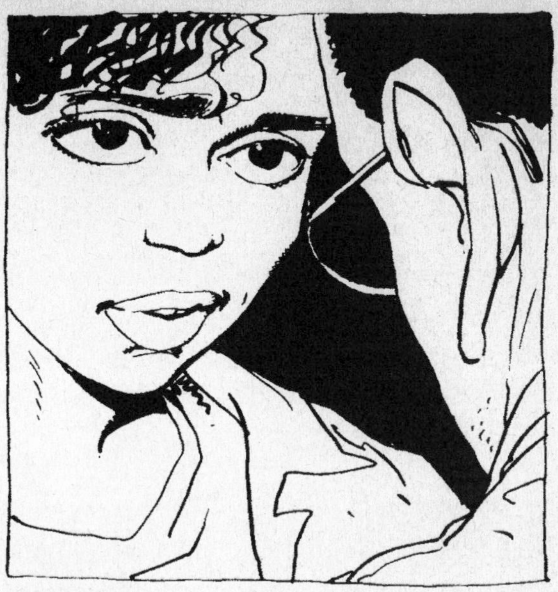

What was the name of the guy who died last night?

Uh . . .

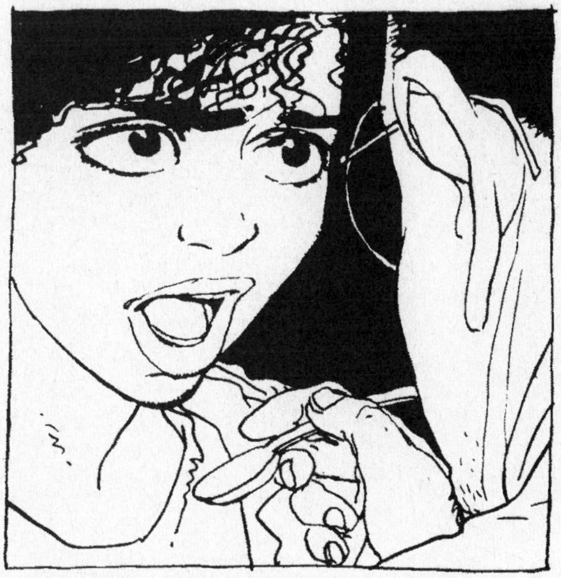

See? He's not famous, and the only reason we even heard about him in the first place is he died! He's dead, and he's *still* not famous! It's amazing what people will do for attention, and it's amazing what people will pay attention to.

Well, to be fair, these people don't die to get on the news.

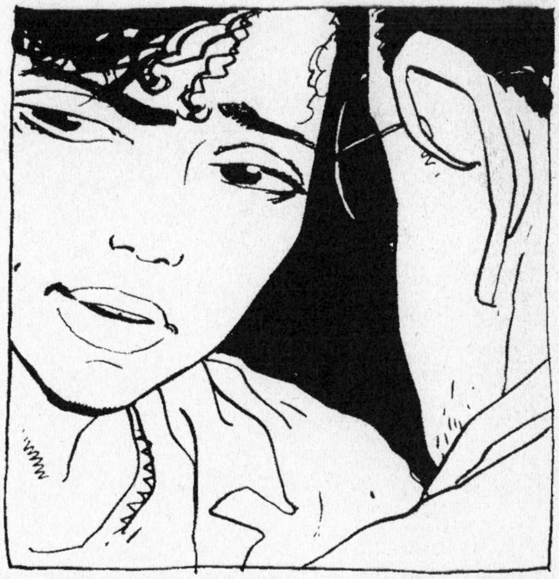

They only *risk* death to get on the news. The news shows up because somebody might die.

Remember that guy who shot himself on TV?

Which one?
I can think
of two.

The
politician.

Oh, yeah, but he
didn't do that just
to get on the
news. Politicians
can get on TV
easy enough.
That was more
of a videotaped
suicide note.

I
guess
so.

Why do people leave
suicide notes, anyway?
Once you're dead, why
should you care? Do
people stick their heads
in the oven and worry
because they left the
gas on? Does the note
say,"Turn off the gas"?
I'm telling you, this
whole thing is just--
What are you doing?

I'm
listening.
Go on.

You're listening.
What are you
doing with your
face?

There's
a baby
behind
you. Go
on, I'm
listening.

I can't talk to you when you're like this. Your eyes are rolling around in your head. If I couldn't see your tongue, I'd be afraid you'd swallow it.

I'm listening. See? I'm not wiggling my ears.

How can you do that? How can you sit there, blinking and spasming with your tongue hanging out, like some short-circuiting pornographic window display, and tell me you're listening? I don't *care* if you're listening!

I knew you'd understand. Hello, baby! Hello! Woop! Woop! Woop!

Oh, good. The noises have started. I'm having lunch with the Macy's Thanksgiving Day Parade.

Woo woo! Pretty baby! Happy baby! Woowoo!

Stop it! Stop it, or I'll kill you! I'll kill you, and your face will be frozen like that! No mortician will touch you.

What's your problem? Don't you like babies?

I *love* babies. I *pity* them. It's bad enough that they can't walk, speak, or use a toilet, but they also probably think they live in a world of pop-eyed freaks!

Gee, I never thought of that.

It must be rough being a baby. Everyone you see is making faces and talking gibberish.

Smiling and waving. People smile and wave at babies all day. I think it must be nice.

You think so? Wherever you go, people just smile and wave and make goofy faces. You have no other interaction with the human race. And all this bizarre attention is directed at you just because you're a baby.

Isn't that great? To be loved universally, and do nothing to earn it! The ultimate free ride.

Free food, free shelter, free clothes . . . If it weren't for the faces, it'd be like Alcatraz. They don't walk much either.

Miss Canon?

Uh,
yeah?

You don't
know me.

Oh, good, I
was feeling
awkward
for not
recognizing
you.
What's
up?

Oh! Nothing!
I just wanted to
meet you. I'll
leave you alone
now. Bye.

Nice
meeting
you.

See what
I'm talking
about?

It's not the
same thing.

You're right.
This one kept
his tongue in
his mouth.
Why do people
do that? Say
"hi" and leave?

Well,
you *are*
famous.

For what? I act
on a bad TV show.
A show I don't
watch. It's just a
job, that's all.

But you do it
in front of
millions of
people.

It's still just a job!
Why don't people go up
to plumbers and say,
"Hey, man, I saw you in
the Yellow Pages. Just
wanted to meet you.
Bye."

You
make
a lot of
people
happy!

So does a working toilet.
I can get along without TV,
but I need my toilet.
I have a very unimportant
job.

Good,
'cause
we're
late.

The History Of Music

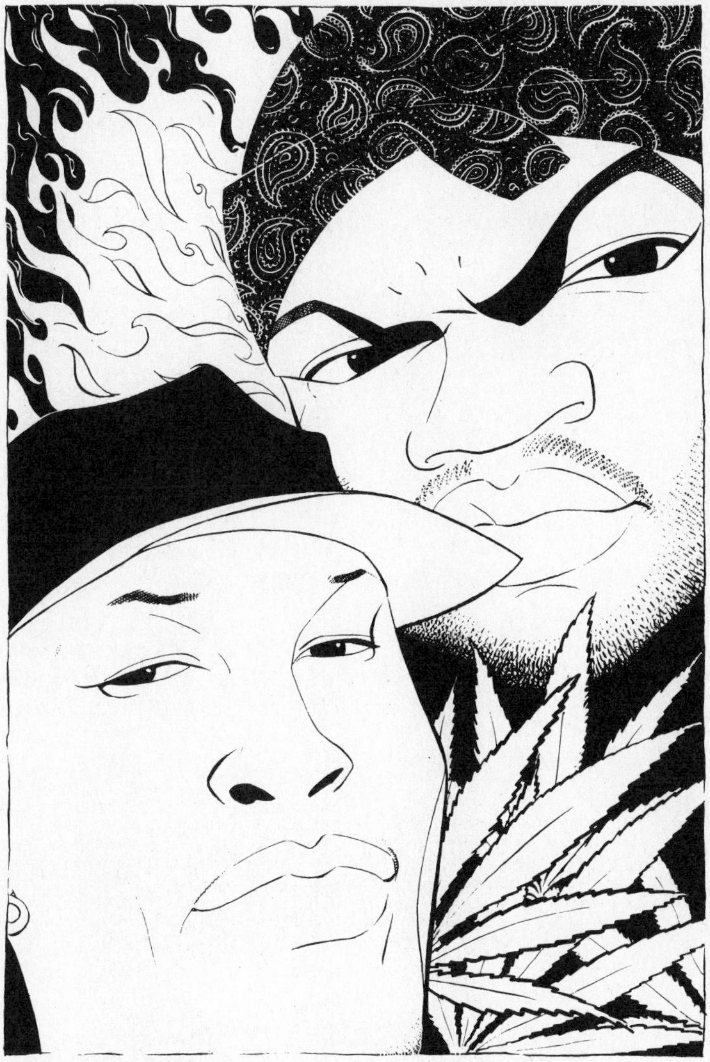

Dr. Dre, Ice Cube

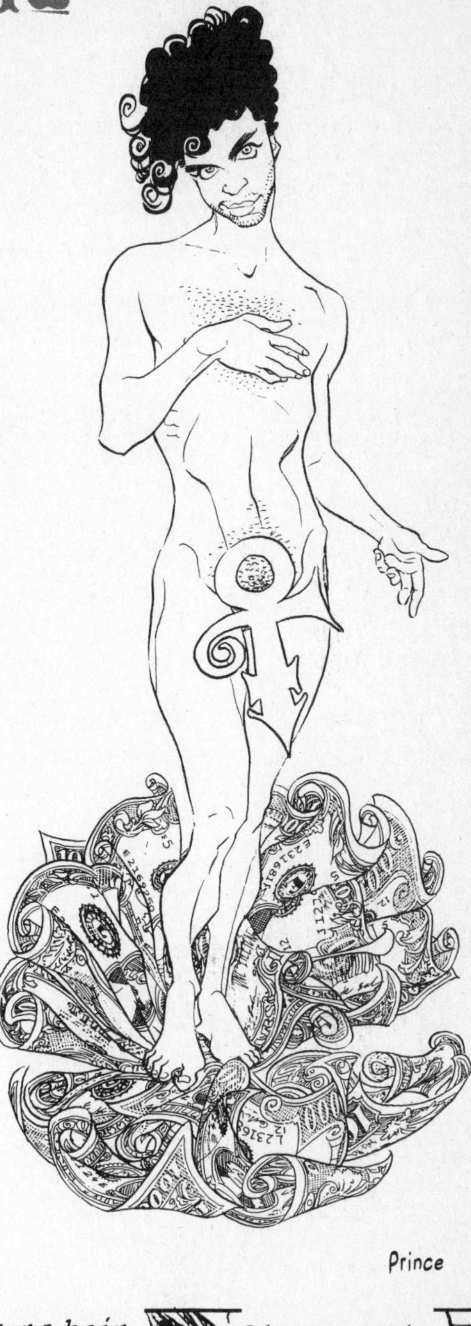

Prince

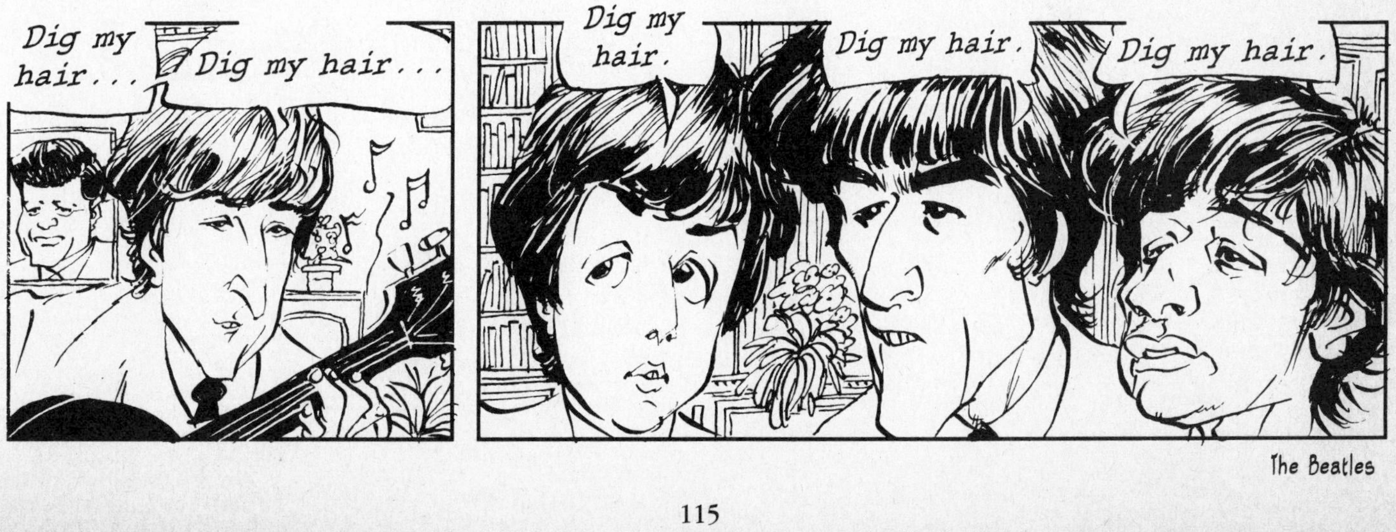
Dig my hair...
Dig my hair...
Dig my hair.
Dig my hair.
Dig my hair.

The Beatles

Guns N' Roses

Billy Idol

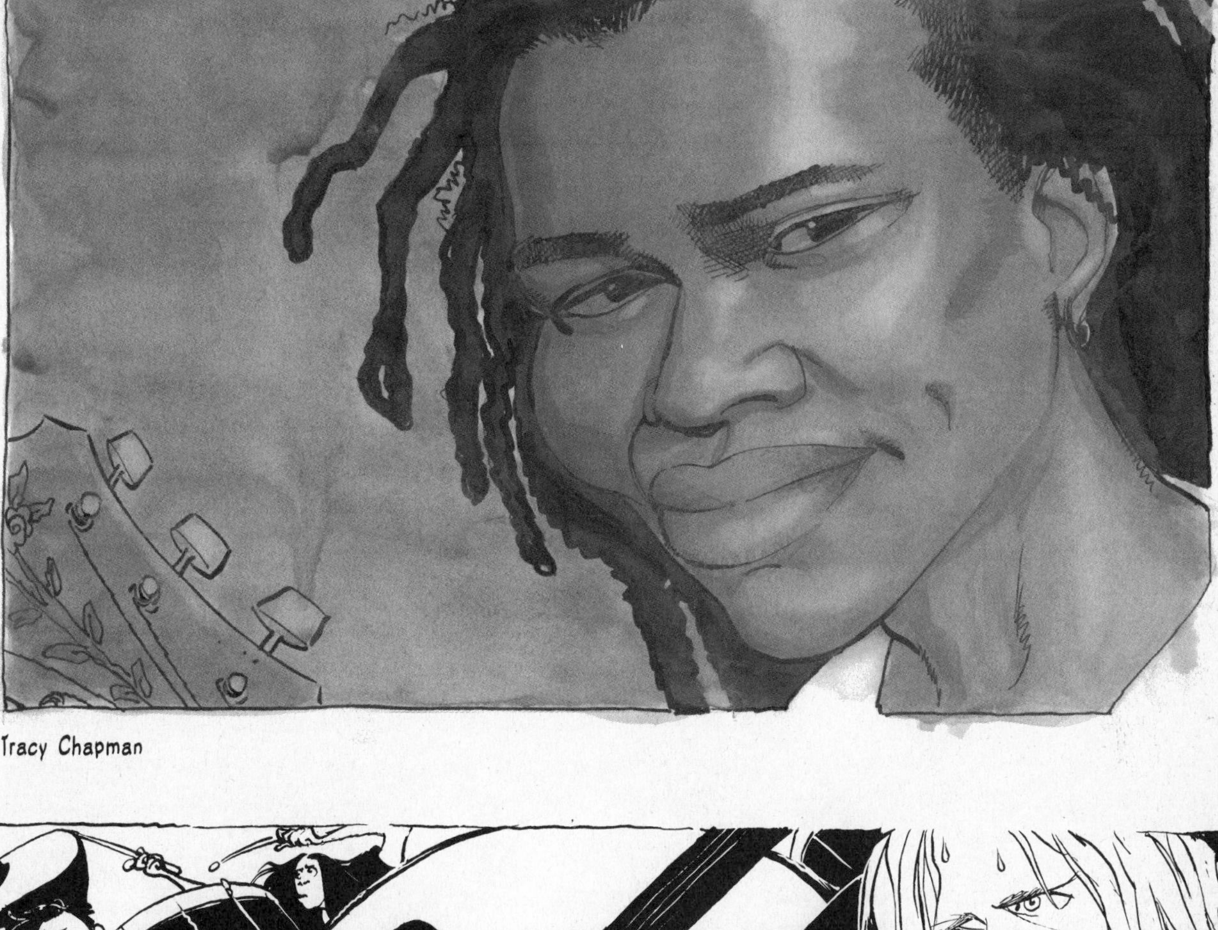

Tracy Chapman

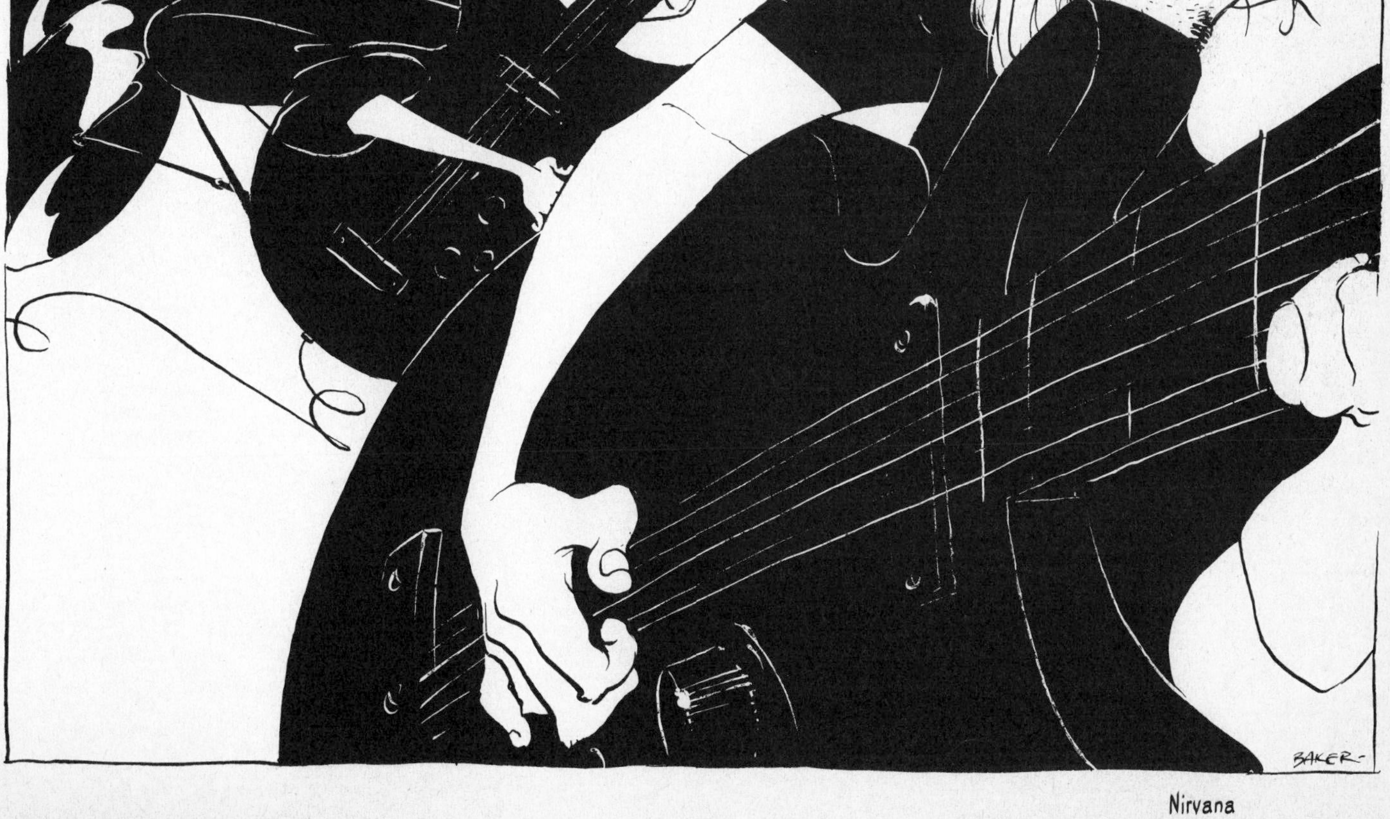
BAKER-

Nirvana

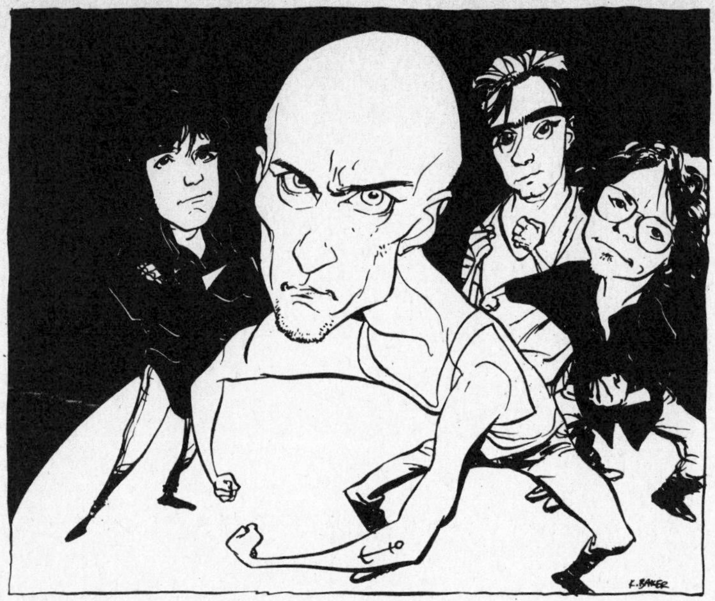
K. BAKER

REM

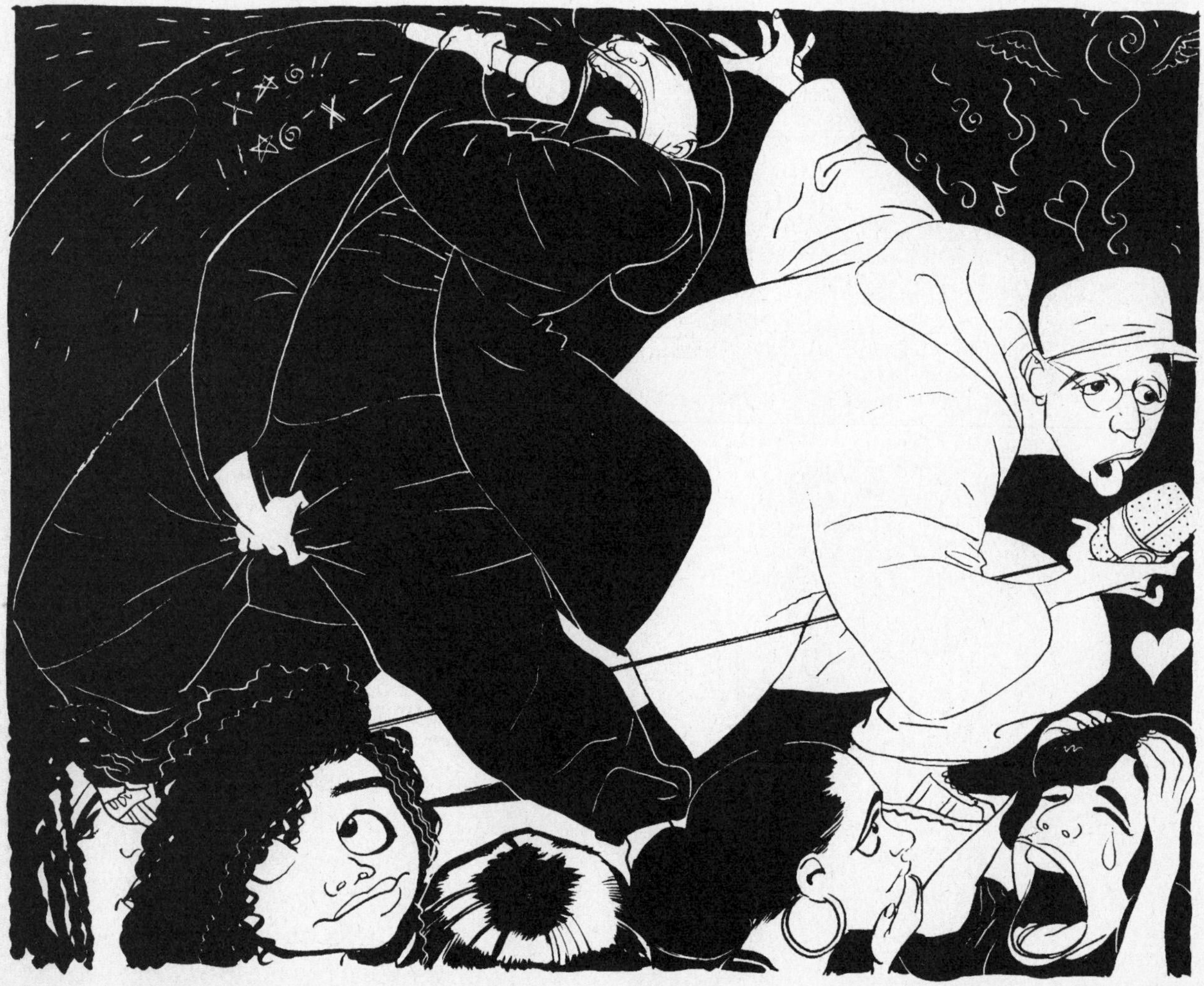

Have you
seen my
burgundy
thing?

It's on
the rack
in the
living
room.

What
a place.
Three
bedrooms
and no
closets.

It's two
bedrooms.
You're
sleeping
in the
closet.

Five floors!
I walked up
five floors!
Shouldn't
this building
have an
elevator?

I hear the landlord had it converted into a studio. It's a bit cramped, but people love the two-hundred-foot ceiling.

God, I can't breathe. I need a cigarette.

Look at my calves. I've lived here six months, and I swear these boots are getting tighter Who's in the bathroom?

Use the mirror in Erica's bedroom.

I'm using the mirror in Erica's bedroom.

I just need the toilet. Can't you use the mirror in the living room?

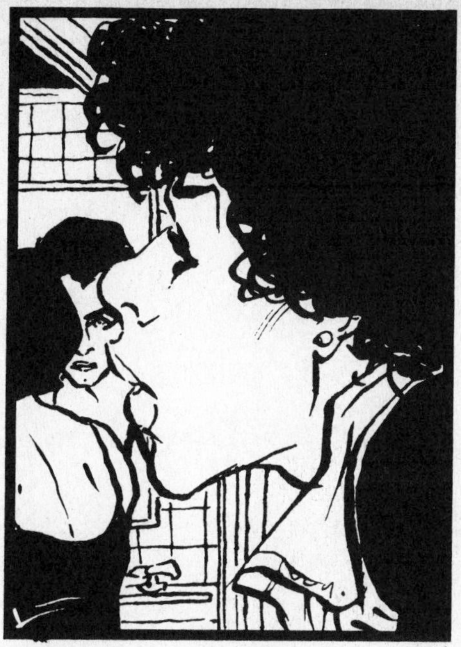

There's no sink in the living room.

There's a sink in the kitchen.

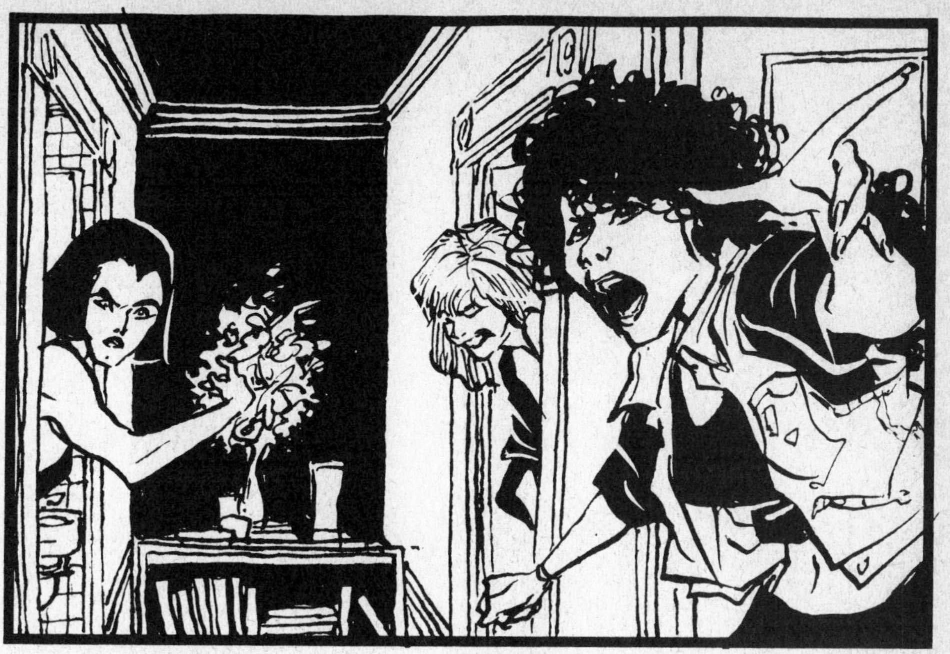

What am I supposed to do, run back and forth between the kitchen and the living room so you can use the bathroom? Just wait two minutes, willya?

No doubt about it, there's too many people living here.

Two minutes? In two minutes, I'll have jumped out that window, I swear to God! Oh, hi, Sally.

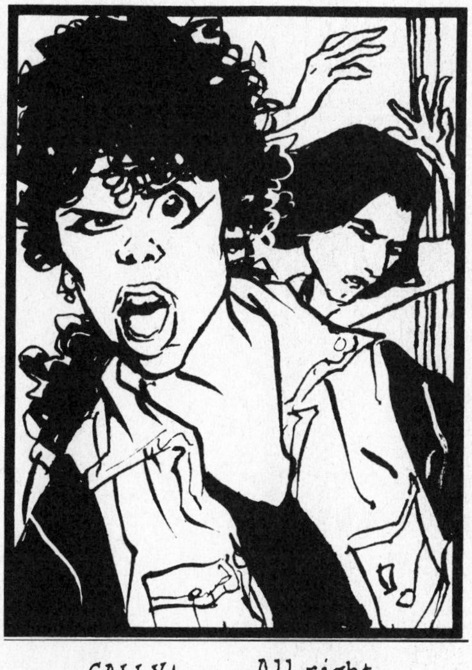

SALLY!

All right, all right, take yer goddamn bathroom!

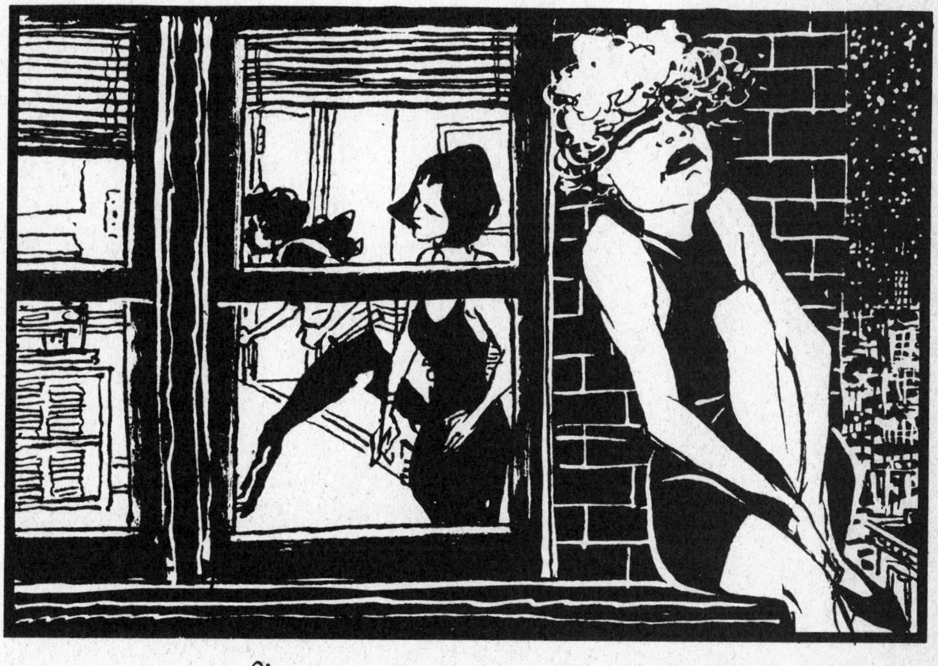

Oh, thank you, Jesus!

Did
she say
something
about
Sally?

Hey,
Sally's
on the
window
ledge!

Yeah, I saw
her. Tell
her we're
supposed
to be
leaving in
fifteen
minutes.

Why's
she
on the
ledge?

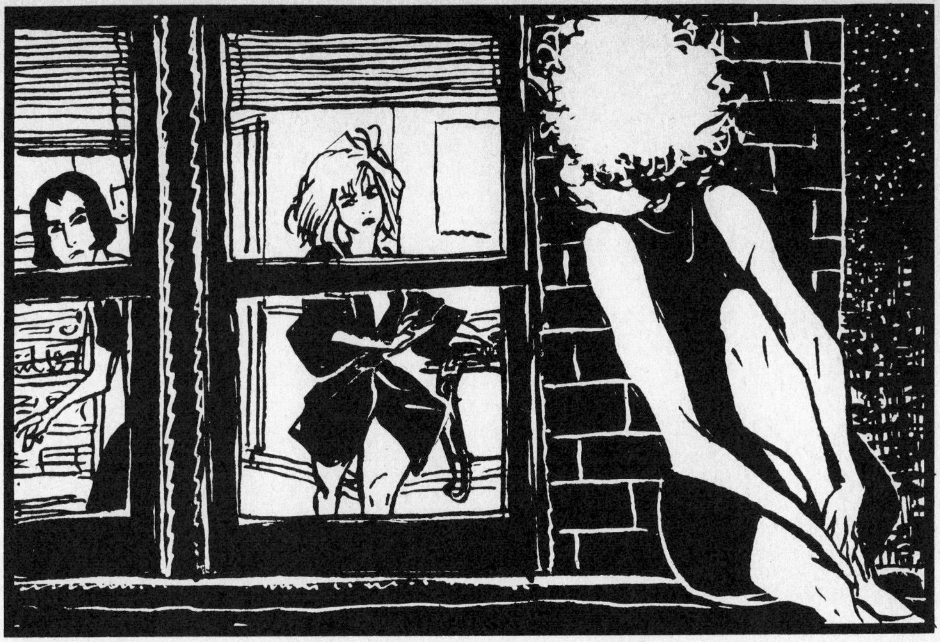

Who knows? She's Sally! She's probably testing a glow-in-the-dark wristwatch.

Sally! What are you doing out there? You say you wanna change, you wanna stop being weird--this is weird, okay?

This is how you talk someone in off a ledge?

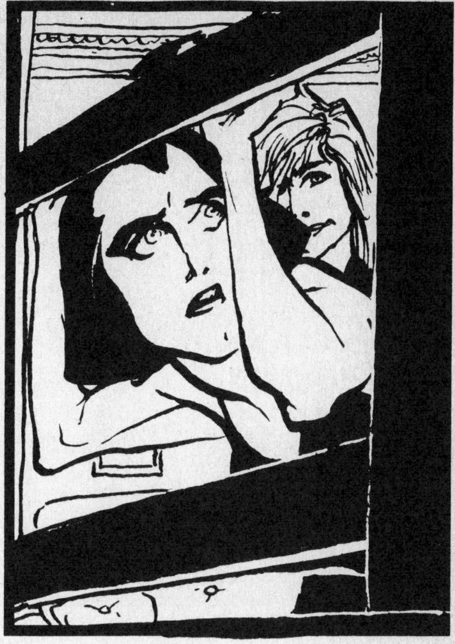

You need talking in? You're really suicidal?

Calm down. She's being funny.

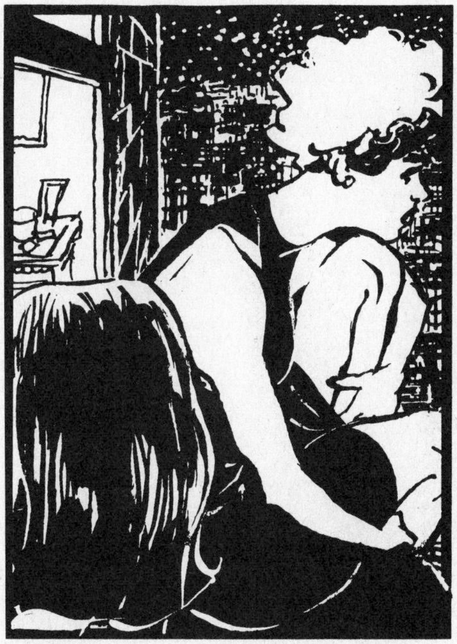

Sally, are you gonna jump?

I just want to be alone right now.

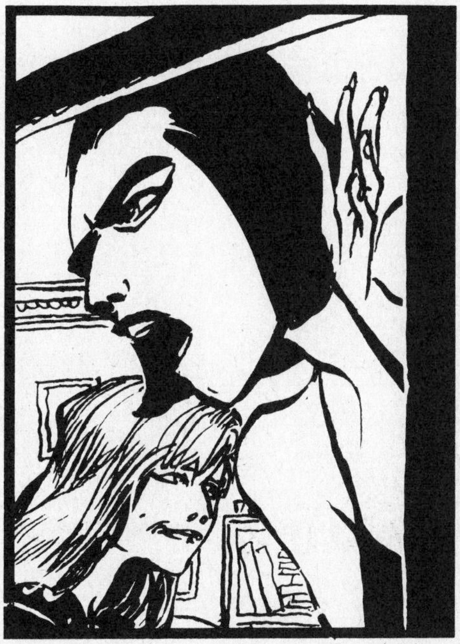

See, it's nothing.

Nothing?! There's a human being in pain on our windowsill!

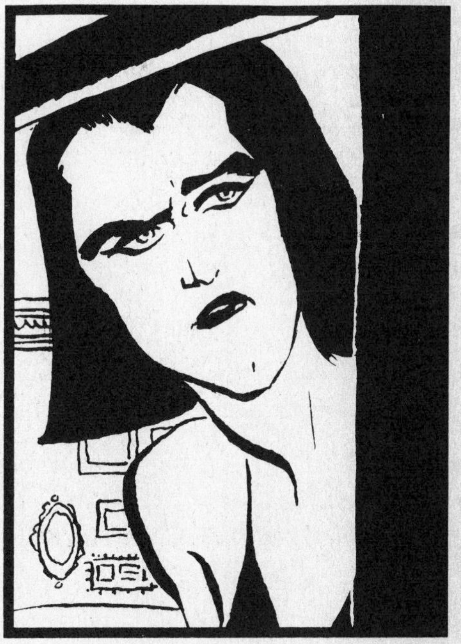

Why are you wearing my dress?

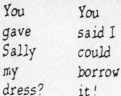

You gave Sally my dress? You said I could borrow it!

You didn't say anything about giving it to Sally to kill herself in! If anything happens to that dress, you owe me fifty dollars! What were you thinking? She wanted to come out with us tonight. She asked me to make her over.

In my dress? I'm a size 5! That's not a makeover, that's a sausage! Hey! Hey! Forget about yourself for a minute, would you? Should we call the police?

What if it's not a suicide? What if it's nothing, like she says? She's weird! Look, Sally, is this a suicide? We'll all find out at the same time, I figure.

See? It's answers like that! You're never serious! That's why nobody likes you!--What is that, sarcasm?

Would I be sarcastic right before killing myself?

Yes!... I give up.

There. You can use the bathroom now.

Thanks-- HOLY CHRIST! What do you eat? Sulfur? I can't stay in there!

It's not that bad.

Not that bad? I'm crying! I'm putting on mascara and I'm crying! I look like Young Tammy Faye! Where's my waterproof stuff?

I've got it out here. I also took some lipstick and a compact.

Why my
makeup?
Julie's
more your
color!
Which
lipstick'd
you take?

What's it matter?
You all wear the
same thing! Red,
black, white.
Red, black,
white. It's like
living with a
pinochle deck!

She's joking
again! See,
that's why
nobody can
figure you out.
You don't seem
to care about
anything!

I'm
on a
ledge,
aren't
I?

So you
are going
to kill
yourself?

Yes
I
think
I am.

I can
never
tell if
you're
serious
or not.

Oh,
for--

p18 screamer, Mike Myers, THE NEW YORKER

Robert DeNiro, THE NEW YORK TIMES MAGAZINE

p20-24, 33-34, ESQUIRE

p62 Shopping At Home, TIME WARNER ANNUAL REPORT

Jim Carrey, Demi Moore, Ovitz, ENTERTAINMENT WEEKLY

Whoopi Goldberg, Will Smith, Denzel, Sam Jackson, Morgan Freeman, Forrest, Angela, Fishburne, Cuba Gooding, VIBE

p90-91, ESPN

p 29-30, AIRWALK ad

p4-7, NATIONAL LAMPOON

p43, COMICS JOURNAL Cover.

p15 Stripper, p18 Cowboy, POV

REM, Prince, Nirvana, Ice Cube, Dr. Dre, Letterman, Idol, Eubanks, p118, VILLAGE VOICE

p41 (illo only), SPIN

p82 Silent Movie Studio, INSIDE

p48 Teens Flip Coin, NY DAILY NEWS

Woody, Ted Turner, Perot, Jerry Lewis, Schwarzenegger, Beatles, Clinton, Helms, Gingrich, Farrakhan, Robertson, Steinbrenner, Stewart, Brosnan, Tarantino, p27 tongue, p35 Monacle, Alien, NEW YORK

Nixon, Arbuckle, Gaines, SNL, SPY

Guns N' Roses, GUITAR WORLD